Computer hardware

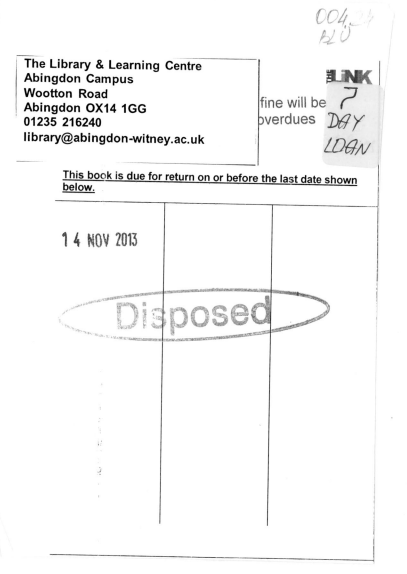

FASTTRACK

Computer Hardware

Barry Blundell

THOMSON

Australia • Canada • Mexico • Singapore • Spain • United Kingdom • United States

THOMSON

Computer Hardware
Barry Blundell

Series Editor
Walaa Bakry, Middlesex University

Middlesex University PRESS

Publishing Partner
Middlesex University Press

Publishing Director
John Yates

Commissioning Editor
Gaynor Redvers-Mutton

Managing Editor
Celia Cozens

Content Project Editor
Leonora Dawson-Bowling

Manufacturing Manager
Helen Mason

Marketing Manager
Jason Bennett

Production Controller
Maeve Healy

Text Design
Design Deluxe, Bath

Cover Design
Matthew Ollive

Typesetter
Keyline Consultancy, Newark

Printer
C&C Offset Printing Co., Ltd, China

For more information, contact
Thomson Learning
High Holborn House
50-51 Bedford Row
London WC1R 4LR

or visit us on the World Wide Web at:
http://www.thomsonlearning.co.uk

ISBN: 978-1-84480-751-2

British Library Cataloguing-in-Publication Data
A catalogue record for this book is available from the British Library.

Contents

The FastTrack Series

Thomson Learning and Middlesex University Press have collaborated to produce a unique collection of textbooks which cover core, mainstream topics in an undergraduate computing curriculum. FastTrack titles are instructional, syllabus-driven books of high quality and utility. They are:

- **For students**: concise and relevant and written so that you should be able to get 100% value out of 100% of the book at an affordable price
- **For instructors**: classroom-tested, written to a tried and trusted pedagogy and market-assessed for mainstream and global syllabus offerings so as to provide you with confidence in the applicability of these books. The resources associated with each title are designed to make delivery of courses straightforward and linked to the text.

FastTrack books can be used for self-study or as directed reading by a tutor. They contain the essential reading necessary to complete a full understanding of the topic. They are augmented by resources and activities, some of which will be delivered online as indicated in the text.

How the series evolved

Rapid growth in communications technology means that learning can become a global activity. In collaboration, Global Campus, Middlesex University and Thomson Learning have produced materials to suit a diverse and innovating discipline and student cohort.

Global Campus at the School of Computing Science, Middlesex University, combines local support and tutors with CD-ROM-based materials and the Internet to enable students and lecturers to work together across the world.

Middlesex University Press is a publishing house committed to providing high-quality, innovative, learning solutions to organisations and individuals. The Press aims to provide leading-edge 'blended learning' solutions to meet the needs of its clients and customers. Partnership working is a major feature of the Press's activities.

Together with Middlesex University Press and Middlesex University's Centre for Learning Development, Global Campus developed FastTrack books using a sound and consistent pedagogic approach. The SCATE pedagogy is a learning framework that builds up as follows:

- **Scope:** Context and the learning outcomes
- **Content:** The bulk of the course: text, illustrations and examples
- **Activity:** Elements which will help students further understand the facts and concepts presented to them in the previous section. Promotes their active participation in their learning and in creating their understanding of the unit content
- **Thinking:** These elements give students the opportunity to reflect and share with their peers their experience of studying each unit. There are *review questions* so that the students can assess their own understanding and progress
- **Extra:** Further online study material and hyperlinks which may be supplemental, remedial or advanced.

The Fastrack Series

How [illegible] evolved

Preface

Successful IT Projects

Computer Hardware is aimed at a first introductory course for computing undergraduates covering the basic principles behind the design of modern computer systems.

Starting with the physical components, this book covers machine-level architectures on which programs and operating systems run, helping readers to understand the respective roles of hardware and software systems.

Coverage in the first half of the book focuses on the binary system, logic gates, bus systems and memory, while the second half looks at storage devices, interaction hardware, connectivity and multimedia.

Using this book

There are several devices which will help you in your studies and use of this book. **Activities** usually require you to try out aspects of the material which have just been explained, or invite you to consider something which is about to be discussed. In some cases, a response is provided as part of the text that follows – so it is important to work on the activity before you proceed! Usually, however, a formal response will be provided at the end of each chapter.

The **time bar** indicates *approximately* how long each activity will take:

short < 10 minutes

medium 10-45 minutes

long > 45 minutes

Review questions are (usually) short questions for each chapter to check you have remembered the main points of a chapter. They are found towards the end of each chapter; feedback is provided at the back of the book. They are a useful practical summary of the content and can be used as a form of revision aid to ensure that you remain competent in each of the areas covered.

About the author

Barry Blundell

Barry Blundell is a physicist with many years of experience in teaching computer and IT-related courses and in developing digital systems. His research interests are multidisciplinary, and he is a leading researcher in the area of emerging 3D display and interaction systems for the advancement of human/computer communication. He is actively involved in forums promoting the ethical usage of computer technologies. Dr Blundell is the author of three research textbooks, several technical and undergraduate teaching books, and he is currently working on an introductory undergraduate computer graphics book.

Visit the accompanying website at **www.thomsonlearning.co.uk/fasttrack** and click through to the appropriate booksite to find further teaching and learning material including:

For Students

- Activities
- Multiple choice questions for each chapter.

For Lecturers

- Downloadable PowerPoint slides.

CHAPTER 1

Computer technologies

OVERVIEW

In this chapter we provide an introduction to computer systems. We begin by identifying the differences between hardware (the electronic components and systems that form a computer) and software (the instructions and data that we use to define how the hardware will behave). This gives a computer tremendous flexibility, as the electronic systems will behave in different ways according to the instructions that we provide. The computer is indeed a 'general-purpose machine'.

We provide some background information relating to computer evolution. As you will see, computers are by no means new – the basic principles date back more than 150 years.

Learning outcomes At the end of this chapter you should be able to:

- Discuss the concept of a computer as a general purpose programmable machine
- Distinguish between hardware and software
- Understand why we use computers, and what they are used for
- Delineate important milestones in the evolution of the modern computer
- Distinguish between the functionality of a traditional calculator and a computing machine.

1.1 Introduction

In this chapter, we begin by distinguishing between hardware and software – these being the two key ingredients that make up a computer. We go on to briefly consider the evolution of the modern computer and describe some of the milestones that have represented major advances in computer technology. Although we tend to consider computers as a modern innovation, pioneering work carried out more than 150 years ago encapsulated many of the underlying techniques employed within the modern machine.

We describe key features of the modern computer within the context of a general-purpose programmable machine, discuss why we use computers and outline some areas of application. Finally, we discuss the confidence that we may place in the veracity of the computed result and consider computability.

In the Glossary we provide a table containing a range of technical terms and acronyms that will be introduced in this book. Beside each entry in the table, space is provided in which you can enter a description of the meaning of each term. You are encouraged to make use of this table. In doing so, you will not only develop a useful source of reference but also the action of writing down the meaning of these various keywords and abbreviations will assist you in the learning process. In activity 1.4 we list some key words introduced in this chapter and suggest you enter their meaning into the table provided in the Glossary.

1.2 Hardware and software

A computer consists of a set of electronic or electromechanical components able to accept some form of input, process this input in a way that we can specify, and produce some form of output – see Figure 1.1.

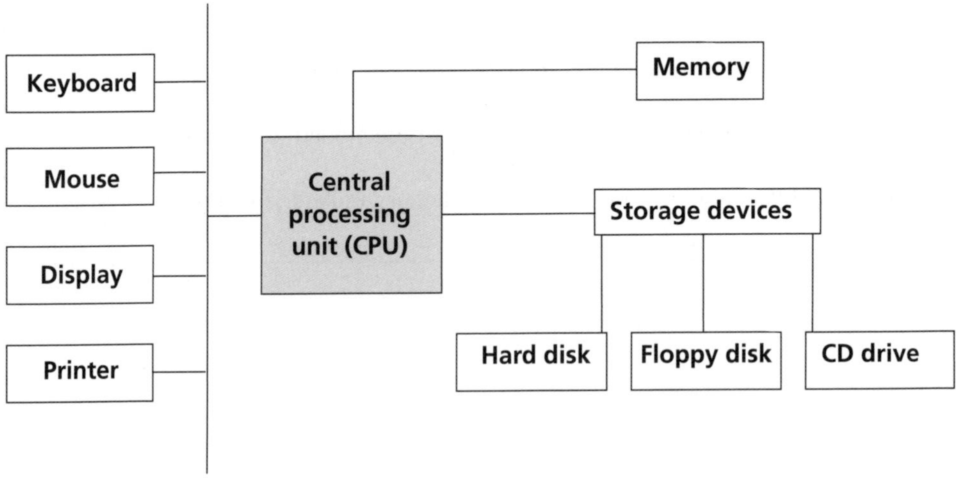

Figure 1.1: Some of the hardware subsystems forming part of a basic computer system

There are two fundamental elements of any computer:

- **Hardware**
- **Software.**

Hardware

This is represented by the electronic or electromechanical components from which the computer is constructed. As was summarised in Figure 1.1, a basic computer system includes the following types of hardware:

- Devices such as a display, keyboard and mouse, through which we interact with the computer. In this respect we provide input to the machine via the keyboard and mouse and observe the results of the computational process by means of the display screen
- A central processing unit (CPU), which is able to follow (execute) a series of instructions and control all activities that take place within the machine
- Memory devices able to store instructions and data during the operation of the computer
- Various storage devices able to store instructions and data even when the computer is turned off.

The most common form of computer in use today is the PC (personal computer). This was the name given to a computer configuration that evolved during the 1970s and which is a desktop machine (we will discuss this configuration in a little more detail shortly). Figure 1.2 provides an illustration of some of the major components within a PC. Typically, a number of peripheral devices are connected to the PC. These may include one or more printers, speakers, scanners etc.

Figure 1.2: Major computer components located on the main circuit board (motherboard)

All computers follow the same fundamental cycle (see Figure 1.3):

- They **accept data** called input
- They **process the data** according to a sequence of instructions (by performing calculations and by making decisions)
- They **produce results** in the form of information or actions called output.

Software

Computer hardware is, in itself, unable to perform any useful tasks – it must be told what to do and how to do it. Consequently it is necessary to provide the hardware with a set of instructions to define the tasks that it is to perform. These instructions (and any necessary data) are contained within programs. Software is a term used to refer to programs in a general way; it encompasses instructions that are to be acted upon by a computer, together with data that may be needed by the instructions.

As we will discuss in some detail during subsequent chapters, software is permanently stored in secondary memory (hard disks, floppy disks, or CD-ROM). Such storage devices do not lose their contents when the computer is turned off (hence they are said to provide long-term storage capability). During the execution of a program, software is temporarily stored in primary memory (also known as random access memory or RAM).

Computer hardware is able to perform a vast range of tasks. These tasks are specified in software. The power of the computer relates to its tremendous flexibility, and so a computer is commonly referred to as a 'general purpose programmable machine'.

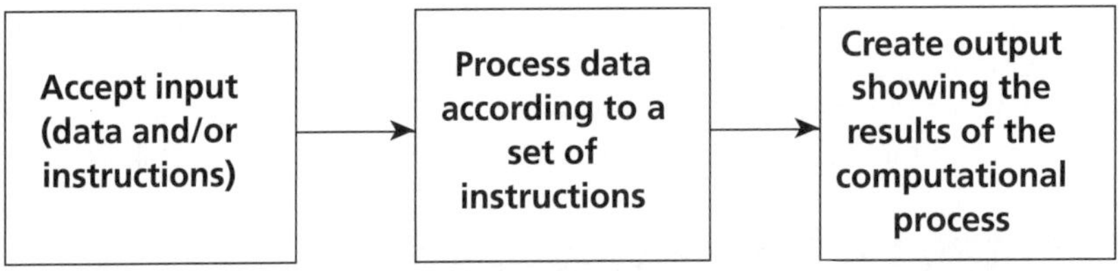

Figure 1.3: Input/process/output cycles

1.3 The evolution of the computer

Charles Babbage (1791-1871) is generally regarded as the first person to have understood the potential of a machine whose operation and purpose may be controlled by the instructions and data contained within a program.

In those days, a major issue was the production of accurate tables (containing, for example, square roots, cube roots, trigonometry functions, interest rates, nautical information, astronomical information, etc.). These tables were calculated manually and the results written out by hand. This process was clearly prone to error and inaccurate tables abounded! Thus, the designs created using these sources of information would be flawed, ships foundered, and end-users became distrustful.

In 1821, Babbage was working with a friend (Herschel) on the checking of a manuscript containing astronomical tables. During the process one of them is said to have exclaimed: 'I wish to God these calculations had been executed by steam' (the reference to steam being made as at that time it represented the power source for automation).

Babbage decided that the future lay in the automatic generation and printing of mathematical tables. In 1822, he produced a first simple demonstration prototype of his 'Difference Engine'.

This was intended to operate on steam power (the technology underpinning the Industrial Revolution). However, his simple prototype used a handle that turned toothed wheels and represented, in fact, a six-digit calculator. This machine proved the validity of the technique.

Babbage's Difference Engine was not only intended to compute data, but also to create printing plates without human intervention whereby the flawed process of transcribing results onto paper by hand would be eradicated. For many years Babbage worked on his Difference Engine. His first problem was the degree of accuracy to which the mechanical components (cogs, wheels and shafts) would have to be machined. At that time, tools of sufficient precision did not exist and so Babbage would frequently design parts of his Difference Engine, subsequently design and produce tools capable of machining the components needed and, during this process, realise that the design of the components within the Difference Engine was not optimal. Being a perfectionist he would therefore redesign the Difference Engine components, and once more begin to consider the tools that would be needed to produce the working machine. Not surprisingly, this was a very time-consuming task.

During this period, Babbage hit upon an alternative and even more revolutionary concept – that of the computer: the 'Analytical Engine'. The Difference Engine may be said to have represented what we today would consider to be the essential features of a calculator. The Analytical Engine was far more ambitious in its scope. Two essential elements were to be the ability of the machine to be programmed to carry out a variety of mathematical computation tasks, and to store numerical information during the computational process. As with the Difference Engine, the Analytical Engine performed its computations mechanically and – had it been completed – it would have been approximately fifteen feet tall and twenty-five feet long (around 5 metres by 9 metres).

In the 1860s, Babbage began to build a scaled-down version of his Analytical Engine. It is hard for us to imagine that some 140 years ago a programmable computer could even have been envisaged. Babbage's machine was certainly not intended to be of low performance – it had the capability to add, subtract, multiply and divide forty-digit numbers, to store values, print, and take input from punched cards (widely used in computers from the 1930s until the 1970s). Babbage's idea of using punched cards for programming and providing input to his computer was in fact not his own, but that of a Frenchman, Joseph-Marie Jacquard, who in 1801 developed punched cards for controlling a textile loom and thereby revolutionised textile manufacture. One important feature of the Analytical Engine was to have been its ability to make decisions during the computational process. This is a vital feature of any computer, and a simple example of this is as follows:

> **If the value we have just calculated is less than 10, do 'this'; otherwise do 'that'.**

This conditional statement allows program flow to be modified during the execution of a program and clearly distinguishes between the abilities of a conventional calculator and our expectations of a computer.

Following the death of Charles Babbage, some years passed before there was any major resurgence of interest in computer technologies – the next generation of machines being electromechanical calculators able to perform data processing tasks. The Hollerith machine – developed by IBM – provides us with one such example. It employed punched cards for the storage of data – the cards being sorted at very high speed according to predefined criteria. The power of this system was demonstrated by its use in Germany during World War Two for managing railways and munitions production. It was also used for far more sinister purposes in connection with the German racially based selections – a machine deciding the fate of vast numbers of people.

Gradually, electromechanical systems (in which, for example, relays were used for the switching of electronic signals) were replaced by valve (vacuum tube) based machines. The ENIAC (electronic numerical integrator and calculator) provides us with an example of one such computer. This contained some 18,000 valves and weighed about 30 tons, although it possessed only a fraction of the computational power of today's PC.

This machine was programmed by manually changing connections between the units of the computer, and each time a new program was executed it was necessary to manually reset up to 6,000 switches. The computer was initially used for solving ballistics problems.

Another important step in the development of computer technology was the 'stored program' concept (often incorrectly accredited solely to Dr. John von Neumann). This involved the transition from programming a machine via the interconnection of cables and the setting of switches, to a paradigm in which the program is stored in the computer's internal memory. Therefore when a new program is to be executed, it can be read into the main memory, obviating the need for the cumbersome reprogramming required with the ENIAC.

A further key advance in the evolution of computers was the introduction of transistors in the 1950s, and the subsequent invention of the integrated circuit (IC), which allows many transistors to be fabricated on the same silicon chip. This enabled circuit densities to be increased (components could be placed closer together) and, as a consequence, computers became smaller, more reliable, faster, and more economic to produce and run.

The late 1960s and early 1970s saw the production of the microprocessor – a single silicon chip containing the central processing unit. Throughout the 1970s, and until the present, the cost of integrated circuits has continued to fall; at the same time, the density at which transistors can be fabricated on silicon has continued to increase. This has led to continual growth in the power of computer technology (in terms of both speed and capability).

Activity 1.1

Computer evolution

Use your local library and Internet resources to research the development of the personal computer. You should focus on the work undertaken at Xerox PARC in the 1970s.

1.4 The computational process

In this section we briefly examine characteristics of the computer, and so gain a better understanding as to why the computer is such a powerful tool.

Let us suppose that you were asked to describe the fundamental characteristics of a computer – where would you begin? Perhaps you would explain the physical characteristics of a computer based upon the most widely used type of machine – the PC. Perhaps you would describe a white/greyish box that sits on a desktop, in front of which is placed a keyboard and mouse, and besides which sits some form of display. Alternatively, you may describe the external features of a laptop machine. This would give a clear impression of the form of today's typical computer, but does not provide us with a fundamental description of the computing machine. In section 1.2 we mentioned two facets of a computer – software and hardware – and certainly all computers comprise these two key components.

In fact, it is the synergy which is generated by the hardware and software combination that leads to the general purpose programmable machine that we have already alluded to.

As discussed in the last section, some 150 years ago Charles Babbage realised the immense power of a machine that could be controlled by a set of instructions. He began work upon the Difference Engine, which is in fact equivalent to today's calculator. Over time his ideas progressed and his interests quickly moved from the calculator to the computing machine. Here he foresaw the possibility of not only a machine that could execute a series of instructions, but also and most importantly a machine that could execute different instructions according to the result of some previous computation. This may sound a little complicated, so let's take a simple example based upon our everyday experiences.

Suppose that you were involved in some cookery. You would perhaps consult a recipe, which contains a series of instructions that you must follow in order to achieve a successful result. Consider how you might follow these instructions:

- You could follow them in sequence: one instruction after another. For example: place some flour in a container, add some water, add three eggs, etc. You are simply following a sequence of instructions
- At times it may be necessary for you to follow a different sequence of instructions depending upon some condition. For example, you may encounter an instruction that says if you prefer margarine, then add 100gm to the mixture, or else add 100gm of butter. Here you can see that you have the possibility of executing two different instructions depending upon some condition (in this case, the condition is your own preference)
- Finally, you may follow a sequence of instructions by iteration. This means repeatedly following the same instructions until some condition occurs. In the case of our baking example, perhaps it is necessary to wait until the oven is at a certain temperature. You might therefore follow instructions of the form:

  ```
  check oven temperature every three minutes;
  when temperature reaches 120 degrees, place mixture in oven.
  ```

  Here, you can see that you are executing the same instruction repeatedly (i.e. checking the oven temperature) until it has reached the required temperature. Similarly, you would repeatedly check on the cake once it is in the oven to verify whether it is cooked.

Computers are therefore able to execute instructions in accordance with the three basic structures mentioned above:

- **In sequence**
- **By selection**
- **By iteration.**

These three simple constructs provide a computer with tremendously powerful capabilities and give a clear insight into the difference between a conventional calculator and a computing machine. The three structures are summarised in Figure 1.4.

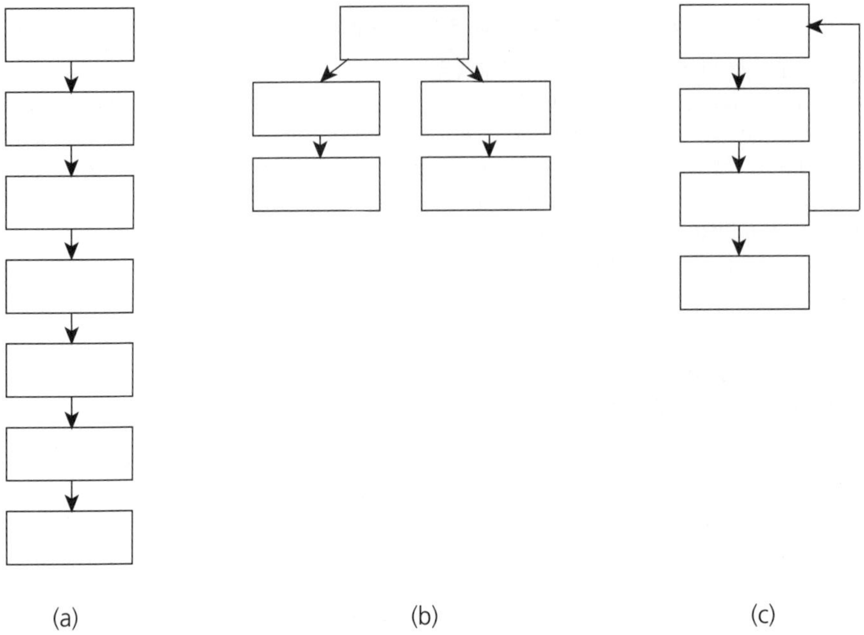

Figure 1.4: A computer is able to execute instructions (a) in sequence, (b) by selection and (c) by iteration

Activity 1.2

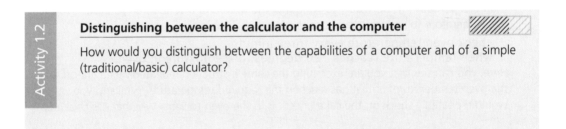

Distinguishing between the calculator and the computer

How would you distinguish between the capabilities of a computer and of a simple (traditional/basic) calculator?

1.5 Why do we use computers?

Since the early 1980s, computers have rapidly advanced and have gained acceptance in practically every area of human endeavour. The computer is a flexible machine able to perform a great variety of tasks and undertake calculations at very high speed. Two important aspects of computer capability are summarised here:

- **Speed and accuracy of processing information:** computers can process data much more quickly and efficiently than humans. Most computers can perform computations in nanoseconds (billionths of a second), and more powerful computers can perform arithmetic operations in picoseconds (trillionths of a second). Therefore, computers can perform vast numbers of calculations in a very short time – this enables them to be used to solve complex problems within reasonable timescales.

- **Storage and accessibility of information:** computers can be programmed to store information on, for example, tapes, disks or CDs. Storage media has continued to advance – enabling ever-greater volumes of data to be stored in a smaller space; furthermore, the speed at which data can be written to, or read from, storage media has continue to increase. Thus information which was previously recorded on paper in many filing cabinets can now be stored on a small number of computer devices in a more condensed way and easily accessed electronically when necessary.

Computer technology is essentially concerned with the processing, storage, transmission and representation of information. The phrase 'information technology' is now used to describe commuter technology in general and the phrase 'information processing' is used to describe what computers do in general – that is, process raw data and produce meaningful information.

1.6 What are computers used for?

The expansion of computer technology over the past two decades has been phenomenal. We now live in an age where almost every aspect of our daily lives is influenced either directly or indirectly by computers. We now highlight just a few of the areas in which computer usage is now commonplace.

General computer usage

The control of virtually all global financial systems including banking and the financial markets: for example, foreign exchange markets transfer billions of dollars every day by EFT (electronic funds transfer). Most bank accounts, credit card accounts, payroll calculations etc. are overseen by computer systems. Millions of people daily use an ATM (automatic teller machine) to carry out transactions on their bank accounts.

Most telephone networks are computer controlled. The advent of the Internet has had an enormous impact on many homes and businesses, facilitating worldwide communication and access to global information.

All main national defence systems are now computer controlled.

Computers control the sale and distribution of goods. Through the use of EPOS (electronic point of sale) shops and other retail outlets are able to record the sale and return of goods. Barcode readers register the sale and return of any item and can automatically reorder stock from suppliers.

Virtually all booking systems for travel and entertainment etc are run on computer systems.

Smaller-scale computer usage

Many domestic appliances such as washing machines and microwaves contain microprocessors that control their function (such dedicated microprocessors are generally referred to as microcontrollers).

Many households own a PC, which can be used for word processing, Internet access, entertainment etc. The connection of PCs to the Internet gives people access to websites across the world enabling them to shop, carry out banking transactions, make travel arrangements, and carry out research from the comfort of their own homes. Internet access also allows people to communicate on a worldwide scale via e-mail for business and pleasure purposes.

Specialised computer usage

- **Healthcare:** computerised devices are now commonly used in healthcare to detect and diagnose illnesses. Some examples are: the medical scanners able to assist in areas such as the imaging of cancerous tumours; automated chemical analysers for evaluating blood samples and detecting mineral and vitamin deficiencies; patient monitoring systems – computerised devices are widely used to continuously monitor patients' vital signs after major surgery or in cases of critical illness
- **Industry:** computers have been used for many years to control industrial processes. Industrial robots are computer-controlled machines, widely used in various production processes where the process comprises tasks which require extreme precision, are repetitive and/or dangerous. Robots are used in areas such as car and aircraft manufacturing for handling nuclear materials etc.

What computers cannot be used for

Computers process data and produce information at exceptionally high speeds and are therefore capable of performing such tasks much more accurately and speedily than humans. However, computers cannot function without human assistance. The type and quality of data input depend upon humans. The way a computer processes data is entirely dependent upon how it has been programmed (with instructions written by humans). Thus in order for a computer to solve a problem, the problem solution must be first devised and instructions conveyed to the computer. Without this human understanding, the computer is powerless.

Although there have been considerable developments in the field of Artificial Intelligence, which attempts to use computers for tasks which require some form of human intelligence (e.g. computers that play chess or undertake medical diagnoses), computers cannot think independently of humans or make moral judgements. Computers are incapable of performing any tasks that involve the application of such human qualities.

The advent of computer networks and the advances that have been made in the development of storage technologies make it possible to store a vast amount of information and this can be rapidly retrieved on a global scale. This introduces various ethical issues, many of which have still to be addressed.

Activity 1.3

Use of computers

List twenty uses of computer systems (don't just focus on the uses of personal computers, but rather consider other types of computing machine).

List ten things that a computer cannot do.

1.7 Computers in problem solving

There is a widespread belief that computers can solve any problem, and that the results generated by computers can be trusted without question – since the computer has calculated the result, it must be accurate. Both of these assumptions are erroneous and we now briefly consider the accuracy of the result derived from the computational process, and the ability of a computer to solve any problem.

Accuracy of result

The result generated by a computer is based on the computer following the set of unambiguous instructions. As we have seen, these instructions and the associated data form the computer program. In order for a computer to obtain a result, we must explicitly indicate to the computer all aspects of the computer program. Creating programs is often a complex undertaking and it is often impossible to prove the correctness of a program. If there are errors in the program, then the computer may still produce a result, but the result could well be incorrect. In addition, in order to create the computer program, the programmer must fully understand the problem that is to be solved. A computer has no innate intelligence, nor can it apply common sense to a problem. If the programmer does not fully understand the problem that is to be solved, then this is likely to lead to the program being incorrectly designed, and again to an erroneous result. Finally, we note that often data must be input to the computer system, and it will be on this data that the program executes and so derives the result. If the data is incorrect, then it is likely that the result will suffer. In short – rubbish in, rubbish out!

Computability

Surprisingly, there are a number of seemingly simple problems that are not actually computable, in the sense that it could take centuries, or thousands of years, to obtain the result. One class of problem that causes particular difficulties as far as the computer is concerned arises when the number of computations that must be performed in order to obtain the result increases as the factorial of the size of the input data set. Let's take a brief, classic example, known as the Travelling Salesman Problem (TSP).

Imagine a salesman who has to make a sales trip involving his travelling by plane between a number of cities. Perhaps he is afraid of flying and therefore wishes to spend the minimum amount of time in the air, or alternatively he may just be in a hurry. Either way, given the set of cities that he has to fly between, he wishes to determine the optimum arrangement of flights in order to minimise his time in the air. If we take a simple case where there are only four cities (denoted A, B, C and D), then he may for example fly from A to B to C to D, or from B to D to C to A, etc. If he is to determine the optimum flight arrangement, then he will need to add up the total flying time for all possible combinations of flight. How many combinations are there?

In fact, the number of combinations is given by **n!** where n indicates the number of cities involved, and the exclamation mark denotes the factorial operation (for example, 3!= 3x2x1=6, 4!=4x3x2x1=24). However, since flying from A to B to C to D will take exactly the same time (in principle) as flying from D to C to B to A, the total number of different flying times is given by n! divided by 2. In the case that we have four cities, there are twelve combinations. A computer would have no problem handling this calculation. On the other hand, as we increase the number of cities, the number of combinations grows rapidly. Suppose that we have *twenty* cities: the number of potentially different combinations is now $1.2x10^{18}$; if we increase the problem to deal with flying between *fifty* cities, the number of potentially different combinations is about $1.5x10^{64}$!!

The difficulty is that the time it takes the computer to solve the problem grows enormously as we increase the number of cities, and so even for a relatively small number of cities it could easily take a computer centuries to look through all possible combinations and so obtain the result. This sort of problem occurs in a number of calculations and provides us with a simple example indicating that computers cannot necessarily solve all problems – there are some problems that are simply not computable.

1.8 Glossary

A glossary is a list and explanation of specialist and/or technical words or phrases. Example glossary entries in relation to this chapter are:

- **Computer:** a computer is a programmable machine used for processing information.
- **Hardware:** the physical components that make up a computer.

Can you think of better, or different, definitions for the words 'computer' and 'hardware'?

On page 191 various technical terms and acronyms are listed. You will find it helpful to regularly make additional entries there, recording the meaning of these terms as required. If it helps you to learn and understand a particular word, you could add simple diagrams.

Activity 1.4

Glossary

Consider the following terms:

- Computer
- Computer architecture
- Input device
- Output devices
- Hardware
- Software
- Computer memory.

Using the listing provided in the Glossary on page 191, write a glossary definition of each term in the list.

If it helps you to understand any of the terms, add appropriate diagrams.

1.9 Summary

In this chapter, we have introduced some basic ideas and have presented some important terminology. You have seen the difference between hardware and software and should have gained an insight into the synergy that can be created by bringing together hardware and software systems. The ability of software to control the operation and functioning of hardware provides us with a machine that is often referred to as a general purpose programmable machine, able to perform a wide range of tasks.

Although we tend to think of computers as a modern innovation, pioneering work into their development was in fact being carried out some 150 years ago. Within this context we have discussed the Difference and Analytical Engines, the former being (in essence) a calculator, and the latter a computing machine. We have also discussed some of the uses of computer technology and have alluded to various limitations.

1.10 Review questions

Review question 1.1

What do you understand by the phrase 'a general purpose programmable machine'?

Review question 1.2

State one fundamental difference between Charles Babbage's Difference and Analytical Engines.

Review question 1.3

State an important advantage of the 'stored program' computer architecture.

Review question 1.4

Explain why the development of the silicon chip denoted a major advance in computer technology.

Review question 1.5

Describe the three ways in which a computer is able to execute instructions.

Review question 1.6

What do you understand by the abbreviation 'CPU'?

Answers to review questions are to be found at the end of the book, starting on page 200.

1.11 Feedback on activities

Feedback on activity 1.1: Computer evolution

Workers at Xerox PARC developed the desktop PC. As a consequence, a computer user no longer had to share resources (such as the CPU and memory) with other computer users – they had at their disposal a computer dedicated to the tasks that they wished to perform. Performance was therefore guaranteed (unless of course they wished to carry out tasks across a network). Although the mouse was first prototyped in approximately 1964, it was refined and first integrated within the computer at PARC. Here the graphical event driven user interface and bitmapped display were also first developed (we will be discussing these later).

Feedback on activity 1.2: Distinguishing between the calculator and the computer

In the case of a simple calculator, we supply some input values and define the operation(s) that is to be performed upon these values. For example, we may enter '3+4='. The data we are supplying to the calculator is represented by the 3 and the 4, and the operation/function that we wish the calculator to perform is indicated as addition. The equals sign is essentially a further instruction that tells the calculator that we wish it to display the result of this calculation. Thus, the calculator is able to perform a set of clearly defined operations. On the other hand, a computing machine provides far greater power for it is able to change the sequence of instructions that are followed during the computational process. This highlights a fundamental difference between a calculating machine and a computing machine.

Feedback on activity 1.3: Use of computers

Compare your list with your colleagues' lists.

Do you agree with the items on the two lists?

Use the knowledge gained from this exercise to answer these questions.

- What are computers used for?
- Why use computers at all?
- For what tasks are they best suited?
- For what tasks are they least suited?
- What can you do with one computer?
- What can you do with a network of computers?

Feedback on activity 1.4: Glossary

Use the book content, your local library or the Internet to develop descriptions that are meaningful and clear. If you use the Internet, be selective as to which sites you use, as some sites (e.g. Wikipedia) may contain incorrect information.

Further reading

- Swade, D (2001), *The Cogwheel Brain*, Little Brown & Co

  This book provides a fascinating account of Charles Babbage's work on the Difference and Analytical Engines. By reading this book you will gain a deeper insight into the differences between the calculator and computer. The book also describes the work undertaken at the Science Museum in London on the construction of Babbage's Difference Engine.
- Black, E (2001), *IBM and the Holocaust*, Crown Publishing Group (NY)

  This book raises many issues in relation to the ethical use of computational systems. An interesting and very topical read for those wishing to learn more about early computational systems and how their use – if not carefully controlled – can lead to disastrous consequences.
- Smith DK & Alexander, RK (1999), *Fumbling the Future: How Xerox First Invented, Then Ignored, the First Personal Computer*, iUniverse.com

  During the 1970s, workers at Xerox PARC in the US undertook a major development programme ultimately resulting in desktop computer systems which closely resemble those we use today. This book describes many aspects of this development process through to the birth of the personal computer (PC). A fascinating and easy-to-read read book that will provide a great deal of useful background information.

- von Neumann, J (1945), *The First Draft Report on the EDVAC*

  This report is available online at the following URL: http://qss.stanford.edu/~godfrey/vonNeumann/vnedvac.pdf and was produced in the 1940s. A central theme is the stored program architecture which forms the basis of the modern computer. Today this is often incorrectly referred to as the 'Von Neumann architectural model'. In fact there is considerable debate as to who should have received credit for this work. By reading this document you will gain a greater insight into the concepts that underpin modern computing.

CHAPTER 2

Maths review

OVERVIEW

In our everyday lives we work in base 10 (the decimal number base). Computers operate in the binary number system (also referred to as base 2). In this chapter we briefly discuss aspects of this number base and also introduce hexadecimal (number base 16). This provides a compact and useful means of expressing binary values. We provide examples showing the conversion of numbers between base 10, base 2 and base 16.

Learning outcomes At the end of this chapter you should be able to:

- Describe why modern computers operate in binary
- Discuss the binary and hexadecimal number bases
- Convert between base 10 and base 2
- Convert between base 10 and base 16.

2.1 Introduction

All values stored within a computer are numerical. Even when we are carrying out a word processing activity, manipulating graphics or playing audio files, the computer is undertaking mathematical operations. In fact the digital world is entirely mathematical.

In our everyday lives, we make use of number base 10 (decimal) with ten different symbols for the representation of numbers. The computer operates in binary – number base 2 where there are only two symbols, '0' and '1'. In the next section, we briefly discuss several reasons for the adoption of base 2 for computer operation and in Section 2.3, we describe aspects of this number base.

Although binary is a very efficient number base for computer operation, it is not particularly efficient when used by human beings. This is because binary numbers tend to comprise many digits (1s and 0s – these are referred to as 'bits'). It is therefore often convenient to represent binary numbers in a more compact form using base 16 (also called hexadecimal – or simply 'hex'). In Section 2.4 we discuss the use of hexadecimal and show how binary numbers may be represented in this form.

2.2 The binary digital computer

Since the 1940s, binary has been the preferred number base for computer operation. There are two very important reasons for this:

The use of binary simplifies and facilitates the mathematical and logical operations carried out within the computer.

In the case of base 10, numbers are represented by means of ten symbols. In the case of base 2, we simply have two symbols (represented as '0' and '1'). In the computer, these symbols are usually represented by voltage levels. Thus, if a computer were to operate in base 10, it would be necessary to have ten different voltage levels and ensure that the electronic circuits could distinguish between these levels.

In the 1940s, computers were either electromechanically based, or made use of electrical components known as valves. Electronics constructed in this way was, by today's standards, relatively primitive and signals were often corrupted by noise. Thus, it was difficult to devise circuits that could reliably distinguish between a multitude of different voltage levels. For this reason, binary became an obvious choice – as here it is only necessary to distinguish between two levels of voltage.

The modern computer is referred to as a digital machine that operates in base 2. The term 'digital' is used to indicate that voltage levels within the computer can only exist in certain states. In the case of a computer operating in binary, there are only two such states – one state representing binary 0, and the other representing binary 1. For example, a binary 0 may be represented by a voltage that is close to zero volts and a binary 1 by a voltage that is close to five volts.

Although voltages are normally used to indicate one or other of the two binary states, it is also possible to represent the states in other ways. For example, current may also be used to represent the two binary states, and these states may also be represented optically (i.e. a binary 0 corresponding to the absence of light, and a binary 1 corresponding to the presence of light). The important point here is that as with a simple light-switch, only two states can exist: the light is on, or the light is off – it cannot be partially on or partially off.

In summary, although since the days of Charles Babbage computers have been proposed and/or produced which operate on number bases other than base 2, for many years now base 2 has been the preferred choice. Today, we see possible advantages of moving to computer systems that employ other number bases. However, such a transition would require an enormous investment in research and development.

Activity 2.1

Analogue and digital signals

Describe the computer in terms of a digital machine that operates in the base 2 number system.

Using your local library or the Internet, distinguish between analogue and digital signals.

2.3 The binary number system

All operations performed by a computer are mathematical and all material stored within a computer is represented numerically. Consequently, when for example we use a wordprocessor to create a text document, the letters and characters that form the document are actually stored and manipulated in numerical form! Since the 1940s, computers have used the binary number base (also referred to as base 2) and in this section we briefly introduce this system.

There are many different numbering systems, each system being based on a limited set of symbols. We normally work in base 10, for which there are 10 symbols. However, in the case of the binary system (base 2), there are only two symbols (0 and 1).

Let us consider the base 10 system. Given 10 symbols, there is no difficulty in representing numbers up to nine – we simply select the appropriate symbol. However, when wishing to represent a number greater than nine, we must employ a scheme that draws only on the ten symbols that are at our disposal. Here we assign a value to each symbol according to its position within the number. For example, consider representing the number twelve:

tens	**ones (units)**
1	2

Here, the symbol '1' represents the number of 10s and the symbol '2' the number of units. Thus twelve is indicated as one ten and (plus) two units. This scheme enables us to represent numbers of any size. Consider another example: suppose that we wish to represent two hundred and fifty-seven:

hundreds	**tens**	**units**
2	5	7

Here the number 257 is represented as:

257=(2*100) + (5*10) + (7*1)

where '*' indicates multiplication. Notice how the values assigned to each place in the number increase.

The number 3782 can similarly be expressed as follows:

$$3782 = (3*1000) + (7*100) + (8*10) + (2*1)$$

or, using powers of 10, as:

$$3782 = 3*10^3 + 7*10^2 + 8*10^1 + 2*10^0$$

(Remember that 10^0 is, by definition, equal to 1). Thus, in base 10, the position values increase by factors of 10, whereas in base 2 (which uses just two symbols, 0 and 1) the position values increase by a factor of 2. For example, the binary number 1011 has the following value:

eights	fours	twos	units
1	0	1	1

This indicates: $1011_2 = 1* 2^3 + 0* 2^2 + 1* 2^1 + 1* 2^0 = 11_{10}$

Notice the use of a *subscript notation* to indicate the number base being referred to (e.g. to indicate that 1011 is in fact a binary number, we place a subscript '2' after it).

A binary digit is called a 'bit'. In computer systems, a group of 8 bits is called a 'byte'. A byte can represent base 10 numbers from 0 to 255:

128s	64s	32s	16s	8s	4s	2s	1s
1	1	1	1	1	1	1	1

Thus, 11111111_2= $128+64+32+16+8+4+2+1=255_{10}$

Alternatively, we can obtain the same result by writing:

$$11111111_2$$

$$= 1*2^7 + 1*2^6 + 1*2^5 + 1*2^4 + 1*2^3 + 1*2^2 + 1*2^1 + 1*2^0$$

$$= 128 + 64 + 32 + 16 + 8 +4 + 2 + 1$$

$$= 255_{10}$$

Conversion from binary to decimal

Consider the number 11011012. To convert this to base 10, we simply need to write out our column (position) values and place the number under these columns. Since the binary number comprises seven bits, we need only seven columns:

64s	32s	16s	8s	4s	2s	1s
1	1	0	1	1	0	1

Thus, $1101101_2 = 64+32+8+4+1=109_{10}$

Alternatively, we can write:

11011012

$= 1*2^6 + 1*2^5 + 0*2^4 + 1*2 + 1*2^2 + 0*2^1 + 1*2^0$

$= 64 + 32+ 0 + 8 +4 +0 + 1$

$= 109_{10}$

By way of a further example, let us convert 1110011_2 to base 10. Again we write out the column values and place the number beneath these:

64s	32s	16s	8s	4s	2s	1s
1	1	1	0	0	1	1

And so, $1110011_2=64+32+16+2+1=115_{10}$

Alternatively, we can obtain the same result by writing:

1110011_2

$= 1*2^6+1*2^5 + 1*2^4 + 0*2^3 + 0*2^2 + 1*2^1 + 1*2^0$

$= 64 + 32 + 16 + 0 +0 + 2 + 1$

$= 115_{10}$

Scientific calculators usually provide the binary to base 10 conversion function. You should examine your calculator and familiarise yourself with this capability. However, it is important that you are also able to carry out this conversion manually. When developing computer programs, this can be very convenient.

Activity 2.2

Binary-to-decimal conversion

Convert the binary numbers 10001 and 11111 to decimal (base 10).

Conversion from decimal to binary

Having reviewed the conversion from binary to base 10, we now turn our attention to the reverse process – the conversion of a base 10 number into base 2. As with the binary-to-base 10 conversion process, most scientific calculators are able to perform the base 10-to-binary function. The ability to make use of this facility is important – but you should also be able to carry out this task manually.

The process is quite simple and is achieved as follows:

- Write out a number of binary column (position) values
- Identify which combination of these values will add together to equal the number that you are wishing to convert
- Place a '1' in each of these columns
- Place a zero in all other columns (excepting any unused columns which are to the left of the left-most 1
- The conversion is now completed.

Initially, this can sound a little complicated and is best understood by means of an example. Let us suppose that we wish to convert the (base 10) number 14 into base 2.

As indicated in the first point above, we begin by writing out column values. Here you may ask how many columns should we write out? The answer to this question is that once the column values become larger than the number that you are wishing to convert, then you have more columns than you will need. Thus to convert 14, we write out the following columns:

16s	**8s**	**4s**	**2s**	**1s**

We have stopped at this point because 16 is larger than the number that we are converting.

We now identify which of these numbers can be added together to form the number that we are to convert (there is only one combination). Thus in the case of 14, this can be obtained by adding together 8, 4 and 2.

Next, we place a '1' in each of these columns:

16s	**8s**	**4s**	**2s**	**1s**
	1	1	1	

We now place a zero in each of the other columns (ignoring the 16s column as this lies to the left of the left-most '1':

16s	**8s**	**4s**	**2s**	**1s**
	1	1	1	0

Thus 14_{10} equals 1110_2

Note that in some situations we may include zeros lying to the left of the left-most '1'. We shall ignore this for the moment.

Let us now consider a second example. Suppose that we wish to convert 44_{10} into base 2. Again we list the column values:

64	32	16	8	4	2	1

Here we have stopped at 64 because this is larger than the value that we wish to convert. We now consider the combination of numbers that may be added together to produce 44. Here we can see that if we add 32 and 16, we will obtain a sum that is larger than 44 – and so this is no good. However, if we add 32 and 8 we obtain 40. Add 4 to this, and we obtain 44. Thus:

64	32	16	8	4	2	1
	1	0	1	1	0	0

Hence $44_{10}=101100_2$

Activity 2.3

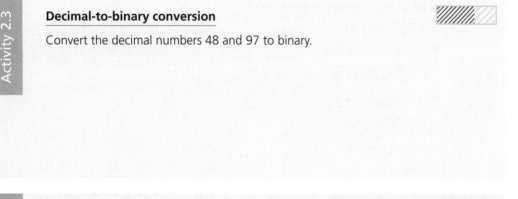

Decimal-to-binary conversion

Convert the decimal numbers 48 and 97 to binary.

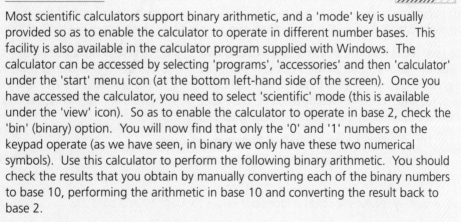

Activity 2.4

Binary arithmetic

Most scientific calculators support binary arithmetic, and a 'mode' key is usually provided so as to enable the calculator to operate in different number bases. This facility is also available in the calculator program supplied with Windows. The calculator can be accessed by selecting 'programs', 'accessories' and then 'calculator' under the 'start' menu icon (at the bottom left-hand side of the screen). Once you have accessed the calculator, you need to select 'scientific' mode (this is available under the 'view' icon). So as to enable the calculator to operate in base 2, check the 'bin' (binary) option. You will now find that only the '0' and '1' numbers on the keypad operate (as we have seen, in binary we only have these two numerical symbols). Use this calculator to perform the following binary arithmetic. You should check the results that you obtain by manually converting each of the binary numbers to base 10, performing the arithmetic in base 10 and converting the result back to base 2.

(a) 11+101=

(b) 1110-11=

(c) 100101*11=

Note '' represents the multiplication operation.*

2.4 Hexadecimal

Expressing numbers in binary often involves writing out long 'strings' of 1s and 0s. This is a very tedious process and is prone to error. Fortunately, there is a simple solution. Rather than writing numbers in binary format, it is convenient to write these in an alternative number base and, most commonly, base 16 is used for this purpose. You'll recall that base 2 is often referred to as binary. Similarly, base 16 has an alternative name – hexadecimal (often abbreviated to 'hex'). In this section we are not going to concern ourselves with why base 16 has been chosen for this purpose, other than to say that it provides a very efficient mechanism for representing binary numbers. (In fact, in earlier years base 8 was also used for this purpose.)

In the next two sections, we briefly describe how to convert a binary number into base 16 (hexadecimal) and also how to convert a base 16 number into binary. However, before we get down to this level of detail, let us briefly discuss base 16 in general terms.

As you will recall, in base 10 we have ten different symbols (0-9). In base 2, we have two symbols (0 and 1). Not surprisingly, therefore, in base 16 we have sixteen symbols. Here we make use of the traditional symbols 0-9 for representing numbers up to and including nine. The remaining six symbols are simply the letters A-F:

A represents 10

B represents 11

C represents 12

D represents 13

E represents 14

F represents 15

Thus, if we wish to write the base 10 number 'nine' in base 16, we have no problem – we simply make use of the same symbol (9). On the other hand, if we want to represent a base 10 number in the range 10-15 in hexadecimal, we simply make use of one of the above symbols (e.g. the base 10 number thirteen is simply represented using the symbol 'D').

You will recall that in the case of both 10 and base 2, it is possible to represent numbers of any value by making use of a digit's position value within the number. For example, if we wish to represent twenty-seven in base 10, then we place the 2 in the tens column, and the 7 in the ones (or units) column. We do similarly in the case of hexadecimal. For all numbers bases, there are only two things that change. These are:

- The number of symbols that we have at our disposal
- The value that we assign to each of the columns (position values) within the number.

Let us quickly review the column (position) values for base 10 and base 2:

Base 10: The column values increase by a factor of 10 – for example:

1000s 100s 10s 1s

Base 2: The column values increase by a factor of 2 – for example:

8	**4**	**2**	**1**

Following this pattern, it is apparent that in base 16, the column (position) values will increase by a factor of 16:

4096	**256**	**16**	**1**

Here, 256 is obtained by multiplying 16 by 16; 4096 is obtained by multiplying 256 by 16. The next column, if we needed it, would be obtained by multiplying 4096 by 16, etc.

Consider now the hexadecimal number A6. Let us suppose that we wish to convert this into base 10. We begin by identifying the column (position) values of the two digits:

16	**1**
A	6

We now multiply the number in each column by its associated column value and add together the results. Here we remember that the symbol 'A' refers to decimal 10 and so:

16*10 + 1*6 = 166

Thus the hexadecimal number A6 equals 166 in base 10. Let us try a further example – suppose that we wish to convert FFFF to base 10, First, identify the column (position) values:

4096	**256**	**16**	**1**
F	F	F	F

Multiply each number by its associated column value and add the results. Here we recall that the symbol 'F' represents 15 in base 10. Thus:

4096*15 + 256*15 + 16*15 + 1*15 = 65535

Activity 2.5

Converting from hex to base 10

Convert the hexadecimal number 4E to base 10.

2.5 Binary and hexadecimal

In this section we briefly explain how to convert from binary to hexadecimal and vice versa. We will look at these two conversion processes in turn:

Binary to hexadecimal

This may be achieved by means of the following four steps:

- Starting from the least significant end of the binary number (this normally means starting from the right-hand end), we split the binary number into groups of 4 digits
- We treat each group of 4 digits separately and insert the column (position) values of each digit within the group
- We multiply each column containing a binary '1' by its column value and add together the results. This is the same as adding together the column values containing a binary '1'. Again we treat each group of 4 digits independently
- In the case that a result obtained in the previous step is larger than 9, we write the number using the letters A-F (where A=10, B=11, etc).

It is perhaps easier to understand the above by reference to a simple example. Let us suppose that we wish to convert the binary number 11000011 to hexadecimal. We begin by dividing the number into groups of 4 bits:

1100 0011

We now assign column (position values) to each group of 4 bits – remember to treat each group of 4 bits independently:

8s	**4s**	**2s**	**1s**	**8s**	**4s**	**2s**	**1s**
1	1	0	0	0	0	1	1

For both of the two groups we now multiply the binary 1s by their column (position) values:

Right-hand group of 4 bits: 8*1 + 4*1 = 12

Left-hand group of 4 bits: 2*1 + 1*1 = 3

12 is larger than 9, and is represented by the letter 'C'. Thus 11000011=C3 in base 16 (hexadecimal).

Activity 2.6

Converting from binary to hex

Convert the binary number 11010101 to base 16.

The conversion process is summarised in Figure 2.1.

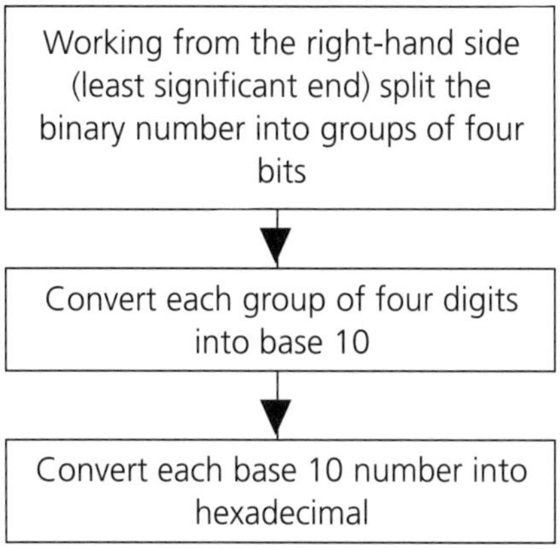

Figure 2.1: The conversion of a binary number into hexadecimal (base 16).

Hexadecimal-to-binary conversion

This process reverses the steps followed in (1) above. The steps followed may be summarised as:

- Examine each digit within the hexadecimal number
- If the digit is represented by a letter rather than as a number in the range 0-9, then the letter should be replaced by its numerical equivalent. For example, in the case of the hexadecimal number F4, we would represent the letter 'F' by the decimal value 15, and make no change to the '4' as this is already represented by a 'conventional' number
- We write out some column (position) values for groups of 4 binary digits. The number of groups that we write down corresponds to the number of digits in the original hexadecimal number. For example, for the hexadecimal number FC3, we would write out three groups of column values:

8	**4**	**2**	**1**	**8**	**4**	**2**	**1**	**8**	**4**	**2**	**1**

- We now enter each digit obtained from the first step within the column value table created in the second step. Thus, in the case of the hexadecimal number FC3, we would have expressed the 'F' as 15 and the 'C' as 12 (the '3' remaining unchanged). We now represent each of these numbers in binary form:

8	**4**	**2**	**1**	**8**	**4**	**2**	**1**	**8**	**4**	**2**	**1**
1	1	1	1	1	1	0	0	0	0	1	1

Thus the hexadecimal number FC3 = 111111000011 in base 2.

Consider a further example – let us suppose that we wish to convert the hexadecimal number 3B2 to binary:

- This number contains only one letter – 'B'. This is used to represent the decimal value of eleven. Thus we consider our hexadecimal number to be represented as a 3, 11, 2.

We now draw up our column (position) values for three groups of binary digits:

8	**4**	**2**	**1**	**8**	**4**	**2**	**1**	**8**	**4**	**2**	**1**

The conversion process is summarised in Figure 2.2

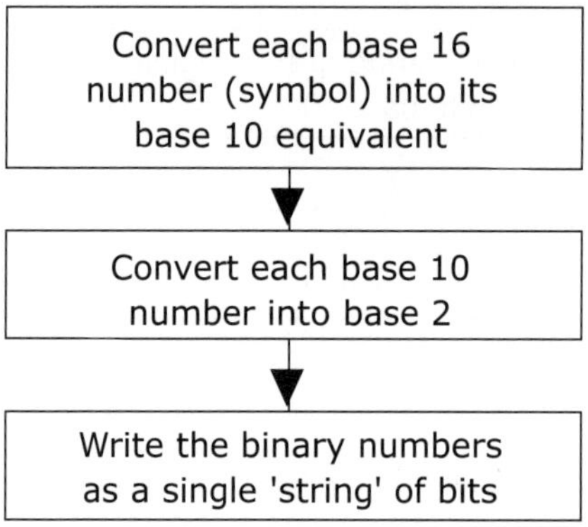

Figure 2.2: The hexadecimal to binary conversion process.

We now convert each of the numbers obtained in the first step, using the column values drawn up in the second step:

8	**4**	**2**	**1**	**8**	**4**	**2**	**1**	**8**	**4**	**2**	**1**
0	0	1	1	1	0	1	1	0	0	1	0

Thus the hexadecimal number 3B2 equals the binary number 001110110010. In some situations we may remove the two zeros that are located at the most significant end (left most).

Activity 2.7

Converting from hexadecimal to binary

Convert the hexadecimal number BA to binary.

2.6 Summary

In this chapter, we have briefly described the use of the binary and hexadecimal number bases. The examples provided coupled with the activity and review questions have given you the opportunity to practise undertaking conversions between these bases.

2.7 Review questions

Review question 2.1

Convert the following binary number to decimal: 11011.

Review question 2.2

Consider a 4 bit binary number. In base 10, what range of numbers could this represent?

Review question 2.3

Why is hexadecimal commonly used for the representation of binary numbers?

Review question 2.4

In hexadecimal, what is the meaning of the symbols 'A' and 'D'?

Review question 2.5

Convert the binary number 10000111 into hexadecimal.

Review question 2.6

What do you understand by the term 'digital signal'?

Review question 2.7

Convert the hexadecimal number B2 to binary.

Review question 2.8

Convert the binary number 110101 to hexadecimal.

Review question 2.9

What is meant by the term 'bit'?

Review question 2.10

What is the maximum number of hexadecimal digits that are needed to represent 24 binary digits?

2.8 Feedback on activities

Feedback on activity 2.1: Analogue and digital signals

A digital signal can only take on certain values. Consequently, it can only exist in certain states. In the case of a computer, which employs base 2, the digital signal can only take on two states, these corresponding to the values 0 and 1. This is rather like a normal room light, which can only take on the two states; that is, it is either turned fully on, or is off. This contrasts with an analogue signal, which can take on any value in a certain range. Again, using the light example, rather than employing a conventional switch, we could make use of an adjustable control which allows us to continuously vary the illumination in a room. Here the bulb may take on any 'brightness' between the range of being fully illuminated and being turned off. Computers have not always been digital machines, and through until the 1970s analogue computer were widely used – particularly in science and engineering. These computers could calculate mathematical functions at extremely high speeds.

Feedback on activity 2.2: Binary-to-decimal conversion

To convert 10001 to decimal:

16s	**8s**	**4s**	**2s**	**1s**
1	0	0	0	1

Thus 10001_2 equals $16+1=17_{10}$

To convert 11111 to decimal:

16s	**8s**	**4s**	**2s**	**1s**
1	1	1	1	1

Thus 11111_2 equals $16+8+4+2+1=31_{10}$

Feedback on activity 2.3: Decimal-to-binary conversion

To convert 48 to binary:

32	**16**	**8**	**4**	**2**	**1**
1	1	0	0	0	0

To convert 97 to binary:

64	**32**	**16**	**8**	**4**	**2**	**1**
1	1	0	0	0	0	1

Feedback on activity 2.4: Binary arithmetic

(a) 11+101= 3+5=8. This corresponds to the binary number 1000.

(b) 1110-11= 14-3=11. This corresponds to the binary number 1011.

(c) 100101*11=37*3= 111. This corresponds to the binary number 1101111.

Feedback on activity 2.5: Converting from hex to base 10

16	**1**
4	E

16*4 + 1*14 = 78

(Here we remember that the symbol 'E' represents decimal 14.)

Feedback on activity 2.6: Converting from binary to hex

8	**4**	**2**	**1**	**8**	**4**	**2**	**1**
1	1	0	1	0	1	0	1

8+4+1=13=D

4+1=5

Thus, the binary number 11010101 = D5 in hex.

Feedback on activity 2.7: Converting from hexadecimal to binary

'B' represents decimal 11 and 'A' decimal 10.

8	**4**	**2**	**1**	**8**	**4**	**2**	**1**
1	0	1	1	1	0	1	0

Thus the hex number BA equals 10111010 in binary.

Further reading

Burrell, M (2004), *Fundamentals of Computer Architecture*, Palgrave.

This book covers many aspects of basic logic circuits.

CHAPTER 3

Logic gates: An overview

OVERVIEW

The electronic circuits comprising a computer are constructed using simple building blocks that are referred to as 'logic gates' – or simply 'gates'. Once the operation of these gates is understood, it is possible to interconnect them and build more complicated circuits. As we discuss in this chapter, a computer comprises very large numbers of gates – each performing a precisely defined but seemingly trivial function. The power of the computer is derived not from the complexity of the individual gates but rather by their collective and combined actions.

Learning outcomes

At the end of this chapter you should be able to:

- Demonstrate a knowledge of logic gates and their associated symbols
- Discuss the operation of basic logic gates
- Understand the functionality of basic combinational and sequential circuits
- Consolidate your understanding of the binary and hexadecimal number bases.

3.1 Introduction

Today's computers are constructed from a small variety of 'building blocks' known as 'logic gates' (or simply 'gates'). Each gate serves a simple but precisely defined purpose. The power of the computer arises not as a consequence of the complex functionality of individual logic gates, but rather because of the power which can be obtained through the interconnection of very large numbers of such gates.

In this chapter we begin by looking at a number of simple logic gates. These comprise elementary circuits which operate upon binary values. We emphasise that the functionality of each gate is extremely simple and provide examples of simple digital circuits that can be constructed from logic gates. Here, you will see that even with a very small number of gates, we can perform a variety of useful tasks.

Additionally, in this chapter we revisit the binary and hexadecimal number bases and provide examples of conversions between base 2, base 10 and base 16.

3.2 Basic logic gates

Consider for a moment the construction of the walls of a building, such as a house. Given that you were faced with undertaking this task, where would you begin? Although the project would commence with the design phase, the actual construction would follow the ordering of the necessary materials. Here you would find that you did not in fact need many different materials. Typically, you would need a great number of bricks, several window frames, door frames and large amounts of cement and sand. Armed with these simple materials, you would be able to make buildings of all shapes and sizes.

When we think of a computer, we often imagine it to be constructed from immensely complex circuits. In fact, a computer can be compared with the example given above – it is essentially constructed by the use of many instances of simple building blocks. These building blocks are referred to as logic gates or, more simply, as gates. A gate consists of a simple electronic circuit which has some inputs and some outputs. We interconnect these gates on a vast scale, and each is responsible for reacting in some way to the binary input values that are presented to it.

The gates used in a computer may be compared to the bricks, cement and other materials used in the construction of a house. Although a single brick is not of any particular value to us, by bringing together many thousands of these bricks we can create buildings of different size and form, with all sorts of functions.

Perhaps it is surprising that something as complicated as a computer can be created by the interconnection of only a small number of different types of gate. The manufacture of various types of gate facilitates the construction and speed of operation of digital hardware. The availability of different types of gate relates therefore to convenience rather than absolute necessity. We will now briefly review the functionality of some key gates:

- **The invertor (NOT gate)**
- **The AND gate**
- **The NAND gate**
- **The OR gate**
- **The NOR gate**
- **The exclusive OR gate.**

Invertor (NOT gates)

The invertor (also commonly referred to as the NOT gate) is the simplest of all gates. As the word 'invertor' implies, the function of this gate is to invert the signal presented to it. It has one input and one output. If a binary 1 (called a logic high) is presented to the input, then the output will be a binary 0 (called a logic low). Conversely, if a logic low is presented to the input, the output will be a logic high.

All gates are represented in circuit diagrams by means of different symbols, and the symbol for an invertor is shown in Figure 3.1. You will note that there is a small circle at the output of the gate. Whenever you see such a circle, it indicates that the gate has an inverting function. In Figure 3.1 we also illustrate the functionality of the gate in the small table, which shows the two possible logic states that can be applied to the input, and the corresponding logic states produced at the output. A table that illustrates the logical function of a gate is referred to as a 'truth table'. Such tables are very convenient and can be used not only to show the logical operation of individual gates, but also to summarise the logical operation of circuits that are constructed from any number of gates.

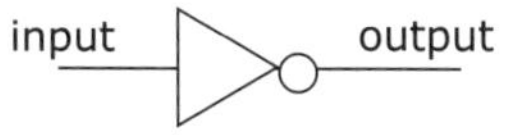

symbol for invertor

input	output
0	1
1	0

Truth table

Figure 3.1: The symbol and truth table for an invertor

A gate is constructed on a silicon chip and consists of simple electronic components. When the input state applied to the gate changes, it takes the components within the gate a certain time to react to these changes and so produce an output. Thus, if the input applied to a gate is changed, it takes a certain (very small) amount of time for this change to be reflected at the output. This delay in the reaction of a gate to an input change is referred to as the gate's propagation delay. These are very small; typically a few nanoseconds (10^{-9} seconds), and it might seem that such small delays are of no significance. However, we must remember that computers operate at extremely high speeds and therefore even very small delays can be significant. It is not the delay associated with a single gate that ultimately counts, but rather the sum of all the delays associated with many gates that form circuits within the computer.

If you have not previously encountered gates, you may well wonder what use an invertor may be. In Figure 3.2 we present a simple circuit diagram showing three invertors connected together. The output of the third invertor is connected back to the input of the first invertor. Let us suppose that when we turn the power on to this circuit, wire A happens to be at a logic high. The output from invertor 1 will then be at a logic low, consequently the output from invertor 2 will be at a logic high, and in turn the output from invertor 3 will be at a logic low. If we now work our way through the circuit again, we will see that wire A will again change state. In short (and in principle) the circuit oscillates – it has no stable state. Each wire switches between being at a logic high and a logic low. This circuit will therefore produce a waveform as indicated in Figure 3.2, and therefore acts as a 'clock' providing pulses which could be used for timing purposes. In fact, the operation of this circuit is somewhat more complex, and in order to ensure that the circuit oscillates, it may be necessary to include additional components.

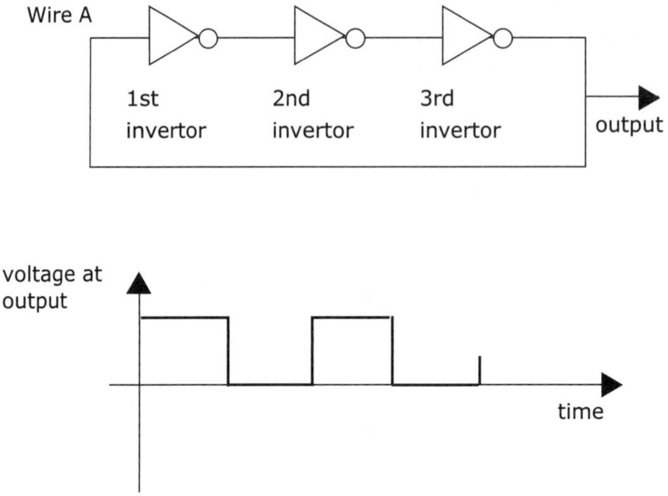

Figure 3.2: A simple oscillator formed from three invertors. In principle, the speed of the clock is governed by the propagation delays of the three gates.

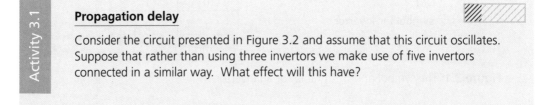

Activity 3.1

Propagation delay

Consider the circuit presented in Figure 3.2 and assume that this circuit oscillates. Suppose that rather than using three invertors we make use of five invertors connected in a similar way. What effect will this have?

Activity 3.2

The action of an invertor

Consider the circuit shown in Figure 3.2. Suppose that it is constructed using an even rather than an odd number of gates. For example, you may consider a circuit comprising two invertors or four invertors, connected together in the manner indicated in Figure 3.2. What will be the behaviour of this circuit?

AND gates

The AND gate is slightly more difficult to understand than the invertor. The AND gate has more than one input (typically between two and eight inputs), and a single output. If any of the inputs are in a logic low state, then the output will also be a logic low. This can be easily remembered as:

- **Any low gives a low.**

The symbol for an AND gate is given in Figure 3.3 with its truth table. Here, we show an AND gate with two inputs, and as can be seen from the truth table, if either of these inputs is a logic low then the output is also a logic low.

Consequently, the output from the gate can only be a logic high if the inputs are all logic highs. As with an invertor, this functionality does not seem particularly complicated, and it is difficult to imagine that such a simple circuit can be of such importance in the implementation of computer systems.

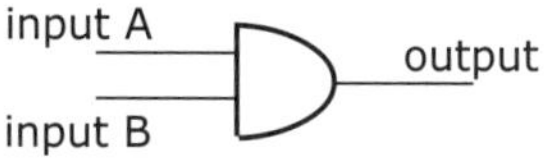

A 2-input AND gate

A	B	output
0	0	0
0	1	0
1	0	0
1	1	1

Truth table

Figure 3.3: A 2-input AND gate and its truth table

As with the invertor and all other gates, there is a propagation delay associated with the operation of the AND gate.

NAND gates

Silicon chips containing NAND gates are readily available, but if one does not have access to a specifically manufactured NAND gate, it can be reproduced by combining an AND gate with an invertor. In Figure 3.4, we provide the symbol for a NAND gate, and its truth table. In Figure 3.5 we show how a NAND gate can be implemented using an AND gate connected to an invertor (which you will recall from above is also referred to as a NOT gate). In fact, the word NAND is created by bringing together the words 'NOT' and 'AND'. Thus, a NAND gate is a 'NOT AND' gate!

As you will see from the truth table, if any of the inputs of the NAND gate are at a logic low, then the output is a logic high. This can easily be remembered as:

- **Any low gives a high.**

If you spend a moment considering the implementation of the NAND gate using a NOT and an AND gate, as shown in Figure 3.3, you will see that in the implementation of the NAND gate we have simply inverted the output from an AND gate. You should verify that the circuit comprising the NOT and AND gates has the same logic functionality as the NAND gate.

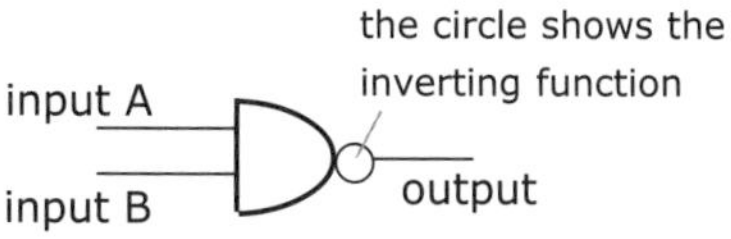

A 2-input NAND gate

A	B	output
0	0	1
0	1	1
1	0	1
1	1	0

Truth table

Figure 3.4: A 2-input NAND gate and its truth table

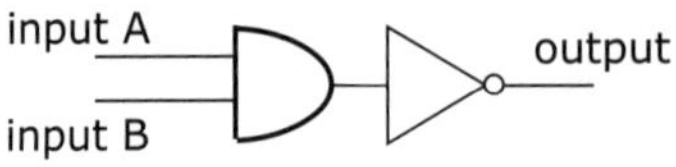

Figure 3.5: A NAND gate may be formed by connecting an AND gate to an Invertor

As with the AND gate, a NAND gate has two or more inputs (typically between two and eight), and a single output. Referring to the symbol for the NAND gate which is illustrated in Figure 3.4, you will see that this symbol is the same as the symbol for the AND gate but has a small circle at the output. As indicated above when we discussed the invertor, this circle indicates that the gate has an inverting function.

By connecting together the inputs of a NAND gate, an invertor may be constructed. This is illustrated in Figure 3.6.

Activity 3.3

Forming an invertor from a NAND gate

Draw up a truth table for the circuit illustrated in Figure 3.6, and hence verify that the circuit acts as an invertor.

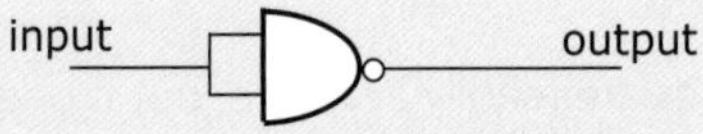

Figure 3.6: When the inputs of a NAND gate are connected together it acts as an invertor

Activity 3.4

A 3-input NAND gate

Draw up a truth table for a 3-input NAND gate.

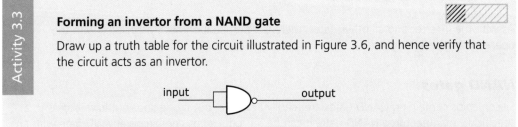

OR gates

As with the AND and NAND gates, the OR gate has two or more inputs. The symbol for a 2-input OR gate is given in Figure 3.7 together with the corresponding truth table.

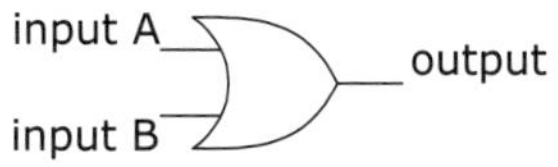

A 2-input OR gate

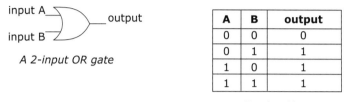

A	B	output
0	0	0
0	1	1
1	0	1
1	1	1

Truth table

Figure 3.7: The symbol for a 2-input OR gate and its truth table

NOR gates

The NOR gate derives its name from the 'NOT OR' designation. This means that it is an OR gate whose output is inverted. The symbol for a 2-input NOR gate is provided in Figure 3.8. Here, you will see that this symbol is the same as that used for an OR gate, but is followed by a small circle which indicates its inverting function. A NOR gate has 2 or more inputs – most commonly between 2 and 8 inputs are provided.

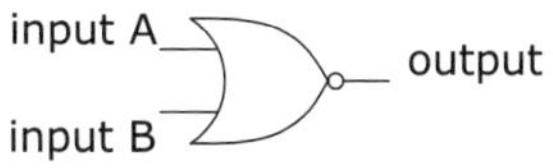

A	B	output
0	0	1
0	1	0
1	0	0
1	1	0

Truth table

Figure 3.8: The symbol for a 2-input NOR gate and its truth table

Exclusive OR gates

The name 'exclusive OR' is usually abbreviated to 'XOR'. Again, this has two or more inputs and, in the case of the 2-input XOR gate, its functionality is the same as the OR gate other than when the two inputs are a logic high. In this case, the output is a logic low. The symbol for a 2-input exclusive OR gate and its corresponding truth table are given in Figure 3.9.

In the case that an XOR gate has more than 2 inputs, the gate generates an output that is a logic high when an odd number of logic highs are applied to the inputs.

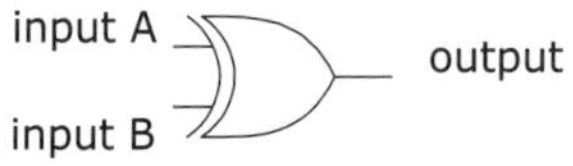

A 2-input XOR gate

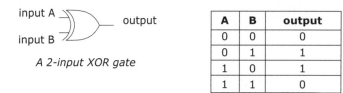

A	B	output
0	0	0
0	1	1
1	0	1
1	1	0

Truth table

Figure 3.9: The symbol for a 2-input XOR gate and its truth table

3.3 Combinational and sequential logic

The gates that we have introduced in the previous section provide the essential building blocks from which the computer is constructed. These gates are fabricated in large numbers on the CPU chip and interconnected to provide the required functionality. They are also used to implement memory devices etc.

The gates may be used to create circuits that are broadly divided into two categories:

- **Combinational logic:** a combinational logic circuit has outputs that are completely defined by the combination of input states. Thus, given a certain set of binary input values, the circuit will produce a certain result (output). For example, the basic AND, OR and NOT gates provide simple examples of combinational logic circuits. As we will see in the next section, these may be interconnected to provide us with more complex combinational logic circuits
- **Sequential logic:** a sequential logic circuit differs from combinational logic in that the outputs depend not only on the combination of inputs but also on the sequence in which they occur (i.e. on some previous state). The concept of sequential logic will be familiar to you but the term may not be. For example, a TV may have a single on/off button and the TV may be in one of two states – 'ON' or 'OFF'. The effect of pressing the on/off button will depend on the state of the TV before the button is pressed. If the TV is already turned on, then the effect of pressing the button will be to turn it off. If the TV is turned off, then pressing the button will turn it on. Thus the output resulting from the input depends on where we are in the on/off sequence. This is a simple example of sequential logic. Sequential logic circuits may be constructed using the combinational logic gates described in the previous section.

3.4 Combinational logic circuits

In this section we briefly examine some simple circuits constructed by means of the logic gates previously introduced. Here, we will examine several circuits and draw up truth tables for them. All circuits discussed in this section fall within the 'combinational' category mentioned in the previous section.

Consider the circuit provided in Figure 3.10. For all possible combinations of input, let us determine the corresponding outputs. This may be readily achieved by drawing up a truth table and including within this table the logic levels that appear on the connections between the gates (in this case there are two – labelled x and y in the illustration).

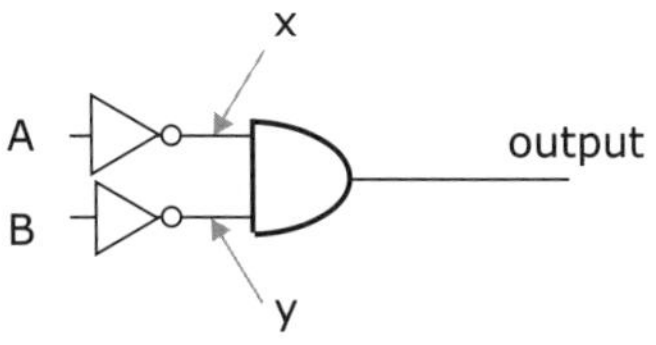

A	B	x	y	output
0	0	1	1	1
0	1	1	0	0
1	0	0	1	0
1	1	0	0	0

Figure 3.10: Example circuit 1

If we compare the input and corresponding outputs given in this table to the truth tables presented in Section 3.2, we will see that this circuit is acting as a NOR gate. Thus a NOR function may be implemented by means of two invertors and an AND gate.

Activity 3.5

Circuit behaviour 1

Consider the circuit provided in Figure 3.11. For all possible combinations of input, determine the corresponding outputs and state the function of the circuit.

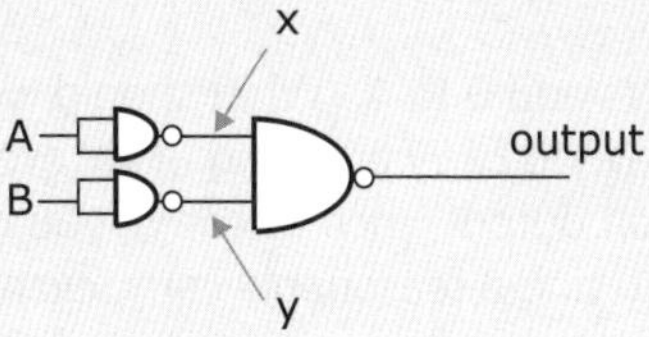

Figure 3.11: Example circuit 2

Activity 3.6

Circuit behaviour 2

Consider the circuit provided in Figure 3.12. For all possible combinations of input, determine the corresponding outputs. Hint: you should employ the same approach that was used in the previous activity.

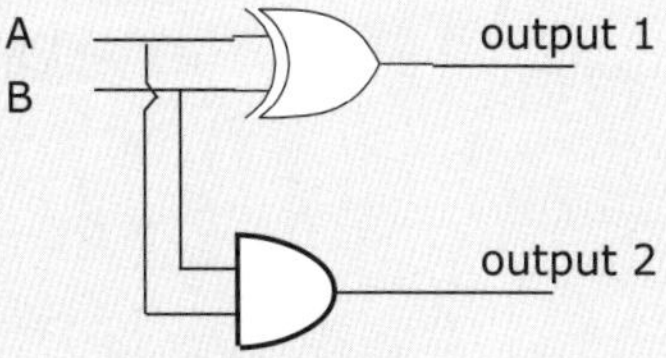

Figure 3.12: Simple example circuit

3.5 The half-adder

Addition of two bits

In this section we will briefly consider the creation of a circuit able to add together two binary digits (bits). However, before we do this, let us briefly look at the process of adding binary numbers. If you are still not confident with binary, further revision of this number base is provided in Section 3.7.

First, let us consider adding two 3-bit binary numbers. For example:

	1	1	0
+	0	1	1

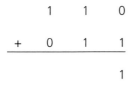

We start the addition process at the rightmost column (the least significant bit) and work our way to the left.

	1	1	0
+	0	1	1
			1

As we add, we may need to carry. We add 0 to 1. What should we carry? You might answer – 'nothing'. Technically, you don't have to carry anything. However, hardware isn't so simple. In general, once you decide there is an output (such as carry), you need to generate that output all the time. Thus, we need to find a reasonable carry, even when there's 'no need' to carry.

In this case, a reasonable carry is to carry a 0 into the next column, and then add that column.

		0	
	1	1	0
+	0	1	1
		0	1

This time, when we add the middle column, we get 0 + 1 + 1 which sums to 0, with a carry of 1.

	1	*0*	
	1	1	0
+	0	1	1
(1)	0	0	1

The final (leftmost) column adds 1 + 1 + 0, which sums to 0, and also generates a carry. We put the carry in parentheses on the left.

Typically, when we perform an addition of two k-bit numbers (such as binary numbers consisting of k binary digits: for example, if k = 2, then the binary numbers would each comprise two binary digits), the result can comprise k+1 bits. To handle that case, we have a carry bit (the one written in parentheses above).

The half-adder

As you look at how numbers are added, it seems to be column by column.

It makes sense to design a circuit that adds in 'columns'. Let us consider adding the rightmost column. We are adding two bits. So, the adder we want to create should have two inputs bits. It generates a sum bit for that column, plus a carry. So there should be two bits of output. This device is called a half-adder.

- **Data inputs:** 2 (call them A and B)
- **Outputs:** 2 (call them SUM, for sum, and CARRY, for carry)

We have already encountered a circuit able to perform this addition task (see Figure 3.12). However, it is more appropriate to label 'output 1' as 'sum' and 'output 2' as 'carry'.

Inspection of the truth table provided in the feedback to activity 3.6 will confirm that this circuit is performing binary addition of B to A (recalling that in binary 1+1 = 0, carry 1). Such a circuit is called a half-adder; the reason for this is that it enables a *carry out* of the current arithmetic operation – but no *carry in* from a previous arithmetic operation.

3.6 Example sequential logic circuits

In Section 3.3 we referred to the concept of a 'sequential logic' circuit. Here, the logic state(s) of a circuit's output(s) depends not only on the present values of the inputs applied to the circuit but also the circuit's previous state. In this section we provide several examples of circuits of this type.

Consider the circuit presented in Figure 3.13. As may be seen, this circuit employs 'feedback' since the outputs of the two NAND gates are 'fed back' to act as inputs. The two outputs are labelled Q and$\overline{Q}$ (generally expressed as 'Q bar'). The use of the 'bar indicates that the two outputs are always (or should be) in opposite logic states (if, for example Q is a logic low, then $\overline{Q}$ will be a logic high).

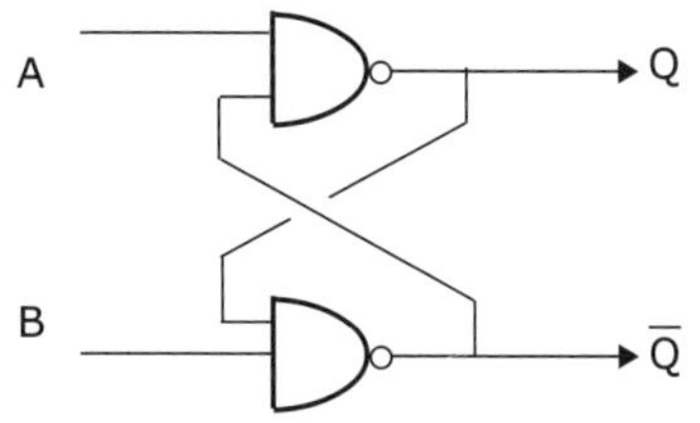

Figure 3.13: A simple example of sequential logic. This circuit is known as the 'RS bistable'

Consider the case that A is a logic low and B a logic high. Using the same approach as was adopted in the previous section, we can readily determine the output states (recall that for a NAND gate 'any low gives a high'). Since input A is low, it follows that the output from the top gate will be a logic high (thus Q is high). Both inputs to the lower NAND gate are high and so its output will be a logic low. Thus Q= high and $\overline{Q}$ =low . If we now change input A to a logic high state (leaving B unaltered) then this will have no impact on Q and $\overline{Q}$ (in fact we can say that the circuit 'remembers' its previous state).

Now consider the case that A is a logic high and B a logic low. Using the same reasoning as was used in the previous paragraph, it follows that Q will be a logic low and $\overline{Q}$ a logic high. If we now change input B to a logic high and leave A unaltered this will have no effect on the outputs. Again the circuit 'remembers its previous state.

Unfortunately, if a logic low is applied to both inputs, then any subsequent change to either one of the inputs has an undefined impact on the circuit. This can be understood by examination of the circuit. If both inputs are a logic low, then the outputs from both NAND gates will be high. If we now change A and B to a logic high, we cannot predict the states of Q and $\overline{Q}$ – this will simply depend on slight differences in the propagation delays of the two gates and so the circuit cannot be viewed as being stable. Consequently, we must avoid simultaneously applying a logic low to both inputs.

The operation of this circuit can be summarised as follows:

- If A=0 and B=1 then Q=1 and $\overline{Q}$ =0. Call this state 1.
- If A=1 and B=0 then Q=0 and $\overline{Q}$ =1. Call this state 2.
- If we now make A=1 and B=1, then the circuit will retain its previous state (state 1 or state 2); that is, it will 'remember' its previous state.

Note that when A=0 and B=1 then Q=1 and $\overline{Q}$ =0. Similarly, when A=1 and B=0 then $\overline{Q}$=1 and Q=0. Thus the output from the circuit corresponds to the inverted input. When Q=1 and $\overline{Q}$ =0 the circuit is said to be 'set' and in the converse case (Q=0 and $\overline{Q}$=1) the circuit is referred to as being in the 'reset' state. Additionally, when both inputs are a logic high the circuit is said to 'latch' (remember) the previous input.

As we have seen, the circuit can latch two input states (1,0 and 0,1) and the output is the inverted input. Since the circuit can exhibit two stable states it is referred to as a 'bistable' device and is generally called an 'RS latch' or 'RS bistable'. Here, the R and S indicate the set and reset conditions in which the circuit is able to exhibit stability and the 'bar' denotes its inversion of the inputs.

Activity 3.7

The RS bistable

Consider the circuit presented in Figure 3.14. Here, the two NAND gates employed in Figure 3.13 have bee replaced with two NOR gates. For this circuit, if A and B are both a logic high the input is said to be invalid. Thus there are three valid combinations of input 0,0; 0,1; 1,0. When the two inputs are a logic low, the circuit will latch the previously applied values (0,1 or 1,0). When A=1 and B=0 and when A=0 and B=1, determine the logic states of Q and $\overline{Q}$. Does this device invert the input values?

..../cont

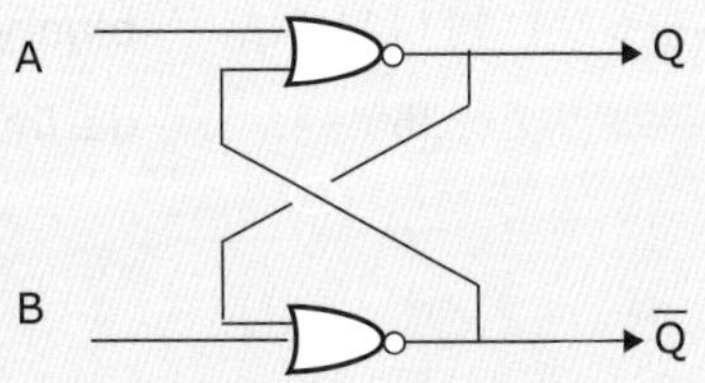

Figure 3.14: The implementation of a bistable using NOR gates

3.7 Consolidation of decimal, binary and hexadecimal number bases

A computer operates in the binary number system. In this section we revise our previous discussion of number bases and provide further examples that will help you consolidate your understanding of both binary and hexadecimal.

There are many different numbering systems; each number system is based on a set of symbols. We normally work in base 10 (decimal number system). As we have seen, the decimal system has 10 symbols. The computer, on the other hand, normally works with the binary system, which only has only two symbols (0 and 1). For convenience, when we are writing down binary numbers, we often represent them in a more compact form by means of hexadecimal (base 16) which has, unsurprisingly, 16 symbols. To make sure that there is no confusion about which base we are using, we will assume that in the absence of other indications it is decimal. We use a subscript for the base for all other systems:

101_2 FF_{16}

Our decimal number system is based on symbols 0, 1, 2, 3, 4, 5, 6, 7, 8, 9. A single 'place' that can hold these symbols is called a digit. To write a number in decimal we make use of these ten digit symbols and also use the method of place value (i.e. the position of a digit affects its meaning). For example, the number 3782 in decimal has four digits; the 2 is filling the *units* place, the 8 is filling the *tens*, the 7 is the *hundreds* and the 3 is filling the *thousands* place.

The number 3782 can therefore be expressed as follows:

$3782 = 3*1000 + 7*100 + 8*10 + 2*1$

or, using powers of 10, as:

$3782 = 3*10^3 + 7*10^2 + 8*10^1 + 2*10^0$

As we have seen, the binary number system uses just two symbols, 0 and 1. A computer carries out all its operations on binary numbers, and all material stored within the machine is represented using 1s and 0s. The binary number system employs the same positional notation as in the decimal number system – although the position (place) values are different.

$1011_2 = 1*2^3 + 0*2^2 + 1*2^1 + 1*2^0 = 11_{10}$

Each binary digit holds the value of increasing powers of 2 from the right to left.

A binary digit is called a bit. In computer systems, a group of 8 bits is called a byte.

A byte can represent numbers from 0 to 255 (i.e. 256 different values).

00000000	00000001	------>	11111111	**binary**
0	1	------>	255	**decimal**

11111111 (binary)

$= 1*2^7 + 1*2^6 + 1*2^5 + 1*2^4 + 1*2^3 + 1*2^2 + 1*2^1 + 1*2^0$

$= 128 + 64 + 32+ 16 + 8 +4 + 2 + 1$

$= 255$ (decimal)

We frequently refer to a certain number of bytes, and in this context when dealing with computers you will often encounter terms such as kilobyte (Kbyte), megabyte (Mbyte) and gigabyte (Gbyte). These terms have the following meanings:

- **Kilo** 1K $= 2^{10} =$ 1,024 bytes
- **Mega** 1M $= 2^{20} =$ 1,048,576
- **Giga** 1G $= 2^{30} =$ 1,073,741,824 (1,024 megabytes)
- **Terra** 1T $= 2^{40} =$ 1,099,511,627,776 (1,024 gigabytes)

1Kbyte is thus approximately 1,000 bytes, 1Mbyte is approximately 1,000,000 bytes, and 1Gbyte is approximately 1,000,000,000 bytes. These approximations are generally used and so, for example, we often interpret 1Kbyte as referring to 1,000 bytes.

Conversion from binary to decimal

Example: Convert 1101101_2 to decimal

To convert a binary number to a decimal number, each binary digit (from the right to the left) represents a power of 2:

1101101_2

$= 1* 2^6+ 1*2^5 + 0*2^4 + 1*2^3 + 1*2^2 + 0*2^1 + 1*2^0$

$= 64 + 32+ 0 + 8 +4 +0 + 1$

$= 109_{10}$

Example: Convert 1110011_2 to decimal

111011_2

$= 1*2^5 + 1*2^4 + 1*2^3 + 0*2^2 + 1*2^1 + 1*2^0$

$= 32+ 16 + 8 +0+2 + 1$

$= 59_{10}$

Conversion from binary to hexadecimal

To convert from binary to hexadecimal, make groups of 4 bits, starting from the binary numbers least significant end (the right-hand side). Add 0s to the most significant end of the number if needed. Then, just convert each bit group to its corresponding hexadecimal digit.

The reason for splitting the binary numbers into groups of 4 digits is that, as shown in the table below, each hexadecimal number can be expressed in terms of a 4-digit binary number.

Decimal numbers	Binary numbers	Hexadecimal numbers
0	0000	0
1	0001	1
2	0010	2
3	0011	3
4	0100	4
5	0101	5
6	0110	6
7	0111	7
8	1000	8
9	1001	9
10	1010	A
11	1011	B
12	1100	C
13	1101	D
14	1110	E
15	1111	F

Table 3.1: Conversion of binary to hexadecimal

Example: Convert 10111111_2 to hexadecimal

- Split the binary number (start from the right) into groups of 4 digits as shown below.

  1111

  1011

- Look at Table 3.1; the value of 1111 is F and the value of 1011 in hexadecimal is B in the table, so: $1011111_2 = BF_{16}$

Example: Convert 0111001_2 to hexadecimal

- Each hexadecimal digit represents 4 binary bits. Split the binary number into groups of 4 bits, starting from the right:

  1001 = 9

  0011 = 3

  Thus $0111001_2 = 39_{16}$

Conversion from hexadecimal to decimal and binary:

Each hexadecimal number can be expressed as a four-digit binary number as was shown in Table 3.1.

Example: Convert $A5_{16}$ to binary and decimal numbers

To convert a hexadecimal number to a decimal number, first we should convert the hexadecimal number to binary, as shown below:

- Converting from hexadecimal to binary is easy: just replace each hexadecimal digit with its equivalent 4-bit binary sequence as shown below:

  A5 = 1010 0101

- Then we can convert $1010\ 0101_2$ (from step 1) to a decimal number: each binary digit holds the value of increasing powers of 2, from the right to the left.

- Multiply each digit with the corresponding powers of 2 and add the multiplications to find the decimal representation of the binary number as shown below:

  $1010\ 0101_2$

  $= 1*2^7 + 0*2^6 + 1*2^5 + 0*2^4 + 0*2^3 + 1*2^2 + 0*2^1 + 1*2^0$

  $= 128 + 32 + 4 + 1$

  $= 165_{10}$

Example: Convert 85_{16} to binary and decimal numbers

- Converting from hexadecimal to binary is easy: just replace each hexadecimal digit with its equivalent 4-bit binary sequence as shown below:

  85 = 1000 0101

- Then we can convert this value, 10000101_2, to a decimal number. Each binary digit holds the value of increasing powers of 2, from the right to the left.

- Multiply each digit with the corresponding powers of 2 and add the multiplications to find the decimal representation of the binary number as shown below:

  10000101_2

  $= 1*2^7 + 0*2^6 + 0*2^5 + 0*2^4 + 0*2^3 + 1*2^2 + 0*2^1 + 1*2^0$

  $= 128 + 4 + 1$

  $= 133_{10}$

3.8 Summary

Our discussion on logic gates demonstrates the simplicity of these 'building blocks'. However, as you will have been able to see from the example circuits supplied, even a small number of gates can be used in a useful manner.

In this and previous chapter we have given considerable attention to the binary, decimal, and hexadecimal number bases. We have provided a number of examples to illustrate how numbers can be converted from one base into another. Although your calculator will probably provide this functionality, and on the Internet there are programs available to undertake these conversions for you, it is strongly recommended that you learn how to manually carry out these processes. With a little practice, you will be able to quickly convert between number bases, and in fact if the numbers are reasonably small you should be able to carry out the conversions in your head without recourse to pen and paper!

3.9 Review questions

Review question 3.1

Draw up a truth table for a 4-input NOR gate.

Review question 3.2

Evaluate the circuit shown here for all possible input combinations and record the results in a truth table.

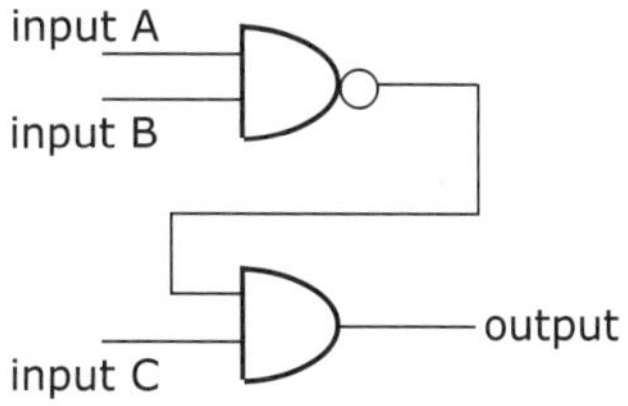

Review question 3.3

What do you understand by the term 'propagation delay'?

Review question 3.4

When a circle is drawn at the output of a gate, what does this signify?

Review question 3.5

How would you describe the purpose of a truth table?

Review question 3.6

Summarise in words the operation of a NAND and an AND gate.

Review question 3.7

Distinguish between the functionality of a 2-input OR and a 2-input XOR gate.

3.10 Feedback on activities

Feedback on activity 3.1: Propagation delay

The speed of oscillation will be reduced because the addition of two further invertors will increase the overall propagation delay of the circuit.

Feedback on activity 3.2: The action of an invertor

This circuit will not oscillate. If the input to the first invertor is a logic high, the output from this invertor will be a logic low, and in turn the output from the second invertor will also be a logic high. This is fed back to the first invertor, thus confirming its state of input. The circuit will then continue in this state. If you assume that the input to the first invertor is a logic low, then you can use the same reasoning to determine that this state will continue. Only circuits of this type which comprise an odd number of invertors will (in principle) oscillate.

Feedback on activity 3.3: Forming an invertor from a NAND gate

The truth table indicated below is formed by remembering that any logic low at the inputs will produce a logic high. Furthermore, since both inputs are connected together, they must both always have the same logic state.

Input	Output
0	1
1	0

The circuit does indeed act as an invertor – when the input is a logic low, the output is a logic high. Similarly, when the input is a logic high, the output is a logic low.

Feedback on activity 3.4: A 3-input NAND gate

In the table given below, A, B and C denote the three inputs.

A	B	C	Output
0	0	0	1
0	0	1	1
0	1	0	1
0	1	1	1
1	0	0	1
1	0	1	1
1	1	0	1
1	1	1	0

Feedback on activity 3.5: Circuit behaviour 1

Again, this is readily achieved by means of a truth table that indicates not only input and output values but also the logic states of the intermediate connections. These connections are denoted as x and y in the circuit and truth table.

A	B	x	y	Output
0	0	1	1	0
0	1	1	0	1
1	0	0	1	1
1	1	0	0	1

From this truth table, it can be seen that the circuit is acting as an OR gate.

Feedback on activity 3.6: Circuit behaviour 2

A	B	Output 1	Output 2
0	0	0	0
0	1	1	0
1	0	1	0
1	1	0	1

Feedback on activity 3.7: The RS bistable

The circuit does not invert the inputs.

Further reading

- Burrell, M (2004), *Fundamentals of Computer Architecture*, Palgrave
  This book covers many aspects of basic logic circuits.

CHAPTER 4

General principles

In this chapter we build on previous discussion and consider a number of aspects of computer hardware. The stored program computer model that dates back to the 1940s is fundamental to the operation of the modern computer. By building on this model we are able to gain an insight into the operation of a simple conceptual computer architecture.

Learning outcomes At the end of this chapter you should be able to:

- Discuss the basic structure of a computer
- Discuss issues relating to the concept of the 'stored program' computer model
- Discuss a basic computer architecture with reference to the address, data and control buses
- Distinguish between various forms of computer.

4.1 Introduction

In this chapter we briefly introduce the 'stored program' computer architecture that appears to have been first proposed in the 1940s, and rapidly became the subject of considerable research activity. This configuration represented a major technical advance and underpins the modern computer architecture. Often in literature this approach is incorrectly attributed to a Hungarian mathematician, John von Neumann, whereas it was in fact the work of a number of people. However, the concept was recorded in a report written by von Neumann and presented under his name. Consequently – as often happens in the reporting of historical events – subsequent writers have tended to exclusively associate von Neumann with the 'stored program' computer model, without making reference to the factual events. In this book we will simply refer to the 'stored program' computer model, and avoid assigning any particular person's name to this computing paradigm.

In Section 4.3, we extend our discussion and introduce the address, data and control buses that are used to connect the central processor unit (CPU or simply 'processor') to peripheral devices such as memory and input/output controllers. We also consider in general terms the way in which the processor is able to perform read and write operations.

In Section 4.4 we briefly introduce key components within the processor and here you will encounter 'registers' that are provided on the processor chip, and which play a pivotal role in its operation. More detailed discussion of elements within the CPU is deferred to Chapter 7.

Other sections of the chapter focus on different forms of computer: specifically the traditional mainframe and minicomputer systems, together with the personal computer (PC). Through until the 1980s, this type of classification was particularly useful. However, as we discuss in Section 4.8, computers and computer-related technologies today are employed in an ever-greater number of forms and used across ever-more areas of application. As a result, the traditional ways in which computers were classified are less meaningful. On the other hand, this type of classification can still be of value – particularly when learning about the diversity and general characteristics of computers. Within this context we briefly discuss the client-server approach which is widely used today.

4.2 The 'stored program' computer model

This general computer architecture was proposed in the 1940s. It represents a major advance in the evolution of computer systems and forms the basis for the modern computer. As mentioned in Section 1.3, until that time computers were configured to perform the desired operations by setting switches and by means of cables that interconnected various components in a particular manner. Naturally, 'programming' a machine in this way is time-consuming, especially as each time that changes are made to the 'program', cables and switches have to be reconfigured. In the case of the 'stored program' architecture, the instructions that are to be executed by a computer are represented as numbers and placed within internal memory (located within the computer).

As may be seen from Figure 4.1, the computer comprises three basic subsystems:

- **The internal memory**
- **The central processing unit (CPU)**
- **Input/output devices.**

- **The internal memory**: this memory stores the program instructions and any associated data as a series of binary numbers. Memory comprises a series of locations and each location is able to store numbers in a certain range. A group of memory locations are illustrated in Figure 4.2. These may be thought of as separate storage compartments, and in the case of a computer's internal main memory, it is possible to change the values stored in each 'compartment' by 'writing' to it a new value, thus overwriting the value previously stored.

  Each location has a unique 'address'. This is used to identify the location that is to be 'written to' or 'read from'. Unlike the postal addresses that we use when mailing a letter, the addresses used when referencing a memory address are entirely numerical. Thus, each memory location has associated with it a unique numerical address.
- **The central processing unit (CPU):** as its name implies, the CPU is central to the computer and is responsible for:
  - fetching instructions from memory
  - executing (processing) these instructions and, when appropriate
  - returning the results of the computation to memory.

  Thus, the CPU reads instructions (and any associated data) from memory, executes each instruction, and when necessary 'writes' the results back to memory.

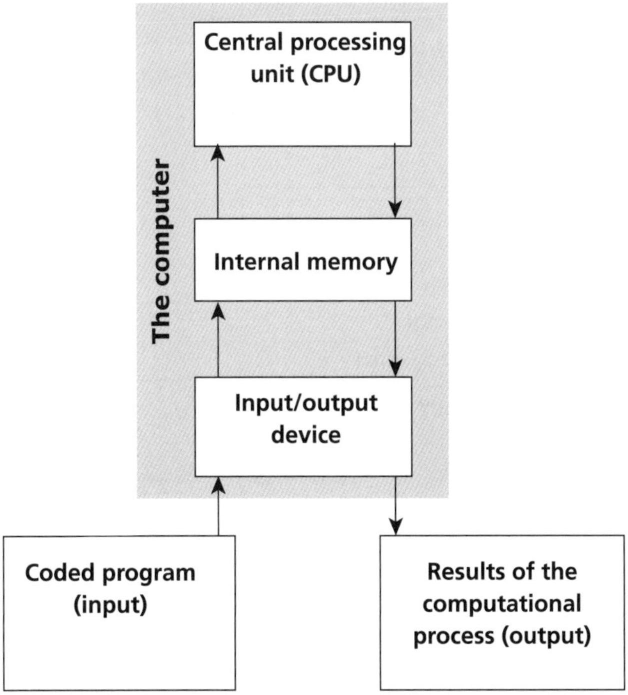

Figure 4.1: The 'stored program' architecture of a computer

- **Input/output devices:** the stored program concept gives rise to a powerful architecture, not only because the CPU is able to rapidly execute a series of instructions, but also because when we wish to change the program (and so have the computer carry out a different task), we need only change the program that is stored in the internal computer memory. The input/output device indicated in Figure 4.1 therefore permits us to load a program into memory, and also provides a way for the computing machine to output the results of its computation.

In the case of early architectures that employed the stored program concept, the program (and any associated data) would have been coded and prepared on special media, such as a set of punched cards or paper tape. An electromechanical reader would then process these cards and load their content into main memory. On completion of the processing task, the results would have been indicated by arrays of lights (which could be interpreted by the operator), or imprinted on paper tape or punched cards. In turn, these cards would have been read by some form of electromechanical machine and their content converted into readable form.

Modern computers also support both input and output – although thankfully we no longer have to work with media such as punched cards! An operator typically provides input to the computer by means of a keyboard and mouse, and the results of the computational process are displayed on a computer monitor (or else hardcopy is produced via a printer).

All computers provide support for both input and output. Naturally, a computer that could not accept input from external sources would have no value, and similarly there would be no purpose in a computer that could not indicate the computed result. An essential difference between the modern computer and earlier machines is the extent to which an operator is able to interact with the system. In the case of earlier computers, once a program was loaded into main memory and began to execute, the operator had little, if any, involvement until computation ended. This type of approach was referred to as 'batch computing'. The modern machine supports a far greater degree of interaction.

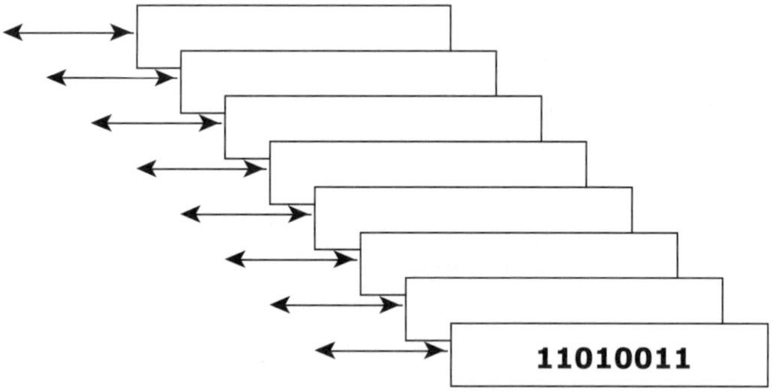

Figure 4.2: A computer's internal main memory consists of a series of memory locations. Each location can hold numbers in a certain range

The modern computer system consists of a number of individual components, including:

- Input devices
- The central processing unit (CPU), which is the heart of the computer system
- Storage devices
- Output equipment that communicates computed results to the user.

The CPU and all input, output, and storage devices are called 'hardware'. For example, as illustrated in Figure 4.3, a personal computer (PC) has a keyboard, mouse and display screen which enables the operator to communicate with the machine, together with additional input/ output (I/O) devices such as hard disk, CD-ROM etc. Additionally, a PC is equipped with a number of 'ports' to which external devices such as printers, cameras, scanners and fax machines can be connected.

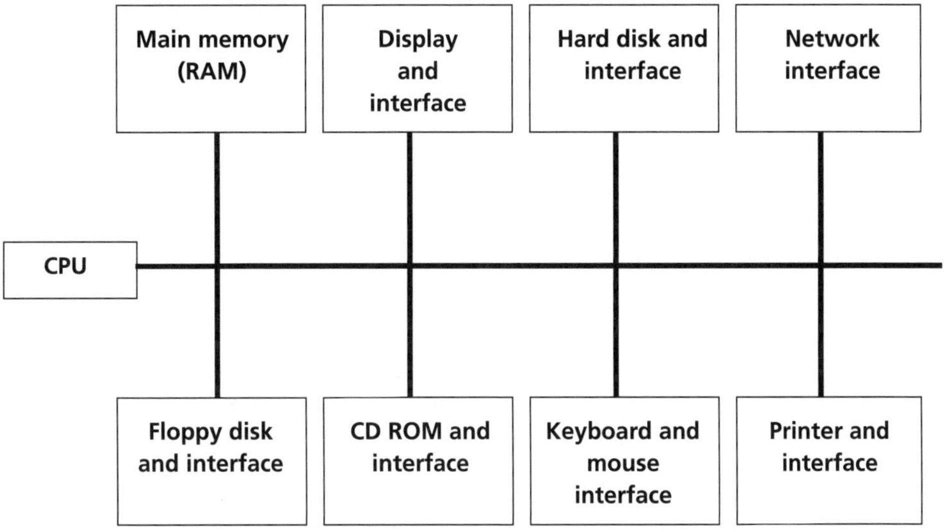

Figure 4.3: The CPU is able to interface with a variety of hardware

Activity 4.1

The computer's main memory

The 'stored program' computer model requires the use of memory able to support both read and write operations. Today this takes the form of RAM (random access memory). Using library or the Internet resources, identify two other forms of memory device.

Activity 4.2

PC hardware: inside a PC

You will need a typical desktop PC (preferably an old and no-longer-used machine). ***Ensure that the computer is not plugged in before proceeding. Additionally, you are advised not to touch any components within the PC, even if switched off, as static electricity, via your fingers, can damage various components.***

Open the PC's case.

Identify the hardware/components inside the PC. Specifically,

the CPU

memory chips

the floppy disk drive

the hard disk drive

the power supply.

In the case that you have access to a machine that is no longer required (i.e. a broken computer), remove the CPU from the motherboard. Note the large number of pins (connections) that link between the chip and the motherboard. As with all connectors within the computer, these pins are gold-plated (this helps to maintain good electrical connectivity). You are strongly advised not to remove the CPU from a working computer – the pins can be easily bent and it may prove quite difficult to re-insert the CPU in its socket!

The modern computer performs its operations in number base 2 (binary) values. As indicated in Chapter 2, a binary value can have one of only two states, represented by any of the following:

- **On/off**
- **True/false**
- **Logic 1/logic 0, etc.**

There is no intermediate state: signals cannot be half 'on', or half 'off'; they are either 'on' or 'off'. As we have seen, individual binary values or 'bits' (the term is derived from the words 'binary' and 'digits') are grouped together, usually 8 bits at a time, to form 'bytes'. The term 'byte' is therefore used when referring to a group of eight bits.

All data and other material held within a computer are stored in the form of binary numbers or codes. This even applies to alphabetic letters!

4.3 The basic computer architecture

In this section we illustrate fundamental aspects of a computer's operation by developing a simple model computer system. In later sections we will extend this model to introduce more complex ideas.

Figure 4.4 illustrates a CPU connected to a memory device. This device takes the form of memory that is able to support both read and write operations (i.e. the processor can read from memory locations and also write to them, so modifying their contents). In our model example, the CPU is connected to the memory device by some 24 connections (wires). These connections are grouped into two different categories – the 'address bus' and the 'data bus'.

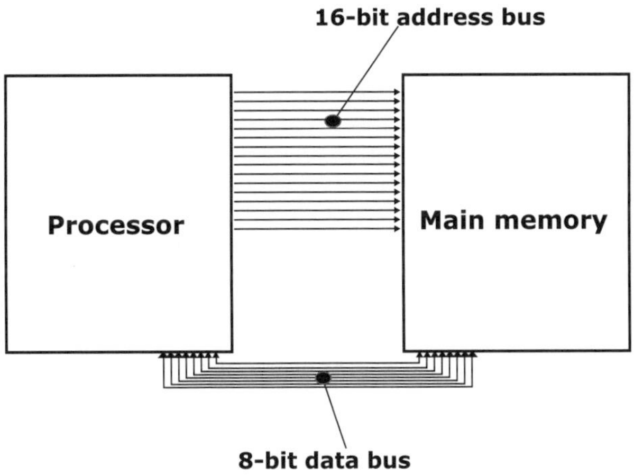

Figure 4.4: The processor connected to memory via an 8-bit address bus and 16-bit data bus

The function of each category is as follows:

- **The address bus:** when the processor wishes to write to or read from a memory location (or other device), it must specify the address of the particular location that it wishes to refer to. The address bus is used for this purpose. The processor specifies an address (using the binary number base) via the wires that form the address bus. Early microprocessors employed 16 wires for the address bus. Today, address buses are typically much larger – an address bus may consist of 32 or more wires (for example the MIPS R4000 processor employs a '64-bit' address bus)
- **The data bus:** as indicated above, when a processor wishes to read from or write to a memory location, it specifies the address of this location by means of the address bus. The data bus enables data to be sent from the processor to the specified memory location, or from the specified location to the processor. When the processor sends data to a memory location, this is called a 'write' operation. When the processor wishes to access data or a program instruction from a memory location, this is called a 'read' operation. Early microprocessors typically employed 8 wires to form the data bus. Today's processors employ many more wires for the data bus – for example, 32 or 64 wires (for example the MIPS R4000 processor employs a '64 bit' data bus). It is important to remember that both the address of the memory location being accessed, and the data that is sent to or read from this address, are always in binary form.

If a processor uses 16 wires for the address bus, this is generally referred to as a '16-bit address bus'. Similarly, if 32 wires are used it would be referred to as a '32-bit address bus'. Similar terminology is used when referring to the data bus – one comprising 8 wires would be referred to as a '8-bit data bus'. The address bus is said to be unidirectional because signals flow along the address bus from the processor to the devices that are connected to the address bus, i.e. signals only travel in one direction. On the other hand, the data bus supports 'bidirectional' signal transfer. Here, data can flow from the processor to other devices (such as memory), and can also flow in the opposite direction, i.e. from devices such as memory to the processor. The direction in which signals travel along the data bus depends upon whether a read or a write operation is occurring.

In Figure 4.4 a processor and a memory device are illustrated, connected together via a simple 8-bit data bus, and a 16-bit address bus. As you can see from this illustration, in the case of the address bus the arrows point in the direction of the memory device. This indicates the direction in which signals travel along the wires; that is, from the processor to the memory device. However, in the case of the data bus there is an arrow at each end of each wire, indicating that signals are able to travel through the data bus in two directions.

Drawing an address bus and data bus by indicating each wire within the buses is tedious and not very helpful. Consequently, address and data buses each tend to be drawn using a single thicker line, as illustrated in Figure 4.5. Again, arrows are drawn on these lines to indicate the direction of signal transfer.

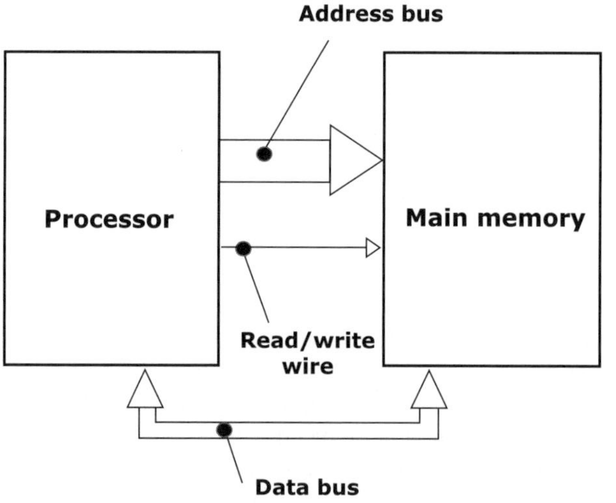

Figure 4.5: The processor and memory are interconnected via address and data buses. These are drawn symbolically. The R/W connection is also shown – see text for details.

The address and data buses are connected to various devices within the computer. Not only do they connect the processor to the computer's internal memories, but also they connect to, for example, the interfaces which enable the processor to communicate with the hard disk drive, a USB port or CD-ROM, etc. This is illustrated in Figure 4.6.

The use of the term 'bus' can cause some confusion. For example, we refer to a computer's 'internal bus', the group of wires that connect the processor to various devices within the computer, and enable the processor to communicate with these devices. However, when we look at a computer's internal bus in more detail, we see that it takes the form of an address bus, a data bus, and various wires through which control and timing signals are passed (the control bus).

Thus, the 'internal bus' is actually made up from three other buses. The easiest way to avoid confusion here is to think of a 'bus' as a collection of wires with a common purpose. Thus, the address bus wires have the common purpose of specifying an address; the data bus wires have the common purpose of supporting data transfer and the control bus specifies the type of operation that is being performed (additionally it provides timing information). However, when we talk of the computer's internal bus we are actually gathering all these wires together and saying that their common purpose is to support internal communication.

As mentioned above, a processor can perform write operations or read operations. Let us suppose that the processor wishes to write to a particular memory location; it sets up an address on the address bus that points to the location to which it wishes to write, and the data on the data bus that is to be written. However, the memory device has no knowledge of whether the processor is wishing to perform a read or write operation – this information must be indicated to it. For this purpose there is a special connection (wire), which is generally referred to as the read/write wire (usually abbreviated to R/$\overline{w}$ – see Figure 4.5. If the processor is wanting to write to a memory location, then this wire is set to a logic 0, and if it is wishing to read from a memory location it is set to a logic 1 (however, this is only one convention and the opposite logic states could be used). Thus, when the processor sets up an address on the address bus and data on the data bus which it wishes to write to a memory location, it will set the R/W wire to a logic low. The memory device interprets the logic low on the R/W wire as an indication that the processor is wishing to write data to the specified location. In turn, the memory device accepts this data and stores it at the appropriate address.

The read/write wire is one of the connections within the 'control bus'.

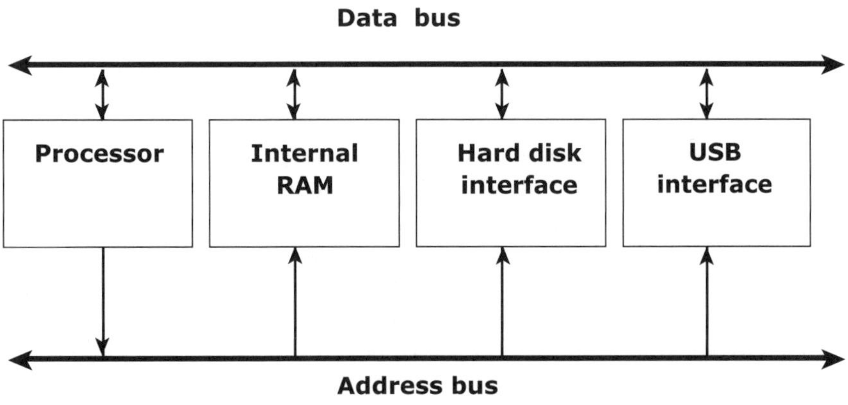

Figure 4.6: The address and data buses connect various devices together

Activity 4.3

A *Read* operation

Explain the events that would take place if the processor wished to read from a particular memory location.

4.4 Structure of the CPU

In this section we briefly introduce several key elements that are contained in the CPU and defer more detailed discussion to Chapter 7.

Three main elements of the CPU are the control unit (CU) and arithmetic logic unit (ALU) and various registers:

- **The arithmetic and logic unit (ALU):** the ALU carries out logical and arithmetic instructions. It is that portion of the computer that performs, among other things, arithmetic operations such as addition and subtraction
- **The control unit (CU):** this coordinates all the low-level activity of the computer. For example, it interprets (decodes) program instructions and directs both internal operations and the flow of data to and from memory (and other devices)
- **The registers:** within the processor there are a numbers of 'registers'. These are special-purpose locations able to store binary values. Early microprocessors contained only a small number of such registers (typically 6) whereas today's processors may contain quite a large number (64). The registers may be grouped into two broad categories:
  - registers that are used by the processor and which should not (or cannot) be directly modified by a program in execution. Such registers support the operation of the processor
  - registers that may be used by a program in execution. For example, an instruction may permit the contents of two registers to be added together and the result of the addition may be stored in a third register. Such registers underpin the operation of a program and, since they are fabricated on the processor chip, they are able to support very high-speed operations.

The size of the registers in the CPU is important in terms of the processor's computing power. If the registers are 16 bits long, then the computer is referred to as having a 16-bit word size. Today, the most common word size is 32 bits.

In our subsequent discussions we will consider the use of registers in some detail and for the present it is sufficient to mention the function of one key register which is usually referred to as the 'program counter'. The purpose of this register is NOT to count the number of programs executing in a computer (although this is perhaps implied by its name) but rather to store the address of the next instruction to be fetched from memory. The program counter thus keeps track of where the processor is up to, in program execution. Should the contents of this register become corrupted, then the processor will not know the address of the next instruction that is to be read from memory and so program execution will fail. The name 'program counter' is often abbreviated to PC.

4.5 Mainframe computers

Mainframe computers were the first type of computer to become commercially available and, during the 1960s and early 1970s, they represented the most commonly used form of computing machine. A mainframe machine was, in its classic form, able to support a number of users who gained access by means of 'terminals' (i.e. the users could simultaneously share computer resources).

A terminal (or visual display unit (VDU)) usually comprised a display screen and keyboard – but did not have any computing ability of its own. It was connected to the mainframe via a cable. Earlier terminals were electromechanical machines known as teletypes. These were equipped with a keyboard and typewriter. Operators' input to the host computer (or output from the host computer) was printed on a paper roll.

These machines were physically quite large and generally housed in a clean, air-conditioned environment. Mainframe computers rapidly grew in size, due to an 'economy of scale' concept that was favoured during the 1960s. This indicated that, by doubling the investment made in a mainframe, the performance of the system was more than doubled. Thus, ever-larger amounts of money were invested in creating mainframe systems able to support greater numbers of users. However, this concept is ultimately flawed as two major problems eventually arise:

- As mainframes grew in size, so did the length of cables connecting the various components that comprise the machine. Since electrical signals pass along cables at a finite speed, it follows that longer cables result in it taking more time for signals to propagate between the devices forming the computer. In turn this reduces performance. In fact so as to maximise computer performance, it is desirable to have all the major components (such as CPU, internal memory and disk drives) in close proximity – the closer they are to each other, the faster the signals are able to travel between them. Thus as mainframes grew in physical size, performance eventually began to be compromised
- As indicated above, mainframes are intended to enable a number of users to simultaneously share the computer's resources. Thus, perhaps hundreds of users would gain access to the machine via their own individual terminals. Naturally, some controls must then be put in place to ensure that each user could not, for example, interfere with a program belonging to another user, or gain access to data belonging to someone else. This was, and still is, a task carried out by a computer's operating system. We will discuss the role of operating systems in more detail in a later chapter and for the moment we will simply consider that it is a program (or set of programs) able to provide computer users with a number of resources, and which in the case of mainframe systems (or other computers that enable multiple users to simultaneously utilise the system):
    - ensures that users equitably share resources (i.e. are given equal access to resources)
    - ensures that a user cannot inappropriately access material belonging to another user (i.e. imposes a level of security).

  As we will see when we consider the operating system (O/S) in more detail, the O/S is responsible for many important aspects of computer operation; in the case of today's PC, Microsoft Windows is the most commonly used O/S.

  As mainframes grew in size and offered to support a growing number of users, the complexity of the O/S continually increased. Ultimately, the O/S programs began to consume a significant portion of the mainframes' resources and in turn this impacted on performance.
- The level of performance offered by the mainframe to each individual user could not be predicted, as this depended on the number of users who were simultaneously accessing the machine, and on the types of activity that they were carrying out. Thus, a user might find that, during standard working hours, computer performance was poor (this compares to our experience when using the Internet at 'peak times'). In order to obtain satisfactory performance, a user might often be forced to make use of the machine in the middle of the night when few other users were accessing resources. It was, in fact, this uncertainty in the performance of a machine that is shared between users that ultimately led to the concept of the PC. In the case of the personal computer, each user possesses their own computer – the machine is not simultaneously used by a number of users and so performance is guaranteed.

The classic mainframe computer is today typically represented by a machine able to perform processing at very high speed and/or offer immense storage capacity, so supporting the processing of vast amounts of data.

4.6 Minicomputers

In the 1970s, a low-cost, scaled-down, version of the mainframe, known as a minicomputer, gained widespread acceptance. As with the mainframe, the minicomputer was able to support a number of users who simultaneously shared the machine's resources through the use of the sort of terminals that we have mentioned above. However, as a result of the lower performance offered by this computer paradigm, the number of users that could share the system was limited (typically up to 30-40). This was a very popular choice for small and medium-sized businesses and for university departments. The minicomputer consumed much less power than did the mainframe installation and it was unnecessary to provide an air-conditioned environment for housing the machine. The PDP-8, PDP11, VAX 750, and VAX 780 were perhaps the most popular minicomputers. As with the mainframe, the O/S not only provided user resources, but was also responsible for equitably sharing computer resources and ensuring that each user worked within a secure environment. It was in connection with minicomputer operation that the well-known UNIX O/S was developed and gained popularity.

4.7 Personal computers

Both the mainframe and minicomputer offer computing resources that are shared between a number of users. Therefore as discussed above (in the context of the mainframe), the performance of the machine as perceived by individual users varied and was determined by:

- **The number of other users** working with the machine
- **The type of applications** currently being run on the machine.

Consequently, there was a lack of predictability; and to obtain satisfactory performance, users would often be forced to carry out computer activities in relation to computationally demanding tasks at unsociable times – perhaps in the middle of the night (when few other people would be using the system).

The 1960s saw the introduction of the integrated circuit and the development of fabrication techniques that enabled the performance of the integrated circuit to increase, while at the same time, production costs fell. Thus, by the late 1960s and early 1970s, it was possible to fabricate complex circuitry on a silicon chip – and at a reasonable price. This led to the birth of the microprocessor – the so-called 'computer on a chip'. In parallel, the cost of memory devices was beginning to fall, and these two vital ingredients made possible the implementation of a cost-effective 'personal computer'.

In the case of the personal computer (PC), the computer system's resources are not simultaneously shared – they 'belong' to a single user. Consequently, performance is guaranteed and is defined by the hardware and software combination that is provided to the user.

Throughout the 1970s, workers at Xerox PARC performed pioneering research not only into the development of computer hardware, but also in relation to the development of software systems that permit us to interact with the computer. Below we briefly review these two aspects of their work:

- **Hardware development:** The workers at Xerox PARC foresaw the benefits of developing a desktop machine whereby each user was given access to a machine that was not simultaneously shared by others. The development of such a computer was made possible by the introduction of the microprocessor, and the gradually falling price of integrated circuits – particularly memory

- **Software development:** The workers at Xerox PARC saw the need to develop new human–computer interaction techniques, thereby supporting more intuitive interaction. In this respect, they developed the graphical user interface (GUI), and incorporated the mouse within the system (although the mouse was first prototyped in the 1960s, it was not commonly used with computer technologies). Thus, at Xerox PARC the interaction modality that is commonly used today, and whereby we move a cursor around the screen with a mouse and select graphical objects depicted on the screen, was first developed. This necessitated the development of new computer graphics techniques.

Although by the mid-1970s the personal computer had been developed (and even included networking capability) it was not until the early 1980s that the PC was widely promoted. Xerox, IBM, and Macintosh almost simultaneously released the PC in one form or another. Users quickly foresaw the advantages of this computer architecture, and sales rapidly grew. Throughout the 1980s and into the 1990s there was a dramatic proliferation of computer technology, and computers began to be used for an ever-increasing number of activities.

Today's PC is largely based upon technologies that were in place by the mid-1970s. More recent developments have tended to refine the original PC architecture, increase its performance, extend its capabilities, and at the same time reduce manufacturing costs.

Activity 4.4

The mainframe, the minicomputer and the personal computer

For the mainframe, minicomputer and personal computer, in each case state one advantageous characteristic, and one disadvantageous characteristic.

Today's PCs seldom operate in isolation and are interconnected using networking technologies. This supports the sharing of resources, communications and the like. Within this context a 'client-server' approach is commonly adopted. Here one or more computers are designated as 'servers' and as the name implies these machines provide resources to other computers in the network (the 'clients'). For example, a computer may be designated as a 'file server', in which case it would be responsible for storing programs, data etc. that may be required by client machines. An authorised client could then request a particular program from the file server and this would subsequently be transferred across the network.

By way of a further example, consider the case that a single printer is to be shared between a number of networked computers. The printer would be connected to a particular machine which would be designated as the 'print server' – see Figure 4.7. Should one of the computers (clients) connected to the network wish to print a document, it would communicate with the print server. Assuming that the computer requesting the print service is an authorised machine, then in due course the document that is to be printed would be transferred across the network to the print server and from this point on the print server would become responsible for the printing task.

4.8 The proliferation of digital computer systems

Traditionally, computers could be readily classified into the mainframe, minicomputer and personal computer categories introduced above. Today the classification of computer systems is far less well defined, and digital computer-based technologies are entering into ever more facets of our daily lives. In this sense the term 'ubiquitous computing' is often used, and in general terms this expression is used to convey the concept of the all-pervasiveness of computer technologies.

Over recent years, computer technologies have, for example, found their place in domestic appliances such as washing machines, video and DVD recorders, toys etc. These computer technologies are able to sense conditions (such as in the case of a washing machine controller, which senses water temperature, etc and in principle makes 'intelligent' decisions so as to maximise efficiency and deal with different forms of fabric in an optimal manner). Such systems are generally based on 'microcontrollers' which are an inexpensive form of computer processor specifically designed for control applications.

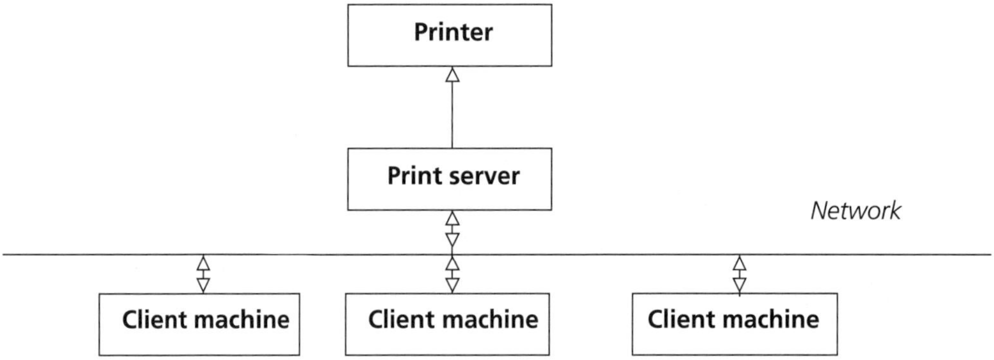

Figure 4.7: A 'print server' provides printing resources to a number of 'clients'.

In the most general terms, ubiquitous computing refers to the all-pervasive use of computer-related technologies which, in principle at least, can sense surrounding conditions and make appropriate decisions. Additionally, wireless communication technologies can allow computer-based systems to communicate and pass data between themselves without human intervention.

One area that has attracted and continues to attract large-scale funding is the application of computer-related technologies for optimising traffic management. For example, computer technologies sense traffic densities, weather conditions and the like, and can at least in theory be empowered to control the actions of the driver. Thus, for example, instead of having conventional traffic lights to which the driver responds, the traffic lights can be replaced or used in conjunction with road-based computer technologies able to communicate directly with computer systems located in vehicles. Rather than simply illuminating a red light to indicate to the driver that the car should stop, the computer systems can be empowered to stop the car. Furthermore, rather than simply indicating via a sign on the motorway the maximum speed at which drivers should travel, given prevailing road conditions and traffic densities, road-based technologies can be used to signal this information to computers within vehicles, and the computer-based technologies could be empowered to impose this restriction – irrespective of the will of the driver.

The example cited above concerning the use of computer-based technologies to change our way of driving is only one simple and easily grasped example of the issues arising, as we move inexorably towards the ever-widening proliferation of digital systems.

Ultimately, it is necessary to decide how much authority we wish to grant to computer technologies – how far we wish them to impact upon our everyday lives. This issue becomes increasingly problematic when we consider the ramifications of simple and effective automatic communication between these 'embedded technologies' and the use of radio frequency identification devices (RFIDs): does having the ability to produce a certain technology make it desirable to do so? By way of a very simple example, and continuing with the above discussion concerning road vehicles, ever-greater numbers of cars are fitted with GPS, and a computer system within a car can be given precise information concerning the car's location. This could be accompanied by information concerning maximum road speeds (and these could be varied according to the time of day, weather etc.). We then have a number of opportunities – for example, the car-based computer technology could simply prevent the driver from exceeding the road speed, and speeding fines would be a thing of the past! Alternatively, if the driver is empowered to exceed the permissible limit, the computer technology in the car could either transmit the overspeed information to the local police authorities, or cut out the middle man and generate the speeding ticket.

There are very many situations in which computer technologies work with people in scenarios where the question does not arise as to whether the individual or the computer technology should have the final say. Pervasive computer systems in an aircraft enable them to fly with great efficiency, leading to savings in both fuel consumption and ticket prices. Patients with heart conditions can make use of wearable computer-based technologies able to continuously monitor the functioning of the heart over a number of days. This provides invaluable data that can assist in diagnosis and treatment planning. On the basis of computer technologies, we are able to implement global communications networks enabling, for example, almost instantaneous Internet access to practically any part of the world.

There can be very few inventions to have gained such widespread usage over such a short period of time. The traditional methods we have encountered and which classify computer systems in terms of mainframes, minicomputers, and the like, worked well in the 1960s and 1970s – perhaps even into the 1980s. Today, things are very different, but the fundamental principles of operation still apply. As you will see in your study of the following chapters, the basic ideas underpinning computer operation have changed very little: a computer is a mathematical machine which operates using the binary number base: we still have a great deal to learn about the power to be derived from such a simple technology.

4.9 Summary

We began this chapter by examining the 'stored program' computer architecture that was first proposed in the 1940s. The great advantage of this approach is that a program to be executed by the computer is stored within the computer's internal memory. This allows the CPU to rapidly execute the program, and when a user wishes to change the program they need simply load a different one into main memory. Such a computer is therefore able to act as a general-purpose machine that can perform a variety of tasks.

We have described the form of the buses that interconnect the processor with other components within the computer and in this context have described the address, data and control buses. Additionally, we have considered the ability of the processor to perform both read and write operations.

Finally, we have considered the traditional mainframe, the minicomputer, and the personal computer (PC). As discussed, although the use of this type of traditional classification scheme can be useful, it does not properly reflect the diversity of computer-based technologies that are in current use.

4.10 Review questions

Review question 4.1

State one major advantage of the 'stored program' computer model.

Review question 4.2

Explain the purpose of the CPU.

Review question 4.3

Explain the purpose of the ALU.

Review question 4.4

Why is it important that components within a computer are located in close proximity?

Review question 4.5

When and where was the basic research carried out in connection with the first personal computer architecture?

Review question 4.6

Why is the address bus said to be 'unidirectional'?

Review question 4.7

In the context of a computer, what do we mean by the term 'bus'?

Review question 4.8

What is the function of the read/write wire?

Review question 4.9

State the purpose of the control unit that is located within the processor.

Review question 4.10

What is a 'byte'?

4.11 Feedback on activities

Feedback on activity 4.1: The computer's main memory

ROM is an acronym for 'read only memory'. This type of memory device supports only read operations – the CPU is not able to write to locations within a ROM chip. The chip is preloaded with material (such as a program(s) and/or data). The contents of the ROM chip cannot be subsequently changed. In the case of RAM, once power is removed from the device, the contents are lost. However, in the case of ROM this is not the case – the contents are retained and cannot be overwritten.

EPROM is an acronym for 'electrically programmable read only memory'. This type of chip can be loaded with program(s) and/or data by means of a special programming device that is known as an 'EPROM programmer'. Once installed within a computer, its contents cannot be altered, or lost when the power is turned off. However, unlike ROM, it is possible to delete the contents of the EPROM and reprogram it (again with an EPROM programmer). The contents are erased by shining ultraviolet light through a small window that lies above the surface of the silicon chip. Typically, it takes a few minutes to erase the chip and then it is ready for reuse.

Feedback on activity 4.2: PC hardware: inside a PC

This activity is designed to help you become familiar with the internal components of a personal computer system. Knowing the components of a personal computer is important when troubleshooting and is important to your success in becoming a computer science graduate.

Feedback on activity 4.3: A read operation

The processor would output on the address bus the address of the location whose contents it wishes to access (read). Additionally, it would set up a logic high state on the read/write wire, thereby signalling that a read operation is to be performed. The memory device will then respond by launching a copy of the contents of the memory location onto the data bus. In turn, the processor will gain access to this.

Feedback on activity 4.4: The mainframe, the minicomputer and the personal computer

Mainframe:

Advantageous characteristic – a centralised repository containing vast amounts of data that can be processed relatively quickly.

Disadvantageous characteristic – the machine supports large numbers of users who can access the resources simultaneously. Consequently, performance for each user cannot be guaranteed.

Minicomputer:

Advantageous characteristic – a relatively low-priced machine that can support a number of users, giving them access to centralised resources.

Disadvantageous characteristic – as with the mainframe, since the computer supports a plurality of users, performance for an individual user cannot be guaranteed.

Personal computer:

Advantageous characteristic – the computer hardware is only used by a single user at any one time, i.e. the hardware and software are usually dedicated to a single user. Consequently, performance can be guaranteed

Disadvantageous characteristic – today, computers are seldom used in isolation but rather are connected to the 'outside world' via some sort of network connection, e.g. via the Internet. Consequently, although the performance of the actual machine can be guaranteed, performance can no longer be guaranteed should a user wish to access outside resources (e.g. some form of server). As we know from our own experience, when we access resources via the Internet, download speeds will vary depending upon current levels of Internet usage. These tend to change during the day.

Further reading

- Clements, A (2006), *Principles of Computer Hardware*, Oxford University Press
  Chapter One - This book provides detailed discussion of many aspects of computer hardware. By reading Chapter One you will gain a greater insight into the basic elements that comprise a computer
- Blundell, BG & Schwarz, AJ (2006), *Creative 3-D Display and Interaction Interfaces: A Trans-Disciplinary Approach*, John Wiley & Sons Inc
  Chapter One - By reading this chapter you will gain a greater insight into the evolution of the modern computer. In addition, it provides a wide range of references through which you can gain further information, and these will be particularly helpful if you undertake a project or group activity in this area
- English, WK, Engelbart, DC, & Berman, ML (1967), 'Display-Selection Techniques for Text Manipulation', *IEEE Transactions on Human Factors in Electronics*, HFE-8 (1) (March 1967)
  This paper is well worth reading as it provides details of the origins and evaluation of several forms of interaction tool, including the prototyping of the first mouse.

CHAPTER 5

Bus systems and memory

OVERVIEW

In order to properly appreciate the operation of the modern computer, it is clearly important to gain an understanding of how the computer's various components work. However, dealing with the individual components (such as the CPU, main memory and hard disk) as standalone entities does not provide us with a complete understanding of the computer system as a whole. We must therefore consider not only the individual components, but also the interaction between these components, and the way in which they are connected.

Learning outcomes At the end of this chapter you should be able to:

- Understand the operation and classification of bus systems
- Describe the use of a system clock, together with synchronous and asynchronous buses
- Describe the function of several types of memory
- Discuss several memory models
- Discuss the benefits offered by cache memory.

5.1 Introduction

We begin by discussing the various general forms of buses used within the modern computer. These form the highways through which instructions, data and other signals travel between the components within a computer . The ability of these highways to support efficient high-speed communication is of vital importance in determining computer performance.

You will encounter the concept of the point-to-point bus and also of the common bus. We also describe the concepts of synchronous and asynchronous buses, and the use of a system clock for timing all operations that are carried out within a computer. The system clock, which consists of a regularly changing waveform, acts as the 'heartbeat' of the machine. One of the major advances over the last thirty years has been the dramatic increase of the system clock frequency. Whereas early microprocessors employed system clocks that operated at around 1MHz, current processors now typically operate in the gigahertz (GHz) region (1GHz=10^9Hz) in the hundreds of MHz region. The faster the system clock, the more rapidly the processor is able to execute instructions. However, the use of a higher clock frequency leads to increased power dissipation and, for example, in the case of laptop machines this can impact on the frequency at which batteries must be recharged.

In this chapter we also discuss several forms of memory device – specifically, random access memory (RAM), read only memory (ROM), non-volatile memory and cache memory. These forms of memory are often said to provide 'primary storage capability'. Here, we also refer to Moore's Law (perhaps more accurately called Moore's Model) which has, over the years, provided a fairly accurate prediction of the way in which memory capacity would increase.

5.2 What is a bus?

A computer bus is a physical link, comprising a number of wires, which connects devices and through which signals can be transmitted. Computer buses enable information to enter the computer via input devices, enable data to be transmitted between different components of a computer system and allow the computer to output the results of the computational process.

The bus connecting the central processing unit (CPU) to memory devices (chips) is called the system bus. The bus connecting the CPU with other devices such as disk drives, keyboard and monitor, etc, is called the I/O bus. The I/O buses connect all I/O devices with the system bus.

A bus, as shown in Figure 5.1, can also be described as:

- A shared communication link, channel or pathway connecting two or more devices
- A single set of wires used to connect multiple subsystems.

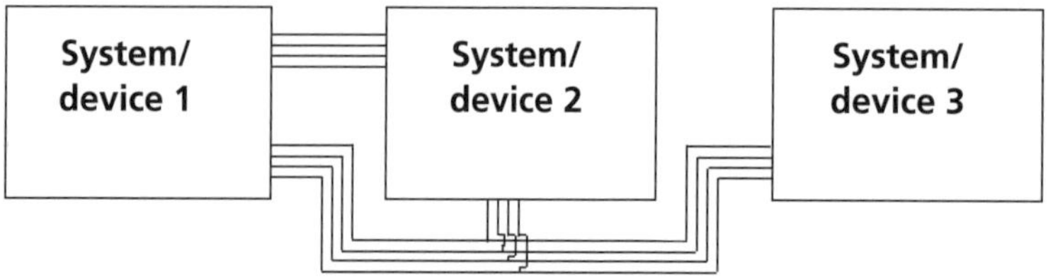

Figure 5.1: A bus transmits data between different devices

As we have seen, memory is used to store both program instructions and data (encoded as sequences of bits). A byte is a sequence of 8 bits; a word is a number of bytes (usually 2 or 4 depending on the design of the computer) and denotes a unit of information – typically the number of bytes that can be transferred between processor registers in one go. In addition to the region of memory used for storing program instructions, the memory used for storing data may be divided into different subregions. For example, one region may be used to store numerical data for use by the program, while another region may be used to store information for display on the computer screen. When any of this information needs to be moved from one place to another within the computer, this transfer is achieved by utilising the computer's buses.

There are two general types of bus arrangement, namely, the point-to-point bus and the common bus.

- **Point-to-point buses** involve a separate connection for each unit (point) pair (transmitter and receiver). This type of bus arrangement is often complex and tends to be expensive to implement
- **Common buses** share connections between units. They are less complex and are more scalable, but require a way of ensuring that only one unit can transmit at any time.

The common bus is generally preferable because it requires less wiring. A further advantage is that it is much easier to add additional components/devices – i.e. the bus can readily accommodate expansion of the number of devices that are connected to it. In this case, the new device/component is simply connected onto the common bus. On the other hand, in the case of the point-to-point bus, when a new device/component is added, it must be connected to each and every other component. Clearly, in this scenario, the number of connections (pathways) grows rapidly as we increase the number of interconnected devices. The number of pathways required to connect every possible pair of n units can be calculated using the following expression:

Number of different pathways = n(n-1)/2

For example, consider the case of five devices (represented as circles in Figure 5.2). Here each circle represents a computer component such as the CPU, memory and input output devices.

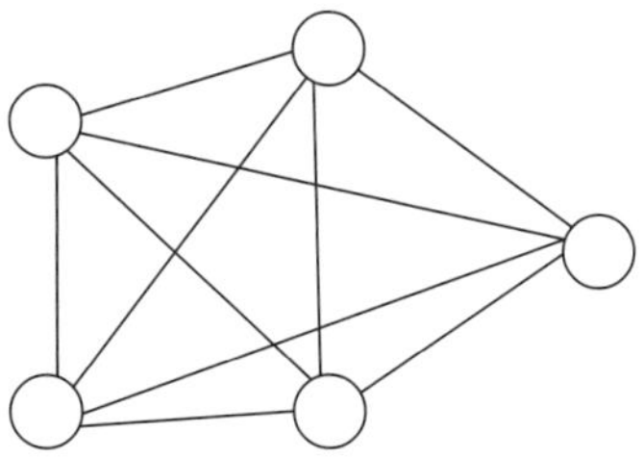

Figure 5.2: The interconnection of five devices using a point-to-point technique.

In this case, ten connections are required to create a fully connected topology. This can be calculated by:

Number of different pathways needed = 5(5-1)/2 = 10

Activity 5.1

Point-to-point interconnection pathways

Complete the following diagram illustrating the point-to-point interconnection pathways required to interconnect the components indicated in Figure 5.3.

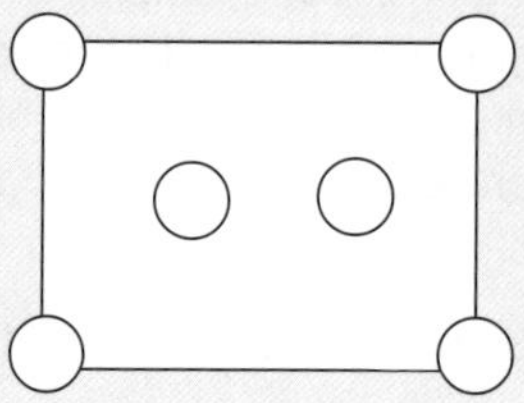

Figure 5.3: Point-to-point connection pathways

Verify the number of pathways that you have drawn by calculating the number of different pathways using the mathematical expression given above.

The disadvantage of the common bus is that, because we are using one bus to transmit information, we have to provide a way of directing the information to its intended destination and also a way of ensuring that the two or more transmissions do not occur at the same time. In this context we need to implement a 'communications protocol'. For example, data or instructions that are to be sent from one component to another must be provided with a destination address (in the same way that we provide an address when mailing a letter or sending an e-mail). Additionally, we must incorporate control mechanisms so that the data only travels when the bus is free from other transmissions. This has resulted in the development of a 'common three-bus system'. All standard computers are built using this approach. Here, the common bus actually comprises three buses (see Figures 5.4 and 5.5). These buses are:

- **Data bus/lines**
- **Address bus/lines**
- **Control bus/lines.**

Note: The term 'lines' is often used when referring to 'wires'.

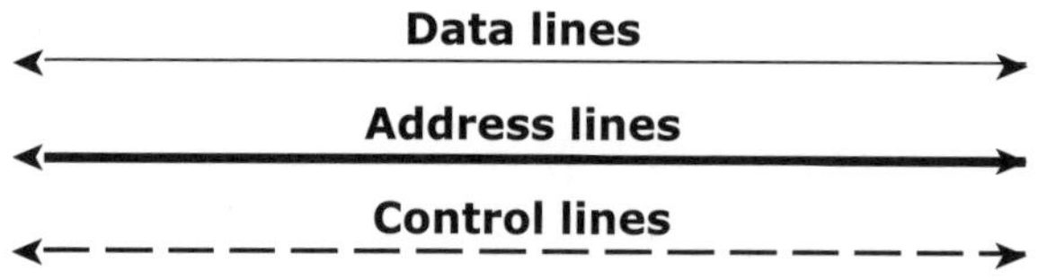

Figure 5.4: Three sets of interconnects used in the implementation of the common bus.

- **The data bus:** the data bus is used to carry both data and instructions. In the case of today's processors, it is typically 32 bits wide (that is, it comprises 32 wires (lines)). In contrast, early microprocessors employed an 8-bit data bus. Each wire in the data bus carries a binary signal (0 or 1 – these two states being represented by two different voltage levels) and thus a 32-bit data bus can either handle 32 separate signals, such as information from 32 separate switches, or it can carry a single group of 32 bits. The 32 wires in the data bus are numbered starting at the least significant bit (D0) to the most significant bit (D31). The data bus is bidirectional – signals can be passed in *both* directions

- **The address bus:** an address bus is a pathway through which source and destination addresses are transmitted between memory, I/O subsystems and the processor. The function of the signals on the address bus is to refer to a specific location (such as a memory location). Once the address of the location is defined by placing signals on the address bus, the CPU can either read data from the location or can write data to that location. Likewise, the input subsystem can write data to the location, or the output subsystem can read from the location. The typical 32-bit address bus is labelled as follows: A0 is the least significant bit and A31 as the most significant bit. When a particular memory location is specified by placing its address on the address bus, all the remaining memory locations are disabled (or deselected). By this we ensure that the computer can talk to one, and only one, location at a time. This bus is usually unidirectional, the addresses being sent in *one direction only* – from the CPU to other devices
- **The control bus:** the control bus carries signals to activate the data/instructions transfers and other events within the system. The control bus is responsible for starting and stopping computer operations. For example, as discussed previously, the CPU has a read/write line (R/W) to tell devices whether it wishes to perform a read or write operation. The R/W line is part of the control bus. For example, when the CPU puts a logic 1 on the R/W line, it tells the computer system that it is about to read data from the location whose address it has placed on the address bus. When it puts a logic 0 on this line, it tells the system that it is about to write or output data to the location whose address is on the address bus.

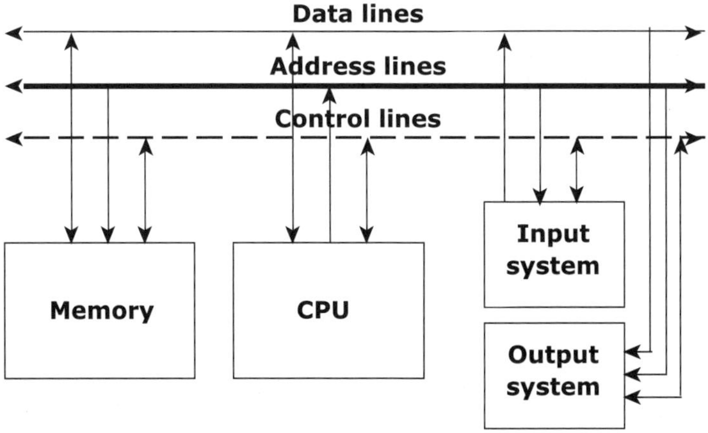

Figure 5.5: A common three-bus system

Activity 5.2

Addresses

Determine the number of different addresses that may be generated by a 32-bit address bus.

Each hardware unit is connected to the address, control and data buses. In this way, each unit of a complex system can communicate with each other. As illustrated in Figure 5.5, a standard computer system is based on the three-bus structure.

Most computers have both internal and external buses. When used in connection with personal computers, the term 'bus' usually refers to the internal bus, which connects all the internal computer components to the CPU and main memory. The internal bus is also referred to as a local bus, because it is intended to connect to local devices – not to those in other machines or to devices external to the computer. On the other hand, an external bus may be used to connect external peripherals to the motherboard. The PC also provides an expansion bus. This enables expansion boards to access the CPU and memory

5.3 Types of buses

The common bus may be implemented in a number of ways:

- **Backplane bus:** This connects processor, memory and I/O devices by a single bus as shown in Figure 5.6. This is a very cost-effective approach as one bus is used to connect all devices. Generally, additional hardware can be plugged onto the backplane bus by means of specially designed sockets that are provided for this purpose

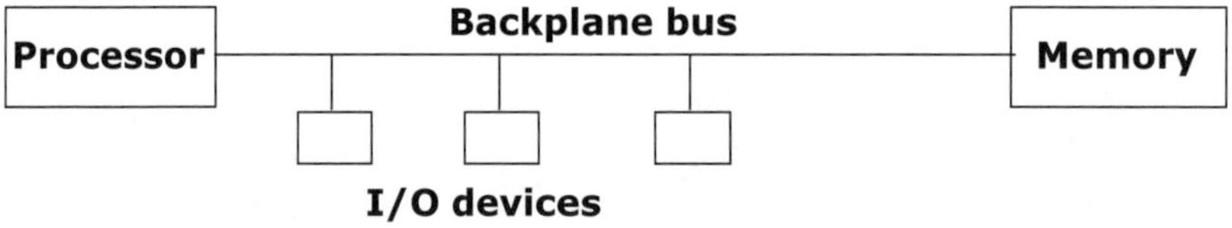

Figure 5.6: The backplane bus

- **Processor memory bus:** this is used to connect the processor and memory. It provides a high-performance communications link
- **I/O bus:** This connects low-speed I/O devices. The I/O bus may be connected to the processor memory bus by means of a bus adaptor as depicted in Figure 5.7.

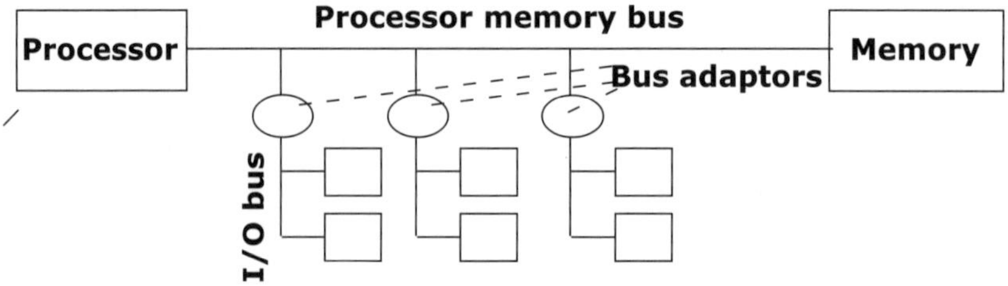

Figure 5.7: Processor memory and I/O buses used in conjunction with bus adapters

5.4 Synchronous versus asynchronous buses

The term 'synchronous', meaning 'coinciding in time', refers to communication carried out at the same time. For example, a face-to-face or telephone conversation, a videoconference, and a chat-room discussion are all forms of synchronous communication.

Literally, the term 'asynchronous' means 'not at the same time' (i.e. not synchronous). In this way, communication does not occur at the same time. Communication via letter, fax or voice mail are examples of asynchronous communication

Buses can be designed to support either synchronous or asynchronous communication. High-speed buses are generally synchronous; low-speed buses asynchronous.

A synchronous bus design uses a common clock signal that is supplied to all communicating devices (in this sense, a 'clock' refers to a repetitive signal, such as a bit pattern that continually changes state – 0101010101...).

Modern computer systems often employ both synchronous and asynchronous buses. The CPU connects to a synchronous memory bus as indicated in Figure 5.8. The bus adaptor provides a connection to an asynchronous bus.

Usually, in such architectures, the synchronous bus is a custom design that is found only on the CPU board itself, and possibly on memory expansion cards, although systems have been designed in the past with such buses on custom backplanes to facilitate memory expansion. In many such applications, the synchronous control scheme is even further simplified by the fact that there are only two potential bus masters.

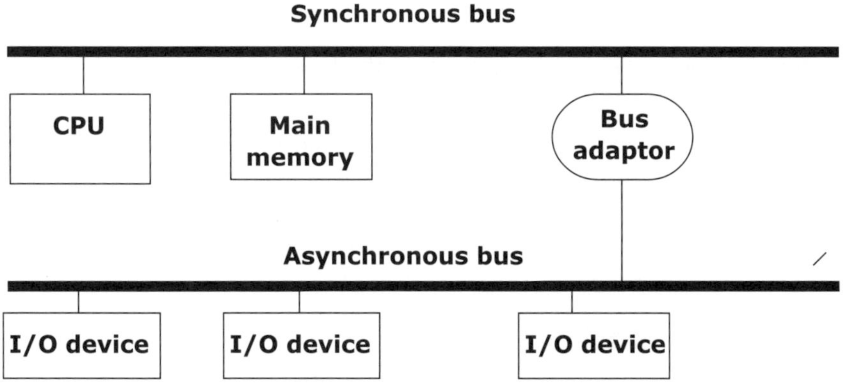

Figure 5.8: CPU connections to a synchronous memory bus and via a bus adaptor to an asynchronous bus

The bus bottleneck is the limitation imposed on the transfer of data within the computer by the bus interconnection system. Only one item can access the bus at any time. To reduce this bottleneck, wider buses are being employed and multiple buses are quite common.

Expansion slots

An expansion slot on a motherboard (the main circuit board within a PC) is used for adding more capability to a computer. They take the form of connection sockets into which expansion cards can be plugged. An expansion slot provides the physical interface for the edge connectors of expansion cards to connect to the system bus. Expansion slots use a unique design of connector type for the different interface bus systems.

Many motherboards use PCI slots with one or two ISA slots. This expansion slot feature ensures the ability to add new hardware capabilities as and when they are needed.

Master versus slave

One of the most important issues in bus design is 'How is the bus reserved by a device that wishes to use it?' The chaos that would be caused by failing to regulate bus access may be avoided by adopting a master–slave arrangement; only the bus master can control access to the bus. The master initiates and controls all bus requests and a slave responds to read and write requests.

Data transfer on a bus consists of a set of control and data exchanges between the bus master and one or more slaves. Electronic systems connected to a bus can act as either (bus) master (in which case they can initiate a bus cycle), or as slaves (which respond to the master's wishes). Some devices can acts as both master and slave – but not at the same time:

The master is the one that starts the bus transaction by issuing a command (and associated address information).

The slave is the one which responds (to read and write requests) by sending data to the master if the master asks for data; or receiving data from the master if the master wants to send data. A master–slave arrangement avoids chaos within the system. When a transfer of data is required, the device sending the data is called the source, and the device which receives the data is called the destination. The complete sequence, from requesting the bus until the completion of the transfer of the data element(s), is termed a bus transaction.

Activity 5.3

Computer performance – the impact of the bus

When purchasing a new computer, we tend to focus on issues such as processor speed and disk size. Often we give less attention to the performance of the internal buses. Why should bus performance be considered with great care?

5.5 The system clock

This defines the time for each basic internal operation of the processor. The clock takes the form of a sequence of voltage pulses (see Figure 5.9) on which components act. The system clock keeps time – just like the regular ticking of a clock. The control bus (part of the system bus) carries the clock signal to interconnected components.

An electronic circuit inside the CPU generates the clock pulses, and accuracy is obtained by means of a quartz crystal. The clock rate is measured in pulses (cycles) per second and is measured in megaHertz (MHz), (i.e. millions of cycles (pulses) per second) or gigaHertz (GHz – 1 GHz=10^9Hz). For example, in the case of a 100MHz processor, the clock 'ticks' 100 million times per second. Different components inside and outside the CPU are kept in step (synchronised) by means of the 'clock signal'.

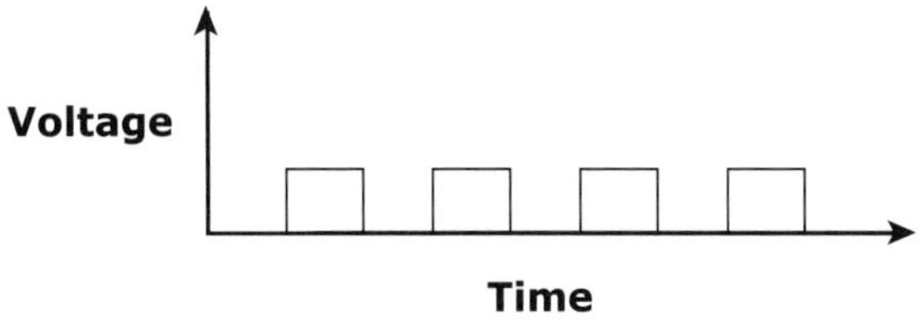

Figure 5.9: A regular clock waveform

Activity 5.4

The processor clock

A clock oscillates at 2MHz. How many clock pulses occur each second, and what is the duration of each individual clock cycle?

5.6 Memory: ROM and RAM

Two general classes of memory chip are used in today's computers. These are referred to as random access memory (RAM) and read-only memory (ROM). Below we briefly discuss these two forms of memory:

ROM

This is an acronym for *read-only memory*. The processor cannot write to this type of memory – it will only support read operations. Special hardware is used to write patterns of 1s and 0s to a ROM chip (these binary values representing instructions and/or data). The ROM retains these bit patterns – even when the power is removed from the device (this is an essential difference between ROM and RAM). In the case of a PC, a special collection of programs called BIOS is stored in a ROM chip. We will discuss the BIOS in a later chapter. Three forms of ROM are outlined below:

- **PROM:** this is an acronym for programmable read-only memory. This sort of memory can be programmed once (and by this we mean that each memory location can be assigned any required bit pattern) and this programming is done with a special machine. Every bit that is stored within the PROM is represented by a transistor. The PROM programming device is used to define whether each transistor represents a binary 0 or a binary 1. This is achieved by destroying (or preserving) minute metallic links which are often referred to as fuses. Once these links have been destroyed, they cannot be reformed, and we can imagine that the binary 1s and 0s that have been programmed into the device have been 'burnt' into it
- **EPROM:** this is an acronym for erasable programmable read-only memory. As with the PROM mentioned above, it is programmed using a special machine. However, unlike the PROM we have just described, the contents of the EPROM can be erased and new contents assigned to it. The erasure process is achieved by shining ultraviolet light

through a small window which is placed just above the surface of the silicon chip. When for a period of a few minutes ultraviolet light is shone through this window, the contents of the EPROM are erased. The EPROM can then be reprogrammed and, as with the description given above for the PROM, when we talk about reprogramming a ROM, we are simply meaning that we assign 1s and 0s to every memory location

- **Flash EPROM:** this has proven to be an extremely versatile and useful form of memory device and is widely used for backing up computers (via 'USB flash cards'), or for the transfer of material between machines. Flash EPROM is also used in MP3 players, digital cameras, and the like. This form of memory is in some ways quite similar to the EPROM mentioned above but there is no need to use ultraviolet light to erase the contents of flash EPROM – erasure is achieved through the application of electrical signals. However, the erasure process does cause some damage to the device, and this can limit the lifetime of this form of memory. Early forms of flash EPROMs may have failed after a hundred or so erasure cycles whereas today's flash EPROM can typically withstand some tens of thousand cycles.

RAM

This an acronym for random access memory and is used as 'main memory' within a computer. The processor may read from or write to RAM. However, when the power is removed (e.g. when the computer is turned off), the RAM chips will lose their contents.) There are many different kinds of RAM on the market, the result of intense competition to satisfy the ever-increasing demands for speed, capacity and low cost. Several types are outlined below.

- **Dynamic RAM or DRAM:** this is the main type of RAM fitted to PCs. It is cheap but not as fast as some other kinds of RAM. In technology there is nearly always a trade- off between conflicting requirements – in this case, it is between cost and speed. DRAM is cheap but relatively slow. It suffers from another problem: many times per second the memory contents need to be refreshed, i.e. the chip will 'forget' or lose its contents unless a refresh operation is carried out. This means that separate refresh circuits are needed, adding to the complexity of the electronics
- **Static RAM or SRAM:** this kind of RAM holds its data without refresh signals and is faster than DRAM, but in the classic trade-off, SRAM loses out on cost. Each bit storage element of SRAM is implemented with between 4 and 6 active components (transistors) whereas for DRAM, it is made from just two. This may not sound to be too much of an issue – but the 6 transistors are for just one bit! A byte is 8 bits, so 1MB of SRAM would take 6*8*1,024*1,024 = 50,331,648 transistors!
- **Non-volatile RAM:** as indicated above, one disadvantage of RAM is that when power is removed from a RAM chip, the contents stored within the chip are lost. One solution to this problem is to equip the memory chip with a small battery so that when the main power supply is turned off, the device can continue to draw current from the battery. For this approach to operate correctly, it is vital that the memory device draws only a very small current from the battery – which is indeed the case for CMOS memory devices (CMOS is an acronym for 'complementary metal oxide semiconductor' and relates to the manner in which circuits are implemented on the silicon chip). This approach provides 'non-volatile' RAM.

When implemented in a PC, a small lithium battery located on the motherboard usually supplies power and, unless the battery is soldered in place, its replacement is simple. This battery supplies power to the real-time clock chip and to memory in which system settings are stored. Should the battery fail, then both these devices will fail to operate – the computer will no longer know the time, and date and system settings will be lost.

Furthermore, if you set a power-on password, this is held in the CMOS memory. Removal of the battery for even a short period of time will force a re-set of the settings to the manufacturer's defaults, thus overcoming the password. For this reason you should not rely on such a password!

5.7 Cache memory

Latency provides us with a measure of the time that it takes for the system to respond to read and write operations. In the case of memory access, latency is not only determined by the performance of memory chips, but also by the speed of the computer bus (in the modern computer, the time taken for electrical signals to propagate along the bus can make a significant contribution to latency).

So as to reduce latency, we require fast memory and short signal paths (thereby ensuring that signals travel the minimum possible distances). Unfortunately, the cost of memory increases with speed. Today's computers attempt to strike a balance between price, performance and memory capacity. This is achieved by including a small amount (in terms of capacity) of very high speed memory that is located on or close to the processor chip. This is referred to as cache memory.

Analysis of a large number of low-level programs reveals that for most of the time the next instruction to be executed will be located at a memory address that is next to, or very close to the address of the instruction currently being executed. This is known as 'spatial locality'. We can make use of this observation by ensuring that when the processor reads an instruction from main memory, it brings into the cache memory other neighbouring instructions. Subsequently, when wishing to read the next instruction from main memory, it first examines the cache memory to see if the instruction is already present. In the case that it is present, it may be accessed very rapidly. On the other hand, if it is not present in the cache memory, the processor will transfer it from main memory together with other adjacent instructions.

The performance improvements that can be gained through the inclusion of cache memory are further increased by the concept of 'temporal locality'. The examination of real programs in execution reveals that if an instruction has been recently executed by a processor, then it is likely that it will be executed again in the near future. The transfer of groups of instructions from main memory to a local high-speed cache memory takes advantage of this principle.

For this approach to provide real benefit, the processor must be able to rapidly determine whether or not an instruction or a data value is already within the memory cache. This is a vital consideration in the implementation of cache memory techniques and can introduce a number of complexities. Furthermore, today's machines incorporate different levels of cache memory – these differing in terms of capacity and access speed.

Activity 5.5

Spatial locality

Suppose that you were in the library researching material for a project that you have been asked to do for one of your courses. How would you make use of the concept of spatial locality?

5.8 Memory and performance

As we have discussed, both ROM and RAM comprise a series of memory locations, each of which is able to store a certain number of bits (for example, each memory location (address) may typically be able to store 32 bits). The processor is able to access each of these memory locations by indicating the address to which it wishes to write, or from which it wishes to read. As we have seen, this is achieved by outputting a binary address on a collection of wires known as the 'address bus'. The number of wires that comprise this bus determines the 'address space' – the number of locations which a processor may access.

Another important consideration when examining memory efficiency concerns access speed. In this context we often consider device 'latency'. This is usually taken as the time for a memory chip to respond to a data request measured from the time of the request to the time the data is made available. This is usually quoted in nanoseconds, which is 10^{-9} seconds – in other words, 1/1,000,000,000 seconds. This is a thousand times shorter than a millionth of a second! In human terms, an impossibly short period of time, but in computing terms it is an 'everyday' unit of time. Table 5.1 below shows some of the powers of both 10 and 2 and the associated names and symbols.

Factor of 10	**Value**	**Prefix**	**Symbol**
10^{-12}	0.000000000001	pico	P
10^{-9}	0.000000001	nano	N
10^{-6}	0.000001	micro	m
10^{-3}	0.001	milli	M
10^{-2}	0.01	centi	C

Power of 2	**Number of bytes**	**Symbol**	**Name**
2^{10}	1,024	KB	Kilobytes
2^{20}	1,048,576	MB	Megabytes
2^{30}	1,073,741,824	GB	Gigabytes
2^{40}	1,099,511,627,776	TB	Terrabytes

Table 5.1: Powers of 2 and 10, together with names and symbols

In 1965, Gordon Moore was the Research Director of the electronics company Fairchild Semiconductor and three years later he became one of the founders of Intel. He made an interesting prediction based on what had happened up to that time with memory chips. He noticed that memory capacity doubled in capacity every 18-24 months. He predicted that this would continue, leading to an exponential growth in size and hence computing power. Market trends have shown this to be generally true. This is known as 'Moore's Law'. However, in terms of current technologies, there is uncertainty as to how long this growth rate can continue.

Note: Moore's 'law' is not a law; it is simply a prediction!

A series grows in an exponential manner when the next term in the series is obtained by the multiplication of the previous term by a factor. For example, if you take a number, say 1 and multiply it by a factor, say 2, you get an answer of 2. If you then repeat this, the number grows slowly at the start but soon rapidly increases.

For instance: if you start with 1 and keep multiplying by 2, you get the series 1, 2, 4, 8, 16, 32, 64, 128, 256, 512, 1,024 and so on. The rate of increase is best displayed as a graph – see Figure 5.10.

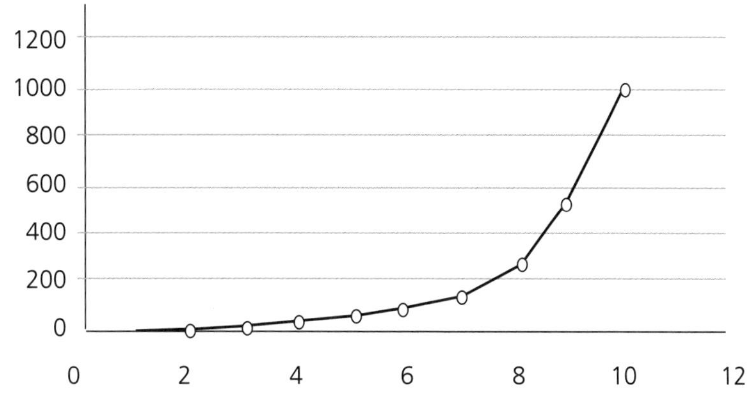

Figure 5.10: An example of exponential growth

Activity 5.6

Memory size and address bus width

Fill in the blanks in this table. Remember, 1KB is 1,024 bytes, 1MB is (1,024*1,024) bytes, 1GB is (1,024*1,024*1,024) bytes.

Address bus width	Address space size	Abbreviation
16		64KB
24	16,777,216	
32		4,096MB

Activity 5.7

Moore's Law

Assume the average size of a hard disk drive in a PC in the year 2000 is 10GB. If Moore's Law (see below) were applied to average hard drive sizes and continued until the year 2012, what would the average size be in that year?

Moore's Law says that it should double every 1.5 years. The answer may surprise you!

5.9 Summary

In this chapter we have outlined various types of buses that are employed within a computer. Here, we encountered both point-to-point and common bus implementations. We also discussed synchronous and asynchronous buses. In the case of the former, all devices connected to the bus are provided with a common clock signal. However, in the case of the asynchronous bus a common clock signal is not required. Both of these approaches have advantageous and disadvantageous characteristics. For example, in the case of a high-speed synchronous bus, the need to distribute a rapid clock signal limits the physical extent of the bus.

As discussed in one of the activity questions, when purchasing a computer we tend to focus on issues such as processor speed, the amount of main memory, and the size of the hard disk. Seldom do we consider bus architecture and bus performance. Hopefully, now that you have an insight into the operation of buses within a computer, you will have a better appreciation of the critical role they play in determining overall computer performance.

In the second part of this chapter, we considered memory devices within the computer system. Here we encountered read-only memory (ROM), random access memory (RAM) and cache memory. We mentioned one limitation of RAM – specifically, its inability to retain its content when power is removed. However, we saw that we can circumvent this problem through the provision of a small battery that enables RAM to retain its content, even when external power has been removed. This type of memory is commonly referred to as being non-volatile.

5.10 Review questions

Review question 5.1

In what way do data and address bus width affect the performance of a computer?

Review question 5.2

Name three different types of buses found in the modern computer.

Review question 5.3

Computers are designed around a three-bus system. Name these three buses and outline their functions.

Review question 5.4

What is the clock signal used for?

Review question 5.5

Is there only one type of bus within a PC? If not – why not?

Review question 5.6

Is a synchronous bus suitable to the high-speed transmission of data over large distances?

Review question 5.7

Moore's 'Law' has provided a useful basis on which to predict increases in processor performance and advances in memory technology. Is it reasonable to assume that this model will continue to be applicable in the future?

Review question 5.8

A clock has a period of oscillation of 1 microsecond. What is its frequency of oscillation?

Review question 5.9

State one major difficulty in implementing a point-to-point bus configuration (a fully connected topology).

Review question 5.10

State one key issue associated with the implementation of the common bus technique.

5.11 Feedback on activities

Feedback on activity 5.1: Addresses

Number of different pathways required:

$$\frac{6(6-1)}{2} = \frac{6 \times 5}{2} = \mathbf{15}$$

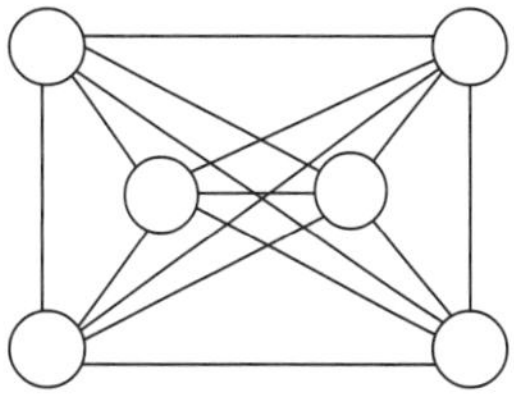

Feedback on activity 5.2: Point-to-point interconnection pathways

Number of addresses= 2^{32}=4,294,967,296

Feedback on activity 5.3: Computer performance – the impact of the bus

The bus architecture impacts on the speed at which read and write operations may be performed. For example, there would be very little point in connecting a slow processor to a high-performance bus. Equally, there is little value in having a high-performance processor if the bus bandwidth cannot sustain the throughput offered by the processor. When considering buses, we should consider their architecture and configuration, the bus width and the maximum data transfer rate of each wire within the bus.

Feedback on activity 5.4: The processor clock

2,000,000 pulses occur each second and therefore a single pulse occupies 1/2,000,000 seconds. This equals 0.5 microseconds.

Feedback on activity 5.5: Spacial locality

Books in a library are usually classified by their general content. Consequently, books that cover similar topics tend to be located close together on the shelves. When researching your project, you will begin by identifying the area of the bookshelves that relates to the general topic that you are working on. It is likely that you will return to this area a number of times to access other books that are relevant to your writing. Here, you are making use of spatial locality in as much as you are accessing books that are in close physical proximity. As we have seen, in the context of a computer, spatial locality refers to the likelihood of the computer executing instructions and data that are stored in close proximity within main memory.

Feedback on activity 5.6: Memory size and address bus width

Address bus width	Address space size	Abbreviation
16	**65,536**	64KB
24	16,777,216	**16,384 Kb**
32	**4,294,967,296**	4,096 Mb

Feedback on activity 5.7: Moore's Law

Moore's Law

Year	**Size in GB**
2000	10GB
2001.5	20GB
2003	40GB
2004.5	80GB
2006	160GB
2007.5	320GB
2009	640GB
2010.5	1,280GB
2012	2,560GB

Further reading

- Cooke, BM & White, NH (1995), *Computer Peripheral*, Edward Arnold, (3rd edn)
  This book provides interesting related discussion. It includes discussion on communication both within the computer and with external peripherals.
- Dowsing, RD, Woodhams, FWD & Marshall, I (2000), *Computers from Logic to Architecture*, (2nd edn) McGraw-Hill
  This is a very readable book and is a good source for general related discussion.
- Clements, A (2006), *Principles of Computer Hardware*, Oxford University Press
  This book provides extremely useful support for the material presented in this chapter, and that presented in other chapters. Strongly recommended for more in-depth discussion.

CHAPTER 6

Programs, numbers and symbols

OVERVIEW

Computers execute a set of instructions in sequence, by selection and by iteration (see Chapter 1). Each instruction comprises an opcode and often an operand. The former tells the CPU of the task that is to be performed and the latter provides data to be used by the opcode. Programs can be written in high-level languages – which are relatively simple for a programmer to read, but must ultimately be converted into low-level machine code prior to execution.

Learning outcomes At the end of this chapter you should be able to:

- Distinguish between high-level languages, assembly language and machine code
- Describe the execution of machine code instructions – with specific reference to the fetch/execute cycles
- Describe ways in which signed (positive and negative) integers may be represented in a computer
- Recognise the use of ASCII and Unicode for symbol representation.

6.1 Introduction

In Chapter 4 we provided an insight into the basic architecture of a computer by describing the stored program model, together with the interconnectivity of key elements – specifically the processor and memory devices using address, data and control buses. By means of these buses the processor is able to perform what is called the 'fetch-execute' cycle. In this respect, the processor is able to input (fetch) instructions and data from memory locations, act on these instructions and where necessary return the results of the computational process back to memory.

In this chapter, we build upon previous discussion and provide a more detailed insight into the way in which a computer is able to execute a program (a program represents a set of instructions together with necessary data). In the next section we begin by distinguishing between high-level and low-level programs, and introduce machine code. Subsequently, in Section 6.3, we examine in closer detail the operation of a computer as machine code instructions are executed. In Section 6.4 we briefly introduce assembly language. This provides us with a convenient means of representing machine code instructions.

In Chapter 2 we described aspects of the binary number system and in Section 6.5 we extend this discussion to show how both positive and negative numbers may be represented within a computer, and consider some simple examples of arithmetic operations that may be performed upon them.

From a user's viewpoint, the modern computer is not simply used to perform complex calculations, but rather to provide a multimedia environment in which documents, images, and the like can be stored and processed. Consequently, in Section 6.6 we discuss the way in which character symbols are represented within a computer. In this context, we introduce the ASCII and Unicode systems by which symbols (such as the letters of the alphabet) are stored by the computer in the form of numbers.

6.2 Concerning programs

It is likely that you will have either viewed the 'source code' within a computer program, or may have actually undertaken some programming exercises. If so, the chances are that you will have seen (or created) what we refer to as 'high-level language' programs. Examples of high-level languages include:

- Basic
- Java
- C
- Fortran
- Pascal.

These programming languages allow us to describe the actions that we would like a computer to perform using instructions that contain words and easily recognisable constructs. For example:

```
For I = 1 to 10
Print 'hello'
```

These are examples of two simple instructions that are commonly found in high-level language programs.

The second instruction causes the word 'hello' to be printed on the display screen and the first instruction defines the number of times that the second is to be executed. The character 'I' represents a variable that is initially assigned the value 1. The print instruction is then executed and the variable I is incremented. Again the print instruction is executed and the process continues until I attains the value of 10, at which point execution terminates (or if there is any instruction following the print instruction, this will be executed).

A high-level language provides us with a way of expressing the actions that we wish a computer to perform, in a straightforward and relatively easily understood way. On the other hand, the processor which is to execute the program does not understand such instructions because all instructions and associated data to be executed by a processor are actually represented as a series of binary numbers.

However, binary numbers are not particularly user-friendly! We would not choose to write a program directly in binary – although in the early days of computing, programs were frequently directly coded this way.

High-level languages provide a relatively straightforward way of expressing ourselves to a computer. On the other hand, the computer is not able to directly execute the statements employed in such a program. Fortunately, it is possible to develop programs able to convert the high-level language statements into the low-level binary codes that can be executed by the processor. This process may be accomplished through the use of special programs known as 'compilers' or 'interpreters'.

These programs take the high-level language code and process it in various ways to generate low-level binary instructions that can be executed by the processor. The low-level binary instructions are referred to as 'machine code' (see Figure 6.1). Thus, machine code for a processor will, when loaded into memory, take the form shown in Figure 6.2. Here, for simplicity we assume the use of a rudimentary 8-bit data bus.

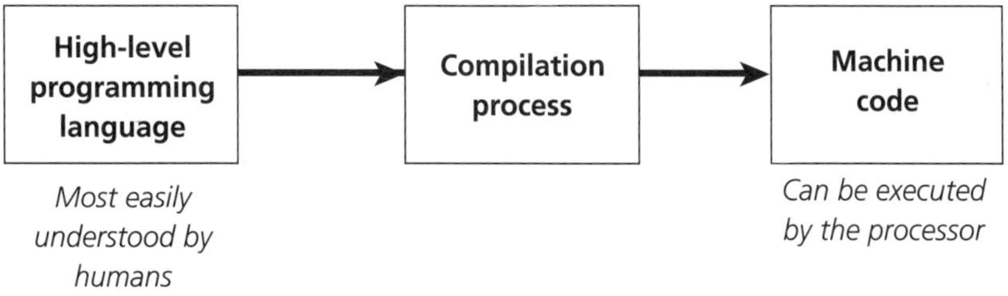

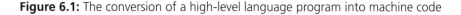

Figure 6.1: The conversion of a high-level language program into machine code

When we consider machine code, it is helpful to avoid its binary representation, and as we saw in Chapter 2, one solution is to represent the binary numbers in base 16. Here it is important to remember that although we represent the binary numbers in base 16, we do this for our own convenience. In Figure 6.2 we also show the hexadecimal representation of the binary codes that are stored in memory. The part of a machine code instruction that tells the processor the task that is to be performed is referred to as 'operation codes' (abbreviated to 'opcodes'). This name originates from the early days of programming when computer researchers and users programmed directly in binary.

In the simplest case, a machine code program is stored in sequential memory locations – as illustrated in Figure 6.2

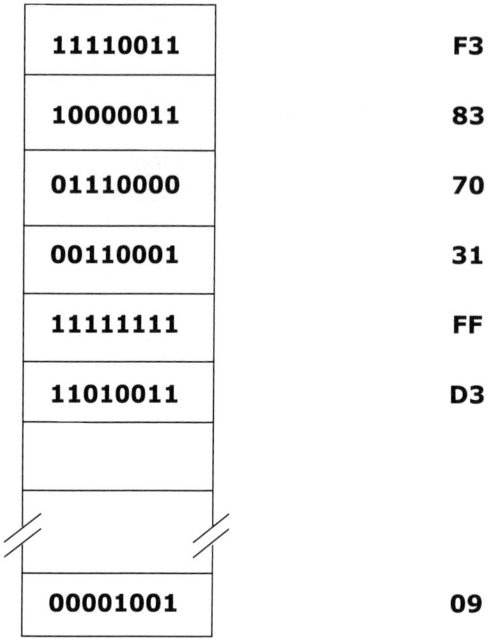

Figure 6.2: Machine code located in a series of memory locations. For convenience, hexadecimal values are also indicated.

An instruction (opcode) may be self-contained in as much as it does not require additional data or information. For example, an instruction may indicate that the contents of a register located in the CPU are to be incremented (i.e. addition of 1). In this case, the instruction is read from memory (we refer to the instruction as being 'fetched'), is decoded and acted upon ('executed'). Alternatively, an opcode may require additional content – upon which it acts in some way. When such an opcode is fetched from memory, the processor 'knows' that it is not self-contained, but rather that additional content is needed (this content is generally referred to as the 'operand'). The operand is obtained by reading from one or more subsequent memory locations. An example of a simple machine code instruction comprising both opcode and operand is one in which we wish the processor to load a certain value into one of its registers. In this case the processor would decode the opcode and find that a register is to be loaded with a particular number. It would therefore undertake a further read (from memory) operation so as to determine the numerical value that should be used (i.e. the value that is to be loaded into the register). As described here, the execution of this instruction would involve two read operations and would therefore take longer to execute than the simple 'increment register value' instruction mentioned above (which involves only a single read operation). Other instructions may require even more memory read (fetch) operations.

Activity 6.1

The operation of compilers and interpreters

Using the Internet or your library, determine a major difference between the operation of a compiler and the operation of an interpreter.

6.3 Instruction execution

Unless instructed to do otherwise, a processor accesses memory locations sequentially: that is, if it is currently addressing a memory location 0010_{16}, it will next access memory location 0011_{16}, then memory location 0012_{16}, and so on. However, as we will see, some instructions can cause the CPU to break away from this sequence.

Consider the simple computer model depicted in Figure 6.3, which shows a processor connected to a memory device in the form of RAM or ROM (recall discussion provided in Chapter 5). We assume that this memory contains a series of opcodes and associated operands. For clarity, each opcode is depicted in bold typeface. Let us suppose that the next address to be accessed by the processor is (in hexadecimal) F000 and that at this address the processor expects to read an opcode. (For simplicity we will assume a very basic processor that uses a 16-bit address bus and 8-bit data bus.)

Following Figure 6.3, the processor reads the instruction contained in this memory location (in this case 86 (hex)) and decodes this instruction. Upon decoding, the processor recognises that it is being told to load a numerical value into one of its registers. It must therefore read the next memory location to determine the actual value of the number to be loaded into the register. It does this, and so completes the instruction.

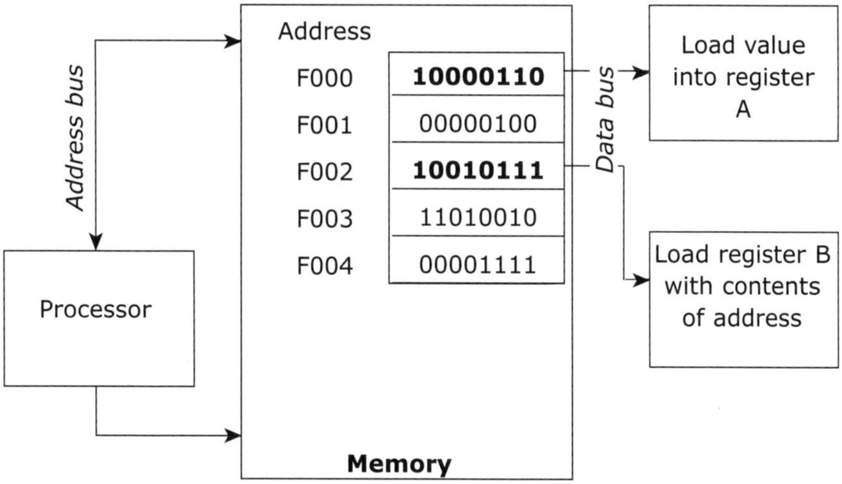

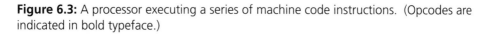

Figure 6.3: A processor executing a series of machine code instructions. (Opcodes are indicated in bold typeface.)

The processor now reads the contents of the next address – in this case, F002 (hex). Here it expects to find another opcode. This is fetched into the processor and duly decoded. In the example illustrated in Figure 6.3, we assume that this tells the processor to load into another of its registers the value stored at a particular memory address. However, to execute this instruction, the processor must read from memory the operand corresponding to the address containing the data it is to load into its register. To obtain this address, it needs to perform two more read operations. Once the address is obtained, the processor must perform another read operation in order to obtain the contents of this address, which can then be loaded into the appropriate register.

Thus, the process goes on as the processor executes a series of very simple instructions. In fact, this underpins the very essence of the modern computer. Machine code instructions are very basic – they do not perform complex tasks. On the other hand, the processor is able to execute these simple instructions at very high speed and can therefore work its way through vast numbers of instructions in a short time. In this way, the processor is ultimately able to carry out extremely complex tasks – but it is important to remember that these tasks are underpinned by the execution of simple instructions at very high speed.

A processor is only able to execute instructions contained within its instruction set. Different processors have different instruction sets; although there is a great deal of commonality between the instructions that can be executed by the processors produced by different manufacturers, these instructions are represented by different binary codes.

Thus, the binary code for an instruction such as 'increment the contents of register A' (this sort of instruction may be found in practically every instruction set) will be different for processors produced by different manufacturers. In turn, this means that machine code is not easily ported from one processor to another – machine code tends to be processor-specific (although the family of processors produced by one single manufacturer may support the same basic set of instructions and associated binary codes).

Activity 6.2

A processor's instruction set

Using the Internet or a library, locate a copy of the instruction set for a microprocessor. Examine these instructions and identify two instructions that can cause the processor to break away from the processing of instructions that are located in a sequential list within memory.

6.4 Assembly language

As indicated above, writing programs using binary numbers is an extremely tedious process. Furthermore, it is very easy to make mistakes by entering a 1 where a 0 should be, and vice versa. It is somewhat ironic that machine code can be executed so efficiently by the processor but is so inefficient as far as the programmer is concerned!

Rather than create programs directly in machine code, it is possible to write them using a special language which is referred to as 'assembly language'. This can be regarded as an intermediate language between at one end machine code, and at the other end high-level languages such as C and Java. Once a program has been written in assembly language, a special program is used to convert this into machine code. This program is referred to as an 'assembler'. Thus, the assembler takes assembly language code and translates this into machine code which can be executed by the processor.

There is a direct correspondence between assembly language instructions and the opcodes and operands that we have discussed above. Let's take a couple of simple examples of assembly language instructions:

Suppose that we wish to load a certain number into a particular register. We will call this register A. Here we may use an assembly language instruction of the form:

```
LDA < value >
```

Here, LDA represents the opcode signifying that a value is to be loaded into register A. This is followed by the numerical value that is to be loaded into the register.

The assembler upon encountering this instruction would translate the LDA to the appropriate binary opcode and would assign the value following this opcode with the value indicated in the assembly language program.

Suppose that we now wished to increment the contents of register A. Here we might use an assembly language instruction of the form:

INC A

Upon encountering this, the assembler would generate the binary machine code instruction which will cause the contents of register A to be incremented. Note that in the first example above, the instruction comprised an opcode and operand, whereas this instruction comprises only an opcode – no operand is needed.

Suppose that we now wish to store the contents of register A at a particular memory address. Here we might use an assembly language instruction of the form:

STA <address>

In this case, STA is recognised by the assembler as representing the opcode for storing the contents of register A at a particular address. The actual value of the address is assumed to immediately follow the STA statement.

As you can see from the very simple examples given above, we represent the opcodes using simple mnemonics which make sense to the person developing the program, or to a person subsequently reading the program. For example, in the case of INC A, it is evident that INC is an abbreviation of 'increment', and that the letter 'A' is intended to name the register whose contents are to be incremented.

An assembly language allows us not only to define opcodes and operands, but also to add text which explains the operation of the program – i.e. comments. These increase readability as far as the programmer is concerned, but are ignored by the assembler when it is creating the machine code 'executable' program. In addition, an assembly language allows the programmer to define various issues. For example, it is possible to include a statement that tells the assembler where in memory the machine code executable should be placed. In this context, a statement is included to define the address at which the first instruction of the assembly language program should be located. Subsequent instructions are then placed at sequential memory addresses (unless the programmer states otherwise).

6.5 Representing positive and negative integers

In Chapter 2 we discussed the representation of positive integers (whole numbers, such as 1, 3, 67, etc.) in binary form. For example, the base 10 number 27 may be represented as the binary value 11011. If this number were to be stored within an 8-bit register, then we would simply pad it out by inserting leading zeros: 00011011. By way of a further example, consider the base 10 number 15. This would be represented within an 8-bit register as the binary value 00001111.

If we have a binary number comprising N bits, then this may represent 2^N different values. For example, an 8-bit number may represent 2^8 (=256) different values ranging from zero through to 255.

Activity 6.3

Number representation

Consider a binary number comprising 16 bits. How many different values may be represented by this number?

A computer must be able to deal with both positive and negative numbers; one simple approach to the representation of negative numbers is to dedicate one bit to indicate a number's sign. This may be achieved as indicated in Figure 6.4 where we show one bit (the left-most bit) as indicating the sign (positive or negative) and the remaining bits as giving the magnitude (size) of the number. For example, we could adopt the convention that if the sign bit is a zero then the number is positive and if the bit is a one, a negative number is indicated. Two examples are illustrated in Figure 6.5.

The use of a sign bit gives rise to the number zero being represented in two ways – see Figure 6.6. Consider a binary number comprising N bits (one of these bits representing the number's sign and N-1 bits the number's magnitude). This enables 2^N-1 different binary values to be represented (the '-1' arises because the number zero is represented in two different ways).

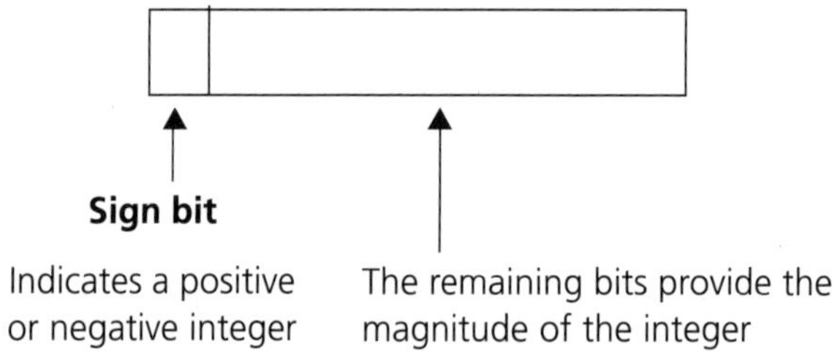
Sign bit
Indicates a positive or negative integer
The remaining bits provide the magnitude of the integer

Figure 6.4: The representation of positive and negative numbers by means of a 'sign' bit. We may, for example, adopt the convention that if the sign bit is a binary zero, then the integer is positive; if the sign bit is a binary one, the number is negative.

In the early days of computing, constructing the electronic circuits that comprise a computer was a difficult and laborious task. As a result, one of the key objectives of the computer designer was to minimise the number of electronic circuits needed to perform arithmetic operations. Although the representation of positive and negative binary numbers in machine code programs using a 'sign' bit (and associated magnitude bits) is a natural choice, it means that addition and subtraction operations have to be carried out by largely separate hardware. In essence, it becomes necessary to implement hardware for the addition of numbers and different hardware for their subtraction. Designers therefore sought other solutions and developed number schemes that would permit both addition and subtraction operations to be performed by the same hardware. Below we review the use of the 2s complement approach.

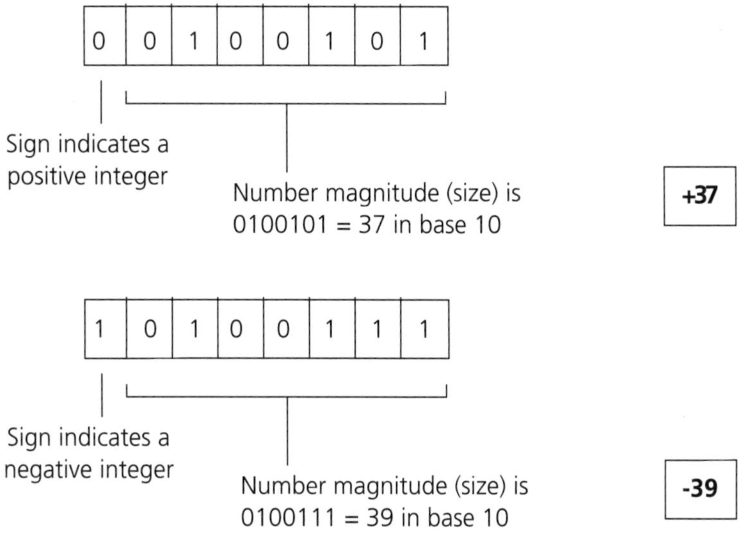

Figure 6.5: The representation of positive and negative integers using a 'sign' bit

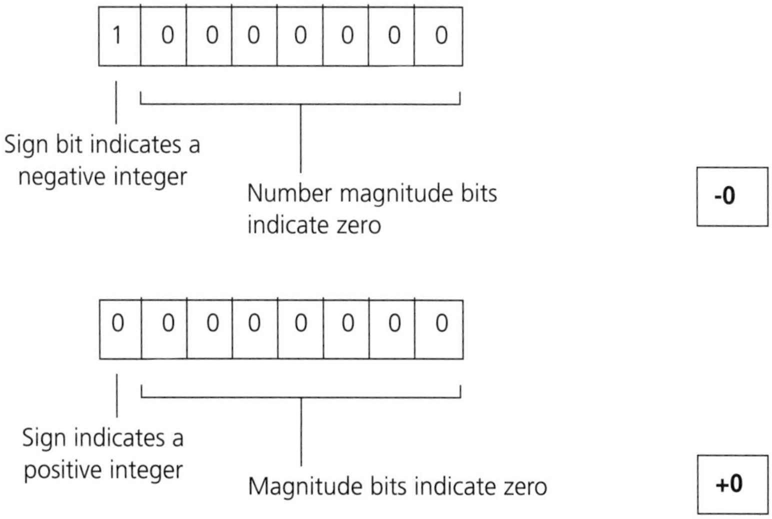

Figure 6.6: The use of a 'sign' bit results in the number zero being represented in two different ways (as +0 and -0). This is non-optimal.

Two's complement arithmetic

Rather than employ a 'sign' bit to indicate whether a number is positive or negative, an alternative approach is to encode the negativity of a number within the number itself. In this context, and when working in the binary number base, we make use of what is called a the 2's complement of a number.

Although at first sight, this may seem complicated, in practice the technique is very simple. To convert a binary number into 2's complement form:

- Change all 1s in the number to 0s
- Change all 0s to 1s
- Add 1.

By way of example, consider the use of four bits to represent the number 5 – 0101. The 2's complement of this number is 1011. This number represents -5.

Note: If you calculate the 2's complement of a number, and then repeat the process on this result, you obtain the original number. This provides a convenient method of checking your arithmetic.

For example, consider the number 1100110.

The 2's complement of this number is 0011010.

And the 2's complement of this number is 1100110 – the original value!

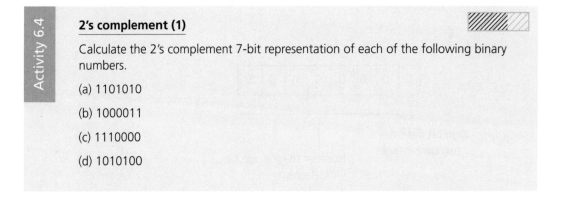

Activity 6.4

2's complement (1)

Calculate the 2's complement 7-bit representation of each of the following binary numbers.

(a) 1101010

(b) 1000011

(c) 1110000

(d) 1010100

In Table 6.1 we indicate the two's complement of various numbers the two's complement value is represented by four bits.

In order to subtract one binary number from another, we can make use of 2's complement arithmetic. Let us suppose that we wish to perform the following calculation:

A – B = C

where A and B represent two binary numbers each comprising N bits. We simply calculate the 2s complement of B (we will refer to this as B') and then compute:

A + B'

Decimal value	Two's complement (binary)
+3	0011
+2	0010
+1	0001
0	0000
-1	1111
-2	1110
-3	1101
-4	
-5	
-6	
-7	

Table 6.1: The two's complement of some exemplar values

Activity 6.5

2's complement (2)

Complete Table 6.1 so as to give the 2's complement (expressed in four bits) representation of -4, -5, -6 and -7.

In other words, by first taking the 2's complement of B, the subtraction of B from A can be performed using addition! There is however one small complication – when performing subtraction operations, the result is sometimes negative. However, when we use the 2's complement approach the sign of the answer (positive/negative) may be determined from the value of the carry (overflow) that occurs. Let's take a couple of examples and see how this works in practice:

Example 1:

Calculate the binary subtraction 11001 – 10011 using the 2's complement approach.

Before we begin, it is convenient to convert both of these binary values to base 10 and see what answer we should obtain for the subtraction. Recall from Chapter 2, 11001 equals 25 (base 10) and 10011 equals 19 (base 10). The subtraction 25-19 = 6 and therefore in base 2 the answer that we obtain should equal 110. (For convenience, we may add two leading zeros so that the result comprises the same number of bits as the two original numbers – i.e. 00110.)

Now let us try the 2's complement approach. In this question A = 11001 and B = 10011. We begin by finding the 2's complement of B (10011) which is 01101 (we will call this B'). We now add A and B' together – see Figure 6.7.

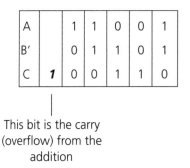

A		1	1	0	0	1
B′		0	1	1	0	1
C	***1***	0	0	1	1	0

This bit is the carry (overflow) from the addition

Figure 6.7: Performing subtraction using 2's complement arithmetic

As may be seen, we obtain a result of 00110 with a carry of one (a carry occurs when the result of the arithmetic operation is one bit longer than the numbers upon which the operation is performed). We simply discard the carry bit and so the result corresponds to the base 10 number 6.

Recall from above that when we performed this calculation in base 10, we obtained an answer of 6 (binary 110). Thus the 2's complement approach provides the correct result.

Example 2:

Calculate the binary subtraction 1100 – 1110 using the 2's complement approach.

As with the previous example, it is instructive to convert both of these binary values to base 10 and see what answer we should obtain for the subtraction. Recall from Chapter 2, 1100 equals 12 (base 10) and 1110 equals 14 (base 10). The subtraction operation gives -2.

Now let us try the 2's complement approach. In this question A = 1100 and B = 1110. We begin by finding the 2's complement of B (1110) which is 0010 (we will call this B'). We now add A and B' together – see Figure 6.8.

A		1	1	0	0	1	0
B′		0	0	0	1	1	0
C		1	1	1	0	0	0

Here, the carry (overflow) is zero

Figure 6.8: Performing subtraction using 2's complement arithmetic

As may be seen, we obtain a result of 1110 with a carry of zero. From Table 6.1, we see that this number corresponds to the base 10 value -2.

When we add or subtract two positive or two negative numbers, overflow can occur. This happens when we have allocated insufficient bits to the representation of the result.

For example, consider the addition of the decimal numbers 4 and 5. If we represent these values using 2's complement form with four bits, we have 0100 and 0101. If we now add these numbers, we obtain 1001. However, this is the 2's complement representation of the number -7 – the answer is clearly incorrect. The problem relates to the range of values that can be represented by a given number of bits. In the case that we have four bits, then in unsigned integer form they can represent numbers in the range 0 through to 15 (base 10). However, in 2's complement form they can represent numbers from +7 to -8 and if the answer to a calculation exceeds this range of values an overflow will occur.

An important point to remember about this method is that it permits both the addition and subtraction of binary integers to be performed by a single hardware unit that performs only addition operations. Booth's algorithm can be used for the multiplication of 2's complement numbers – see, for example Dowsing et al [2000]. Details of this reference are given at the end of this chapter.

6.6 Coding symbols

So far we have confined our discussion to the representation of numbers within a computer. However, for many applications (such as word-processing) the computer must also be able to handle symbols (e.g. alphabetic characters, punctuation characters and the symbols that we use to represent numbers). As we have seen, the digital world knows of only two states – logic high and logic low (binary 1 and binary zero). Consequently, in order to process characters, we must represent them as binary codes.

The most widely used technique that is employed for the representation of symbols is based on the use of ASCII codes. ASCII is an acronym for the 'American Standard Code for Information Interchange' – this standard was originally developed by the American National Standards Institute. Traditionally, it is based on the use of seven bits to represent each character – as illustrated in Table 6.2. An alternative coding scheme is known as EBCDIC (Extended Binary Coded Decimal Interchange Code).

Since standard ASCII uses a 7-bit code, 128 different characters may be represented (only 96 of these are normal printing characters – the remainder carry out special functions , such as 'backspace'). When an ASCII character is stored as a byte, the most significant bit is generally zero.

ASCII codes have been extended to the 8-bit ISO 8859-1 Latin code, thereby enabling support for accented characters. However, 8 bits are insufficient for the representation of the symbols used for the world's languages. Unicode provides a solution by supporting 16-bit character representation, thereby permitting a vast range of symbols to be incorporated.

Decimal	Hex	Binary	Value
000	000	00000000	NUL (Null char.)
001	001	00000001	SOH (Start of Header)
002	002	00000010	STX (Start of Text)
003	003	00000011	ETX (End of Text)
004	004	00000100	EOT (End of Transmission)
005	005	00000101	ENQ (Enquiry)
006	006	00000110	ACK (Acknowledgement)
007	007	00000111	BEL (Bell)
008	008	00001000	BS (Backspace)
009	009	00001001	HT (Horizontal Tab)
010	00A	00001010	LF (Line Feed)
011	00B	00001011	VT (Vertical Tab)
012	00C	00001100	FF (Form Feed)
013	00D	00001101	CR (Carriage Return)
014	00E	00001110	SO (Serial In)
015	00F	00001111	SI (Serial Out)
016	010	00010000	DLE (Data Link Escape)
017	011	00010001	DC1 (XON) (Device Control 1)
018	012	00010010	DC2 (Device Control 2)
019	013	00010011	DC3 (XOFF) (Device Control 3)
020	014	00010100	DC4 (Device Control 4)
021	015	00010101	NAK (Negative Acknowledgement)
022	016	00010110	SYN (Synchronous Idle)
023	017	00010111	ETB (End of Trans. Block)
024	018	00011000	CAN (Cancel)
025	019	00011001	EM
026	01A	00011010	SUB
027	01B	00011011	ESC (Escape)
028	01C	00011100	FS (File Separator)
029	01D	00011101	GS
030	01E	00011110	RS (Request to Send)
031	01F	00011111	US
032	020	00100000	SP (Space)
033	021	00100001	!

.../cont

Table 6.2: The ASCII codes used to represent symbols (part 1)

Decimal	Hex	Binary	Value	Decimal	Hex	Binary	Value
034	022	00100010	'	081	051	01010001	Q
035	023	00100011	#	082	052	01010010	R
036	024	00100100	$	083	053	01010011	S
037	025	00100101	%	084	054	01010100	T
038	026	00100110	&	085	055	01010101	U
039	027	00100111	'	086	056	01010110	V
040	028	00101000	(	087	057	01011111	W
041	029	00101001	)	088	058	01011000	X
042	02A	00101010	*	089	059	01011001	Y
043	02B	00101011	+	090	05A	01011010	Z
044	02C	00101100	,	091	05B	01011011	[
045	02D	00101101	-	092	05C	01011100	\
046	02E	00101110	.	093	05D	01011101	]
047	02F	00101111	/	094	05E	01011110	^
048	030	00110000	0	095	05F	01011111	_
049	031	00110001	1	096	060	01100000	'
050	032	00110010	2	097	061	01100001	a
051	033	00110011	3	098	062	01100010	b
052	034	00110100	4	099	063	01100011	c
053	035	00110101	5	100	064	01100100	d
054	036	00110110	6	101	065	01100101	e
055	037	00110111	7	102	066	01100110	f
056	038	00111000	8	103	067	01100111	g
057	039	00111001	9	104	068	01101000	h
058	03A	00111010	:	105	069	01101001	i
059	03B	00111011	;	106	06A	01101010	j
060	03C	00111100	<	107	06B	01101011	k
061	03D	00111101	=	108	06C	01101100	l
062	03E	00111110	>	109	06D	01101101	m
063	03F	00111111	?	110	06E	01101110	n
064	040	01000000	@	111	06F	01101111	o
065	041	01000001	A	112	070	01110000	p
066	042	01000010	B	113	071	01110001	q
067	043	01000011	C	114	072	01110010	r
068	044	01000100	D	115	073	01110011	s
069	045	01000101	E	116	074	01110100	t
070	046	01000110	F	117	075	01110101	u
071	047	01000111	G	118	076	01110110	v
072	048	01001000	H	119	077	01110111	w
073	049	01001001	I	120	078	01111000	x
074	04A	01001010	J	121	079	01111001	y
075	04B	01001011	K	122	07A	01111010	z
076	04C	01001100	L	123	07B	01111011	{
077	04D	01001101	M	124	07C	01111100	|
078	04E	01001110	N	125	07D	01111101	}
079	04F	01001111	O	126	07E	01111110	~
080	050	01010000	P	127	07F	01111111	DEL

Table 6.2: The ASCII codes used to represent symbols (part 2)

Let's write the word 'chocolate' in ASCII and decimal code. To do this we find the decimal and the binary code of each letter of the word 'CHOCOLATE' from Table 6.2:

Letter	Decimal	Binary conversion
C	067	0 1 0 0 0 0 1 1
H	072	0 1 0 0 1 0 0 0
O	079	0 1 0 0 1 1 1 1
C	067	0 1 0 0 0 0 1 1
O	079	0 1 0 0 1 1 1 1
L	076	0 1 0 0 1 1 0 0
A	065	0 1 0 0 0 0 0 1
T	084	0 1 0 1 0 1 0 0
E	069	0 1 0 0 0 1 0 1

Activity 6.6

Find the word written in decimal and ASCII

Let's find the word written in the decimal and ASCII codes in the table provided below:

Decimal	Binary conversion	(ASCII) Letter
066	0 1 0 0 0 0 1 0	
065	0 1 0 0 0 0 0 1	
078	0 1 0 0 1 1 1 0	
065	0 1 0 0 0 0 0 1	
079	0 1 0 0 1 1 1 1	
065	0 1 0 0 0 0 0 1	

Activity 6.7

Write your name in ASCII

Using the ASCII table, write your name in ASCII and decimal code.

6.7 Summary

In this chapter, we have introduced a range of important concepts which will form the foundation for our subsequent discussions. We have discussed the general form of instructions that can be executed by a processor (machine code) and in this context have distinguished between high-level and low-level languages. At the most basic level we see the computer as a machine in which the processor continually reads opcodes and operands from memory, acts upon these and, where appropriate, returns the results to memory. Although a machine code instruction set comprises a set of simple instructions, great power can be obtained from a machine able to execute large numbers of these instructions in a very short time.

We are able to represent various forms of numbers and symbols within a computer. In this chapter we have focused on the storage of signed integers and have introduced the use of 2's complement arithmetic. Although the processor operates wholly on numbers and manipulates these numbers by means of arithmetic and logical operations, we can also represent symbols (such as the letters of the alphabet) within the digital world. Here, we make use of codes (e.g. ASCII and Unicode) that associate with each symbol a numerical value and the processor has no knowledge of the actual meaning that we ascribe to these codes.

6.8 Review questions

Review question 6.1

Why do we generally use high-level languages for programming?

Review question 6.2

What is the meaning of the term 'opcode'.

Review question 6.3

Does a processor always execute instructions which are sequentially stored in memory?

Review question 6.4

Suppose that you determine the 2's complement of a binary number and that you the repeat the process on the value obtained (i.e. you take the 2's complement twice). What is the overall result?

Review question 6.5

State one advantage associated with the use of the 2's complement representation of an integer.

Review question 6.6

Write down the 2's complement (six-bit representation) of the binary number 110100

Review question 6.7

State the meaning of the abbreviations ASCII and EBCDIC.

Review question 6.8

With reference to Table 6.2, determine what mathematical operation should be performed on an upper-case letter (e.g. A, B, C etc.) so as to convert it into its lower-case equivalent (e.g. a, b, c etc.).

6.9 Feedback on activities

Feedback on activity 6.1: The operation of compilers and interpreters

A compiler processes a high-level language program in its entirety with the objective of ultimately producing an executable program (containing machine code instructions). On the other hand, an interpreter translates each individual high-level language instruction into a set of executable machine code instructions – as and when required. Thus the interpreter performs the translation task gradually – each instruction being converted into machine code as execution progresses.

Feedback on activity 6.2: A processor's instruction set

Various possible instructions may cause this to happen. For example, the 'jump' instruction may be used to tell the processor to go to a particular address. Another example is the 'jump to subroutine'. This causes the processor to begin executing a self-contained piece of code which is referred to as a subroutine. A further example is the 'branch' instruction that will cause a change in the sequence of instruction execution on the basis of some condition that has been evaluated.

Feedback on activity 6.3: Number representation

16 bits may take on 216 different values – i.e. 65,536 values.

Feedback on activity 6.4: 2's complement (1)

0010110

0111101

0010000

0101100

Feedback on activity 6.5: 2's complement (2)

-4 1100

-5 1011

-6 1010

-7 1001

Feedback on activity 6.6: Find the word written in decimal and ASCII

Letter	Decimal	Binary conversion (ASCII)
B	066	0 1 0 0 0 0 1 0
A	065	0 1 0 0 0 0 0 1
N	078	0 1 0 0 1 1 1 0
A	065	0 1 0 0 0 0 0 1
N	079	0 1 0 0 1 1 1 1
A	065	0 1 0 0 0 0 0 1

Feedback on activity 6.7: Write your name in ASCII

Write your full name (first and last name) in both decimal and ASCII – using both upper-case letters and lower-case. Don't forget to insert codes for spaces!

Further reading

It is suggested that you further study the way in which numbers are represented and manipulated within a computer. In this context, you may be interested in reading about the floating point representation of numbers. Additionally, you are advised to read further in relation to machine code instructions. This material is contained within most basic computer architecture/computer systems books. Three useful works are:

- Clements, A (2006), *Principles of Computer Hardware*, Oxford University Press
- Patterson, DA & Hennessy, JL (2004), *Computer Organization & Design: The Hardware/ Software Interface*, (3rd edn) Morgan Kaufmann
- Dowsing, RD, Woodhams, FWD & Marshal, I (2000), *Computers from logic to architecture*, McGraw Hill

CHAPTER 7

The processor

OVERVIEW

The central processing unit (CPU) forms the central resource within a computer and is responsible for controlling practically all aspects of a computer's operation. Specifically, the processor fetches instructions and associated data from memory, executes these instructions and where appropriate returns the results to memory. In this chapter, we take a brief look at aspects of the processor's internal hardware and differentiate between several forms of processor – specifically, microprocessors and microcontrollers.

Learning outcomes At the end of this chapter you should be able to:

- Describe several functional units within a simple processor model
- Describe the purpose of various processor registers
- Distinguish between microprocessors and microcontrollers
- Distinguish between general purpose computers and embedded controllers.

7.1 Introduction

In the next section, we introduce an elementary processor architecture. Here, our emphasis is on general considerations and we therefore employ a simple processor model. This enables us to provide a basic insight into processor operation without the need to come to terms with the complexities of the advanced processors that are employed in current computer systems. However, many of the concepts that are described within this chapter are scalable in so far as they can be further developed and applied to high-performance processors. By way of an analogy, given a basic understanding of the operation of a simple internal combustion engine, the basic ideas can be scaled and extended in order to describe the operation of a high-performance engine used in a racing car. Therefore, in this chapter we direct our attention to fundamental issues and provide references that can be used to obtain more detailed information concerning specific processor embodiments.

We describe various 'sub-units' within a simple processor model, and introduce several types of register that are usually encountered in one form or another within the majority of processors. Discussion includes the use of the instruction register, condition code register, and program counter.

In Section 7.3 we consider embedded controllers which are based upon microcontroller technology. An embedded controller is the name given to a type of digital hardware that is found in many appliances, such as washing machines and TVs. Here we distinguish between the embedded controller (which is produced with a certain application in mind) and the standard computer that, as we have seen, is a general-purpose programmable machine.

7.2 Within the CPU

The central processing unit ('CPU') controls and organises activity within the computer. As we have discussed, one of the basic functions performed by the CPU is to fetch instructions from the system's RAM or ROM and to execute them. As indicated above, the architecture of the modern processor is generally quite complex and so, to most readily describe some key aspects of a processor's internal features, we confine our discussion to a simple processor model. Figure 7.1 illustrates various key elements that comprise this model (and which are found in typical 'real' processor implementations).

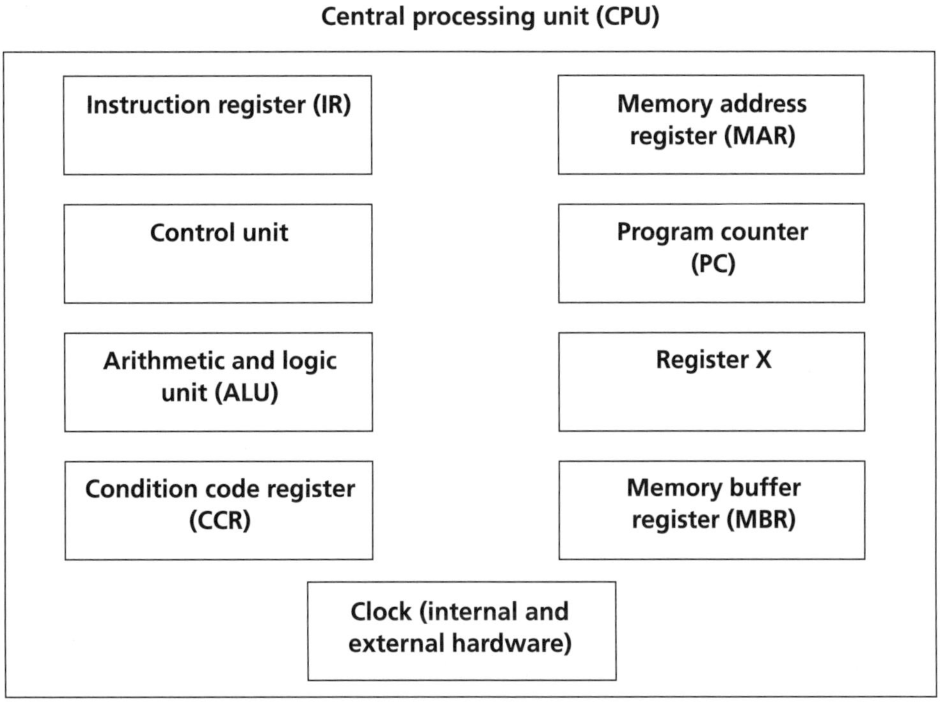

Figure 7.1: Key 'sub-units' within the simple model processor

In the pages that follow we outline the functionality of these sub-units.

The program counter and memory address register

The program counter (PC) acts as a pointer to where the processor is up to in the execution of a program. If the contents of the PC are lost (or in some way corrupted), then the processor would have no record of the next memory address that is to be accessed and so program execution would fail. Figure 7.2 shows the PC connected to the Memory Address Register (MAR) which acts as the interface (or gateway) between the PC and the address bus.

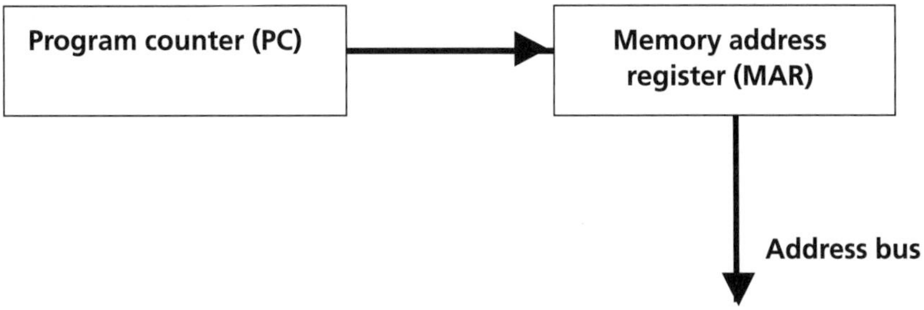

Figure 7.2: The memory address register interfaces the program counter to the address bus

As we have seen, a computer is able to execute instructions in sequence, by selection, and by iteration. In the case that instructions are executed sequentially (and if we assume that each instruction (opcode together with any associated operand) occupies a single memory location, see Figure 7.3), then as the processor moves on to execute each subsequent instruction it is only necessary to increment (add one) to the value stored in the PC, see Figure 7.4.

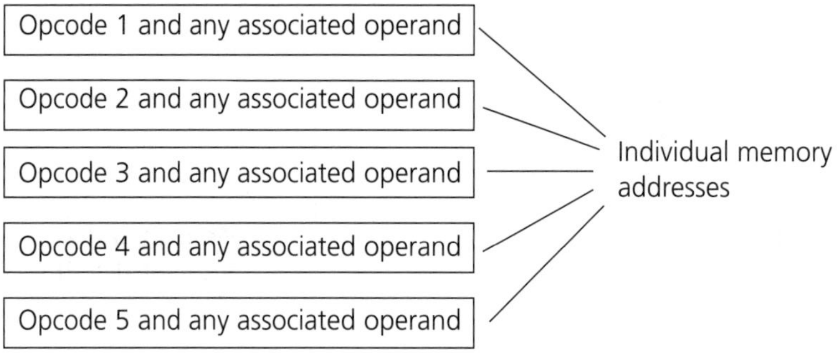

Figure 7.3: Here, we assume that each opcode (together with its associated operand) is stored in a single memory address – i.e. that an opcode (and associated operand) does not span more than a single memory location.

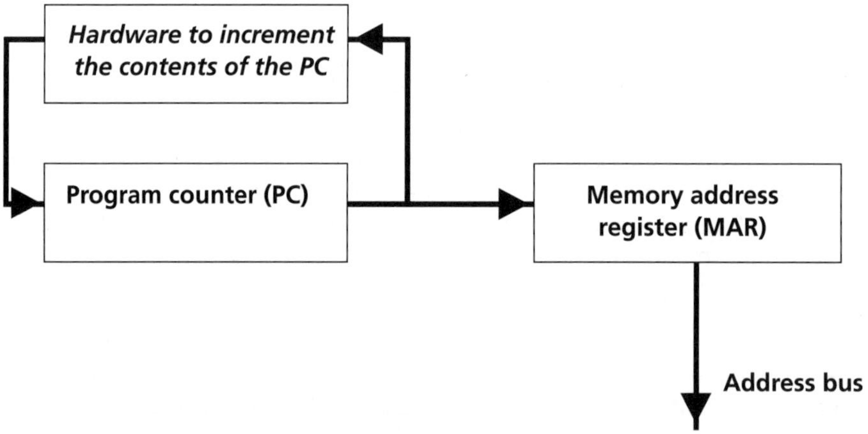

Figure 7.4: If we assume that each instruction (opcode and any associated operand) is contained within a single unique memory location (i.e. that they do not span more than one memory address), then when executing instructions in sequence it is only necessary to increment the value stored in the PC.

In the case that instructions are executed by selection and by iteration, we need to provide hardware that will enable a completely new value to be loaded into the PC. For example, consider the repeated execution of a set of instructions (i.e. by repeated iteration) as indicated in Figure 7.5. In this simple example, the processor executes an instruction at address $0000 (this is a value that we have arbitrarily chosen) – note our use of a dollar symbol, which indicates that we are specifying a number in hexadecimal form.

The next instruction is at address $0001 – followed by address $0002, etc. This process of sequential instruction execution continues until we reach address $0005. Here, we assume the processor encounters a 'Jump' instruction. This instruction is equivalent to the contentious 'GoTo' statement encountered in many high-level programming languages (it is also known as an 'unconditional branch') and we will assume that it instructs the processor that the next instruction to be executed is at address $0000. Thus program execution 'loops back' and within the processor this necessitates the loading of a new value into the PC (the address $0000).

In Figure 7.6 we advance Figure 7.4 to indicate the need for additional hardware that will enable the PC to be loaded with a particular binary value. This load operation may occur when, for example:

- A 'jump' instruction is encountered
- A branch instruction is encountered. (Branch instructions enable the processor to execute instructions by selection; the action taken depends on the outcome of some computation. By analogy, the branch instruction may be considered to parallel the 'if… then…else…' instruction employed in high-level languages.)
- Program execution is initiated
- The processor is to commence execution (enter) an interrupt service routine – see Chapter 8.

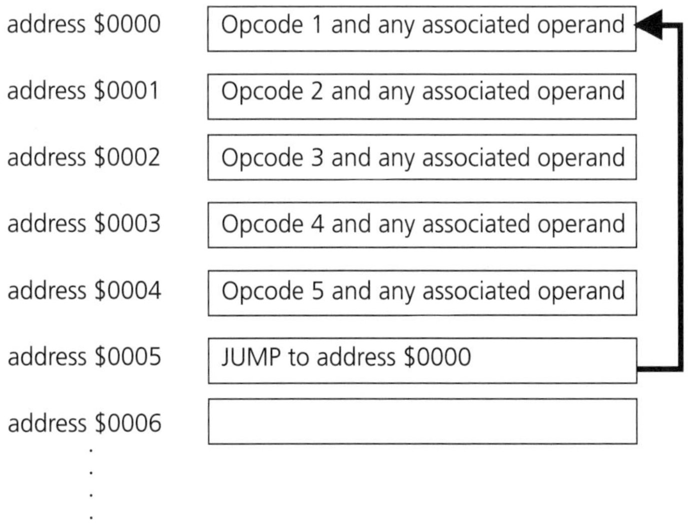

Figure 7.5: The use of a 'jump' instruction that results in the repeated execution of a set of instructions (i.e. the execution of instructions by repeated iteration)

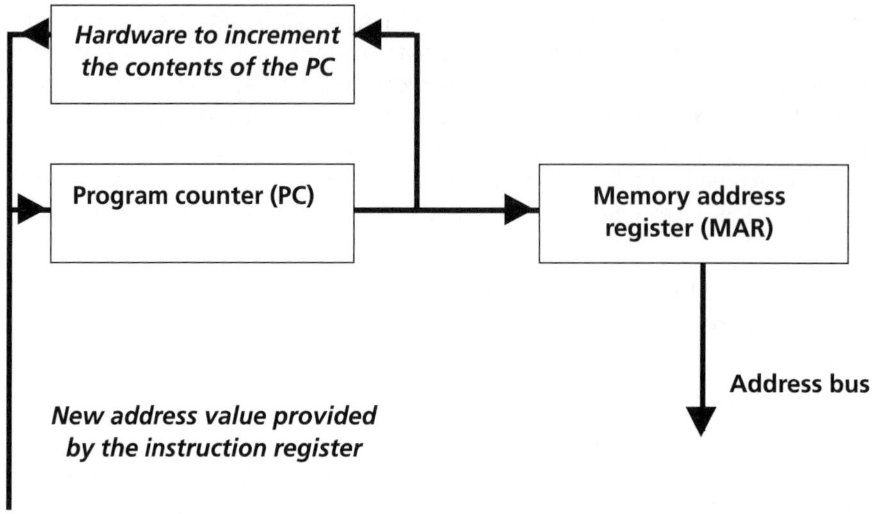

Figure 7.6: As discussed, we need to provide a mechanism whereby a new address may be loaded into the program counter. As will be discussed shortly, in the case of 'jump' and 'branch' instructions, this address may be generated by the instruction register.

- **The memory buffer register (MBR):** in the previous description, we focused on processor 'sub-units' that operate on the generation of addresses and, as we indicated, the MAR acts as the interface between the address bus connections and the PC. The memory buffer register performs a similar function in relation to the flow of opcodes and operands into and out of the CPU. In fact, the MBR interfaces the data bus connections with several sub-units within the CPU that deal with the processing of opcodes and operands. Thus when data is to be written to memory or when a read operation is performed, the MBR serves as a temporary buffer
- **The instruction register (IR):** in the case of our simple processor model, we have assumed that each opcode (together with any associated operand) is stored in a single memory location. In the case of 'real' processors this is often not the case and an opcode/operand combination can span two or even more memory locations – however, for simplicity we overlook this complication. Furthermore, we will assume that an opcode can have a maximum of one operand (i.e. an opcode has no associated operand or one operand).

  When an instruction fetch occurs, the opcode and operand are passed through the MBR to the instruction register. Here (as in memory) the opcode and operands are segregated, see Figure 7.7.

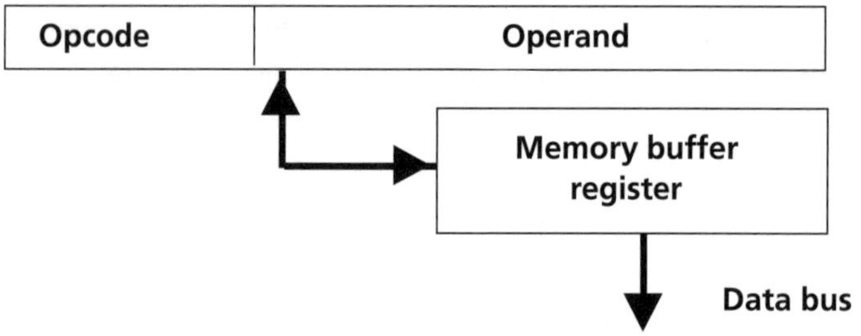

Figure 7.7: The instruction register allows hardware within the processor to extract opcode and operand information from the instruction currently in execution

- **The arithmetic and logic unit (ALU) and register X:** As its name implies, the arithmetic and logic unit is responsible for the arithmetic operations (e.g. addition and subtraction) and logic (e.g. shifting a binary number so many places to the left or right). Register X (or simply 'X') is the name that we will use when referring to a register used for the temporary storage of a value during a mathematical operation. For example, a program fragment may contain instructions of the form illustrated in Figure 7.8.

Load X with the contents of a particular memory location (address)
Add to X the value 23 (hex)
Shift the contents of X one place to the right
Store the value contained in X at a particular memory location (address)

Figure 7.8: Indicating the use of Register X as a temporary store during arithmetic and logical operations

As each instruction is executed, appropriate signals are applied to the ALU to indicate the mathematical operation to be performed, together with the source of input data and the destination of the result. In this context, it is important to remember that the source and destination referred to here relate to registers within the CPU. For example, the MBR and Register X are possible source and destination registers, see Figure 7.9.

- **The condition control register (CCR):** the individual bits (commonly referred to as 'flags') that comprise the CCR have different meanings and are set or reset according to the outcome of the last operation performed by the ALU. For example, one bit within the CCR is used to indicate whether an arithmetic operation generated a carry. Thus, for example, if the processor were to perform an addition instruction this may or may not generate a carry of 1 (e.g. in the case that the binary value 00000011 is added to 11111111 a carry of 1 would occur). If the next instruction to be executed is a conditional branch (in which the condition for branching depends on whether or not a carry of 1 has occurred), a check would be made to determine the status of the carry bit within the CCR. Other bits in the CCR may be used to indicate that an ALU operation has generated a negative result and to indicate a result of zero. The CCR is sometimes referred to as the 'processor status register' (PSR)
- **The control unit (CU):** This is responsible for orchestrating and managing all operations performed by the processor (such as register transfers and defining each arithmetic operation to be carried out by the ALU). All timing and synchronisation of signals, register transfers and other activities are derived from a clock signal generated by hardware within, and external to the processor. As we have discussed, the instruction register (IR) holds the opcode and operand of the current instruction that has been fetched from memory. The control unit must decode each opcode to identify the signals that must be generated to permit successful instruction execution. In the case of a conditional instruction (conditional branch) the control unit will also take input from the condition control register (CCR). This interconnectivity is indicated in Figure 7.9.

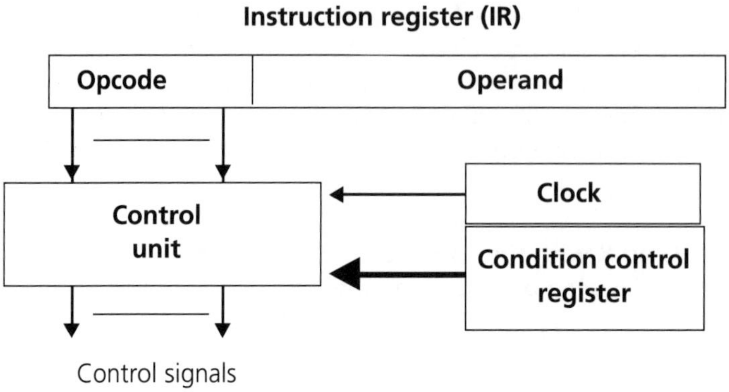

Figure 7.9: The control unit is shown taking input from the IR and CCR

Microprocessors vary in processing power and this may be categorised according to word size, processing speed and memory capacity. Word size refers to the number of bits the CPU is able to manipulate at one time and is based on the size of the CPU's registers. A CPU with a 32-bit word size is called a 32-bit processor. Most PCs are today are powered by 32-bit or 64-bit processors.

Activity 7.1

The program counter

What is the purpose of the program counter and what do you believe would be the effect of the contents of this register being corrupted?

Activity 7.2

A typical processor

Using the library or Internet facilities, research the architecture of at least one CPU. For example, use a search engine to obtain information on the Intel Dual Core series of processors.

Activity 7.3

Address space

A processor has a 16-bit address bus.
How many different addresses may it access?

Activity 7.4

Condition Control Register

Describe two functions of the condition control register

7.3 Microcontrollers

Computer-based technologies are playing an ever-increasing role across a very wide variety of applications. For example, many domestic appliances such as washing machines, refrigerators or televisions, make use of computer technologies. Even the average car is typically equipped with a number of computer systems. Such computers perform specific tasks and are, therefore, not the general-purpose programmable machines that we have referred to in previous chapters. Consequently, such systems are commonly known as 'embedded controllers'. In a washing machine, for example, the embedded controller is able to control the washing and drying cycles, and (in principle at least) optimise the conditions under which garments of a certain type are washed. In the case of a car, embedded controllers may be used to optimise the efficiency of the engine, adjust the temperature within the car, and even sometimes provide irritating audio warning messages. Thus, embedded controllers perform specific functions and at the heart of the embedded controller is a 'microcontroller'. This is a special form of microprocessor which is particularly suited to control applications. Often a microcontroller chip will contain ROM and RAM, and will make available to the designer a number of connections that are used for control purposes. When referring to the ROM and RAM located on the microcontroller chip, we generally use the terms 'on-board ROM' and 'on-board RAM'. (In fact, some microprocessors also make use of on-board RAM.) The on-board ROM contains the program to be executed by the microcontroller, and this is programmed when the embedded controller is manufactured. The control connections offered by a microcontroller typically allow control signals to be passed from the microcontroller to peripheral hardware, or vice versa. This peripheral hardware often takes the form of 'transducers' – these are electrical components able to convert some physical stimulus into an electrical signal. For example, a temperature transducer measures the temperature of some physical entity and converts this into an electrical voltage.

There are a number of differences between microprocessors and microcontrollers. For example:

- To be operational, the microprocessor has to be part of larger system comprising other components such as memory and input/ output devices. It is this collection of components that make up a complete computer system. The microcontroller, on the other hand, is largely a self-contained unit, having its own internal memory and other additional features on one chip. It can therefore function as a computer without the assistance of major external parts
- A microcontroller dedicated to a particular application will be pre-programmed solely to fulfil the needs of that particular application. In many cases, such as washing machines or DVD players, the programming is very basic and the software is stored in the microcontroller's ROM. This will not change throughout the lifetime of the system. From a software point of view, the microcontroller does not therefore need a facility for secondary memory. A microprocessor/CPU used in a general-purpose programmable machine such as a PC has a far more complex role to play. Not only does it execute the programs of the PC's operating system software, but it also executes any number of different applications software programs. Unlike the microcontroller, the microprocessor does not permanently store programs, which are located separately in the system's memory
- The microprocessor/CPU is usually both physically and functionally separate from the system's memory. One of the microprocessor's main functions is to move program code and data from the system's external memory to the CPU. The microcontroller has its own internal RAM and ROM and is designed to use a much smaller range of instructions to move code and data from the internal memory to the ALU.

The amount of on-chip memory in a microcontroller is, of course, vastly smaller than the memory of the most basic PC. That is because the microcontroller only requires a limited memory as its primary purpose is to control a specific application.

Activity 7.5

The embedded controller

Identify four appliances in your home or place of work that employ embedded controllers. In each case identify the main function(s) of the embedded controller and comment upon the advantages (or disadvantages) that are associated with the inclusion of computer-based technology within the device.

7.4 Summary

In this chapter we have introduced various functional units contained within a typical CPU. In addition we have also discussed embedded controllers. These employ computing technologies that are put together with a specific application in mind (usually this is a control application). In addition we have distinguished between microprocessors and microcontrollers.

7.5 Review questions

Review question 7.1

What is the major function of the ALU?

Review question 7.2

State three aspects of a microcontroller that distinguish it from a microprocessor.

Review question 7.3

Why is a microcontroller equipped with on-board ROM?

Review question 7.4

State the purpose of the MBR.

Review question 7.5

State the purpose of the CCR.

7.6 Feedback on activities

Feedback on activity 7.1: The program counter

The program counter holds the address of the instruction currently being executed. Should the contents of this register be corrupted or otherwise lost, then the CPU would not know the address of the next instruction that is to be fetched from memory – program execution would fail (or possibly continue in an unpredictable and unstable manner).

Feedback on activity 7.2: A typical processor

No feedback on this activity.

Feedback on activity 7.3: Address space

Number of addresses equals 216=65,536.

Feedback on activity 7.4: Condition control register

One bit within the CCR is used to indicate whether an arithmetic operation generated a carry. One bit in the CCR may be used to indicate that an ALU operation has generated a negative result.

Feedback on activity 7.5: The embedded controller

Many different appliances may be selected – TV, washing machine, security systems etc. In considering the advantages and/or disadvantages, you should consider these not only from the perspective of the appliance to which they interface but also from their interface with the human operator. Do they enhance simplicity of use, do they increase complexity (by providing too much functionality) etc.? Also, do they increase reliability – or otherwise?

Further reading

- Englander, I (2003), *The Architecture of Computer Hardware and Systems Software: An Information Technology Approach*, John Wiley & Sons
- Stallings, W (2003), *Computer Organization and Architecture: Designing for Performance*, Pearson Education Inc

CHAPTER 8

Interrupts

OVERVIEW

The processor needs a way of efficiently identifying when hardware within the computer needs its attention. To this end, a system of interrupts is employed whereby a device that seeks to gain processor access sends a special signal to hardware that is connected to the processor. This causes the processor to stop its current activity and run a special program known as the interrupt service routine. Once the device that generated the interrupt has been dealt with, the processor continues with its original activity.

Learning outcomes At the end of this chapter you should be able to:

- Discuss the handling of interrupts from both single and multiple sources
- Describe the importance of assigning interrupt priorities and the efficiency issues relating to the interrupt technique
- Distinguish between maskable and non-maskable forms of interrupt.

8.1 Introduction

To understand the nature of interrupts it is convenient to use a brief analogy. Suppose that you are working on a computer at home and expecting somebody to visit. How do you know when the person has arrived? You could regularly walk to the front door, open it and see if anybody is there. Naturally this isn't a very efficient approach! Within a computer, this type of technique is referred to as 'polling'. If, for example, a CPU wishes to know whether a keyboard key has been pressed, it may regularly 'poll' a particular memory location to see if a character code has appeared at this location. However, as with the human example of going to the door, regularly polling locations is not efficient as time is needlessly used in checking to see if a particular event has occurred. A system of *interrupts* provides an alternative solution. Returning to our analogy of expecting a visitor, rather than regularly polling the front door, we could buy a doorbell. When the visitor arrives, they press the doorbell, we hear the sound and break off from what we are doing to go to the door. In short, the doorbell 'interrupts' us from our work. Of course, we may be carrying out some fairly critical task when the doorbell rings. Perhaps we are engaged in reading a chapter of this book when the visitor arrives and so, before we get up from the table to answer the door, we may mark in our notes exactly where we are up to (say, by placing a cross in the margin) so that when our visitor has left we can easily pick up from where we have left off.

In a PC, the CPU must deal with many tasks, such as detecting keyboard input (and dealing with it), detecting that one of the disk drives needs some form of attention, etc. To deal with these by regularly polling (checking to determine whether or not devices need attention) would be extremely wasteful of CPU time. As we shall see, the interrupt approach is generally much more efficient.

In this chapter we outline techniques used to enable the processor to handle interrupts from both single and multiple sources.

8.2 Dealing with a single interrupt

An interrupt is a special signal that is applied to one of the pins (connection) of the processor chip. When the logic state of this connection is changed, an interrupt is said to have occurred. The processor then carries out several tasks. These are as follows:

- The processor completes the execution of the current instruction
- The processor stores the contents of all its registers at a special location within main memory (RAM)
- The processor accesses the 'interrupt vector' and uses this to locate a special program known as the 'interrupt service routine'. This program has been written to tell the processor the instructions it should follow when an interrupt occurs
- When the processor has completed executing the 'interrupt service routine', it restores the register contents that were previously saved in RAM
- The processor continues with the task it was performing prior to the interrupt occurring.

This may sound a little complicated. For example, you may wonder why the processor saved the contents of its registers to RAM. Using the analogy presented in the introduction to this chapter, this is just like marking a page of the book prior to getting up from the table to answer the doorbell. If the processor does not save the contents of its registers, then they will be lost and the processor will have no way of picking up from where it left off once it has serviced the interrupt.

Here you will recall, for example, the 'program counter'. As previously discussed, this register stores the address of the next memory location that a processor is to access as it executes a program. If the contents of the program counter are lost, then the processor has no idea of where it is up to in program execution. Saving the registers in memory before servicing the interrupt enables them to be subsequently restored – and enables the processor to continue its normal activities once it has serviced the interrupt.

The interrupt vector is a pointer to the address of the first instruction that a processor should execute when an interrupt occurs.

A program called the interrupt service routine (ISR) tells the processor what to do when an interrupt occurs. A special location in memory is used to store the 'interrupt vector'. This corresponds to the address of the first instruction in the interrupt service routine (see Figure 8.1). Once the contents of the processor's registers have been saved, the processor accesses the interrupt vector and uses this to locate the first instruction contained within the interrupt service routine. The execution of the interrupt service routine now begins.

Suppose that the pressing of a keyboard key gives rise to an interrupt. To deal with this, the processor:

- Completes the current instruction
- Saves the contents of its registers
- Accesses the interrupt vector
- Uses this to locate the interrupt service routine.

The program would read the code corresponding to the keyboard key that has been pressed, and use this in some way. Subsequently, the process restores the contents of its registers and is then able to pick up from where it left off – prior to the key being pressed. The events that take place when an interrupt occurs are summarised in Figure 8.2.

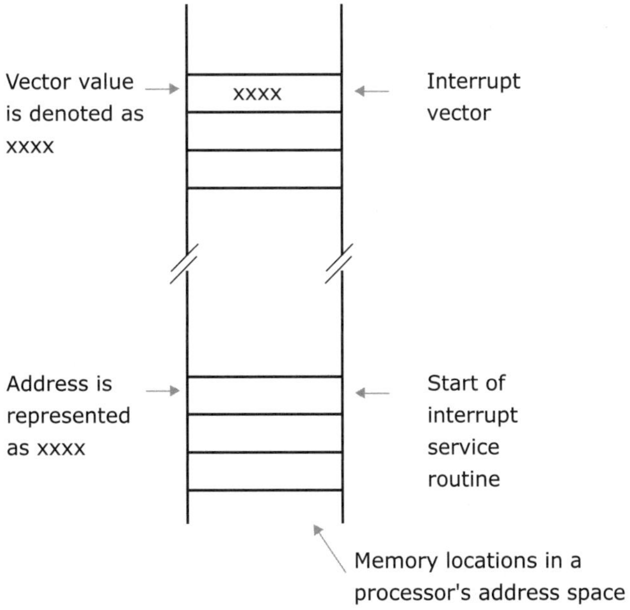

Figure 8.1: The use of an interrupt vector to point to the start of the interrupt service routine

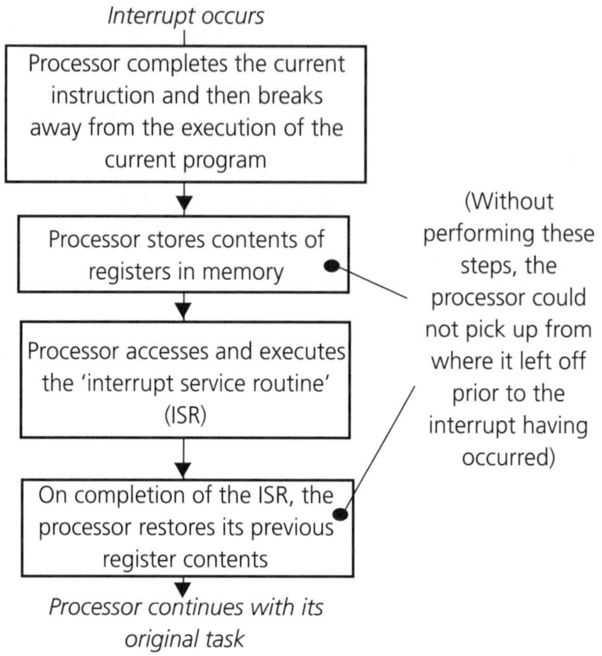
Interrupt occurs
Processor completes the current instruction and then breaks away from the execution of the current program
Processor stores contents of registers in memory
Processor accesses and executes the 'interrupt service routine' (ISR)
On completion of the ISR, the processor restores its previous register contents
Processor continues with its original task
(Without performing these steps, the processor could not pick up from where it left off prior to the interrupt having occurred)

Figure 8.2: Illustrating the events that take place when an interrupt occurs. Note that if the contents of the registers (i.e. the 'context' of the current program) are not saved prior to the interrupt being serviced, then it is not possible to resume normal activity once the interrupt service routine has run to completion.

8.3 The need to handle multiple interrupts

The discussion provided in the previous section allows us to understand the way in which interrupts can be used, but does not explain how a processor is able to handle interrupts from multiple sources. The ability to handle multiple interrupts is vital in the operation of the modern computer, as there are many devices that generate them. Let's consider the hard disk and the interface chip which allows the computer to communicate with the printer.

Hard disk

Suppose that the processor wishes to read material that is stored on the hard disk. To do this, it must set up a 'read' request, whereby the CPU informs special hardware called the hard disk controller (see Chapter 9), not only that it wants to perform a read operation, but also of the exact details of the information that it wishes to access. Having provided this information, the hard disk controller is then responsible for locating and retrieving the relevant information, and making it available to the processor.

There would be little point in the processor idly waiting for the hard disk controller to complete this task – a read operation will in fact take some significant time. It is therefore better for the processor to make the read request, and then carry on with some other activity until the required information becomes available. At this point, the hard disk controller will generate an interrupt informing the processor that the read operation has been completed.

Printer

We generally think of a printing activity as being 'unidirectional'. When we consider the processor sending characters and symbols to the printer, it seems that the flow of data is from the computer to the printer. However, there is also a need for a flow of data in the opposite direction – from the printer to the processor. There can be a number of reasons for this flow, one of the simplest of which occurs should the printer run out of paper. As we know from experience, when this happens an 'out-of-paper' message usually appears on the computer screen. This is as a result of a signal generated by the printer which is sent back to the computer. The flow of data is, thus, not unidirectional, but rather bidirectional.

The computer sends characters or symbols to the printer by writing these to a special chip which appears in the processor's address space – quite simply, the processor performs write operations to a particular memory location. In turn, values written to the location are passed to the printer. Should the printer run out of paper, it passes a signal to the chip in the computer to which it is interfaced, and in turn this chip generates an interrupt. If properly handled, this interrupt will then cause the 'out of-paper' message to appear on the computer screen.

As you can see from the above two scenarios, the two forms of interrupt described need to be dealt with in quite different ways by the interrupt service routine. In the modern PC, interrupts can be generated by a variety of hardware. In the text that follows, we briefly describe the way a computer handles interrupts from multiple sources.

Activity 8.1

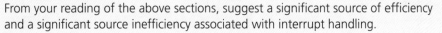

Interrupt efficiency

From your reading of the above sections, suggest a significant source of efficiency and a significant source inefficiency associated with interrupt handling.

Activity 8.2

The interrupt service routine (ISR) 1

Why is it necessary to save the contents of the CPU's registers prior to executing the interrupt service routine?

8.4 Handling multiple interrupts

As indicated in the previous section, a variety of hardware may generate interrupts; each must be handled in an appropriate way. For example, if we return for a moment to our earlier analogy of being at home, engaged in some activity, when either the phone or doorbell rings. These represent two different sources of interrupt. Clearly, should the phone ring, there would be no point in going to the front door – and when the doorbell rings there would be no point in picking up the phone! Fortunately, the ringing of the phone and the doorbell are likely to correspond to two different sounds that we can readily distinguish and so it is easy for us to identify the specific interrupt source.

In the case of a computer system, a special-purpose integrated circuit known as an 'interrupt controller' is commonly used to allow the system to handle interrupts from a variety of sources.

In Figure 8.3, we illustrate a CPU connected to an interrupt controller. As can be seen from this illustration, the CPU and interrupt controller are interconnected via the address and data buses. Furthermore, a wire from the interrupt controller is connected to the interrupt pin or the processor. The interrupt controller is responsible for generating the interrupt signal which is applied to the CPU. Various devices (each able to generate interrupts) are connected to the interrupt controller.

In Figure 8.3, we show the hard disk and CD-ROM controllers connected to the interrupt controller. In reality, there would be many other devices connected to a single interrupt controller. We also indicate the presence of a register, which is labelled 'interrupt ID register'. Let us now have a look at how this configuration could operate:

- Suppose that the hard disk controller generates an interrupt. This signal is applied to the interrupt controller
- The interrupt controller will now perform two tasks: it will load into the 'interrupt ID register' a binary code that will shortly allow the CPU to identify the source of the interrupt – it will also generate an interrupt signal which is passed to the CPU
- The CPU receives the interrupt signal, completes the current instruction that it is executing, saves the contents of its internal registers and accesses the interrupt vector. It then begins executing the interrupt service routine (recall this is the special program that is responsible for handling interrupts)
- On commencement of execution, the interrupt service routine will perform a 'read' operation from the register (which we have called the interrupt ID register), and read the binary code contained therein. This code is used by the processor to identify the source of the interrupt. Once this source is known, the processor can perform the appropriate actions.

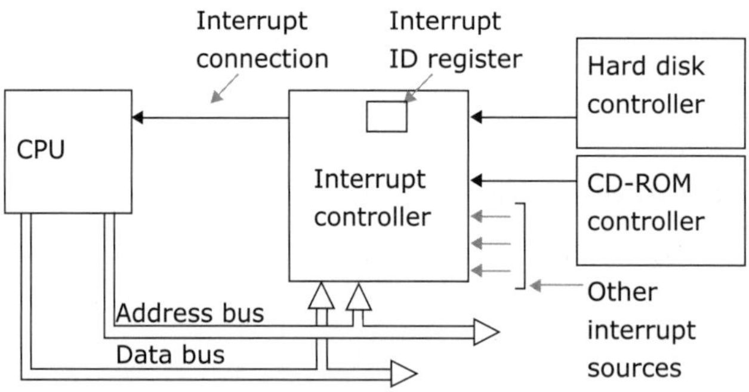

Figure 8.3: The use of an interrupt controller to handle multiple interrupt sources

The above description is straightforward and should be fairly easy to follow. However, we have made some simplifications and have so far overlooked one important scenario: what happens if while the processor is servicing an interrupt, a second, or even third interrupt occurs from other sources? Returning for a moment to our earlier analogy, we can imagine a scenario in which we are talking on the phone (i.e. servicing the first interrupt) when the doorbell rings. Naturally, the way we deal with this situation will depend upon the relative importance that we attach to dealing with the phone call, as compared with answering the door.

In the case of the modern PC, interrupts occur with great frequency and it is common for the processor to have to handle many interrupts that occur in close succession.

One of the additional tasks of the interrupt controller is to help with such situations. The interrupt controller contains additional registers and it is possible for the processor to write to these registers and so assign priorities to the different sources of interrupt to which the interrupt controller is connected. Here, it is important to remember that:

- A lower priority interrupt cannot interrupt a higher priority interrupt
- A higher priority interrupt can interrupt a lower priority interrupt.

Suppose that a higher priority is assigned to the hard disk controller than to the CD-ROM controller. In this case, if the processor was handling an interrupt generated by the hard disk controller, when a further interrupt arrived from the CD-ROM controller, this latter interrupt will be ignored until the processor has completed handling the interrupt generated by the hard disk controller.

The above approach provides considerable power and flexibility in the handling of interrupts and, most importantly, the hardware required is straightforward. In Figure 8.4, we summarise the handling of multiple interrupts.

Before concluding this discussion on interrupts there is one other important point that you should note. A modern computer employs more than one type of interrupt. Below we briefly consider maskable and non-maskable interrupts.

Let us return for a moment to our analogy and suppose that, while we are speaking on the telephone (i.e. handling an interrupt), a fire breaks out within the building and the fire alarm sounds. Naturally, the fire alarm is of great importance and it would not be sensible to ignore it! In short, the fire alarm (which represents another form of interrupt) should be regarded as a 'non-maskable' interrupt, inasmuch as the fire alarm itself should never be turned off (in computer terminology: it should never be 'masked'). In comparison, we may choose to turn off other potential forms of interrupt because we are doing something of importance and the interrupt source is deemed to be of less importance. We may, for example, occasionally unplug the phone so that we will not be disturbed. In this sense, the phone is representing a source of maskable interrupt.

Activity 8.3

The interrupt service routine 2

A programmer decides to relocate the interrupt service routine. What actions must the programmer perform?

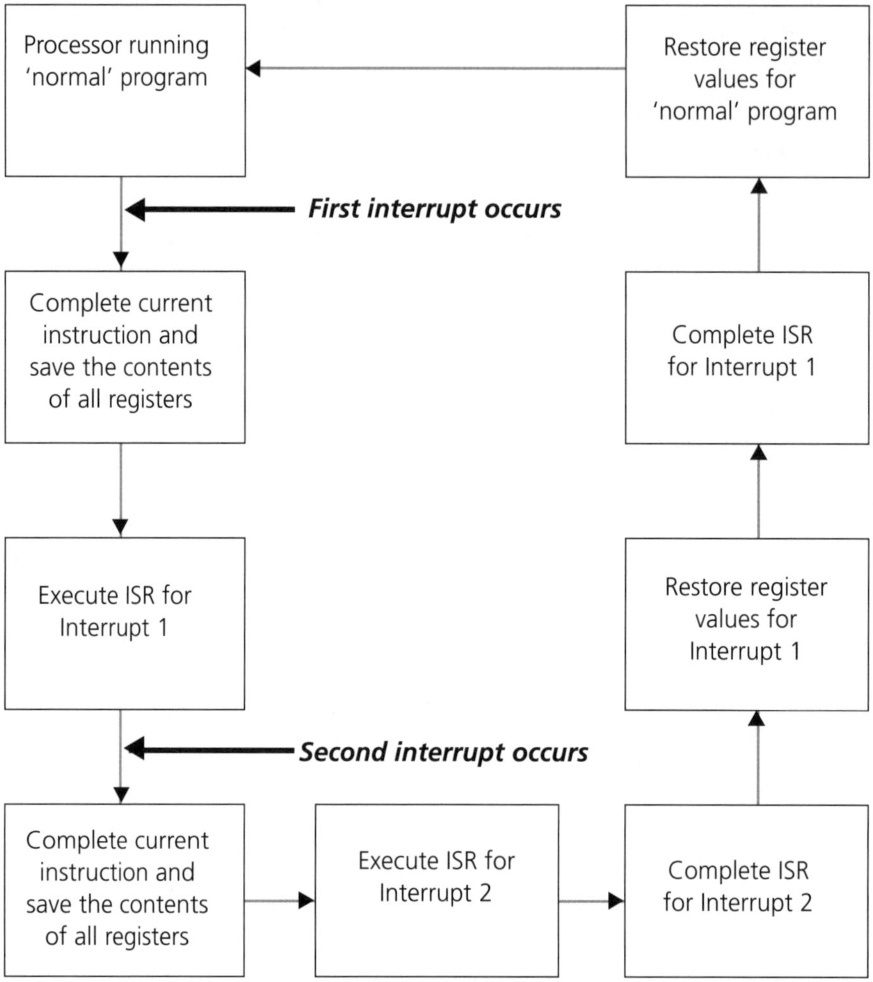

Figure 8.4: A processor is running its 'normal' program when an interrupt occurs (Interrupt 1). It stores registers (the 'context' of this 'normal' program) and begins to run the 'interrupt service routine' (ISR) for Interrupt 1. While this is executing, a second higher priority interrupt occurs (Interrupt 2). The processor breaks off from servicing Interrupt 1, stores registers (the 'context' of the interrupt service routine for this interrupt) and runs the ISR for Interrupt 2. On completion it restores the context of Interrupt 1 and runs the ISR for this interrupt. Once this is completed, it restores the context of its original ('normal') program and returns to running this code (from the point at which it broke off when Interrupt 1 occurred).

A non-maskable interrupt can never be ignored by the processor and is used to deal with critical events. However, maskable interrupts may be disabled, while (for example) the CPU is performing some critical function.

8.5 Summary

In this chapter, we have examined the use of interrupts and have provided an insight into the way in which a CPU is able to accept interrupts from both single and multiple sources. Although the interrupt technique provides us with a simple method of achieving I/O, it does have associated overheads which detract from the method's overall efficiency. These specifically relate to the time taken to save and restore the contents of the processor's internal registers.

8.6 Review questions

Review question 8.1

What do you understand by the abbreviation 'ISR'?

Review question 8.2

What is the purpose of the 'interrupt vector'?

Review question 8.3

State two functions of the interrupt controller.

Review question 8.4

What is a maskable interrupt?

Review question 8.5

What is a non-maskable interrupt?

Review question 8.6

Can a lower-priority interrupt interrupt a higher-priority interrupt?

Review question 8.7

Within the context of a computer, what do you understand by the term 'polling'?

8.7 Feedback on activities

Feedback on activity 8.1: Interrupt efficiency

From a hardware point of view, an interrupt-based system is easily implemented – the hardware required is very simple. Consequently, the interrupt paradigm is very efficient when viewed from a hardware perspective. However, each time the processor services an interrupt, it must carry out a number of tasks, such as saving and restoring register contents. This occupies some time – while saving and restoring registers, program execution is delayed. This represents the greatest inefficiency associated with the interrupt approach.

Feedback on activity 8.2: The interrupt service routine (ISR) 1

If the contents of these registers are not saved, then it will be impossible for them to be restored once the execution of the interrupt service routine has been completed. In this case, the processor would have no way of knowing where it was up to in terms of program execution prior to the interrupt occurring, and could not therefore recommence program execution from the place at which it left off. By saving the registers prior to servicing the interrupt, it is possible for the register contents to be restored at the end of the interrupt service routine and so the processor is able to continue seamlessly with its earlier activities.

Feedback on activity 8.3: The interrupt service routine 2

The programmer may freely relocate the ISR but must also appropriately update the interrupt vector. The interrupt vector is found at a certain (defined) memory address – the location of the interrupt vector cannot be changed. However, the ISR may be relocated – as long as the interrupt vector is also updated.

Further reading

- Clements, A (2006), *Principles of Computer Hardware*, Oxford University Press
- Patterson, SA & and Hennessy, JL (2004), *Computer Organization & Design: The Hardware/Software Interface*, (3rd edn) Morgan Kaufmann

CHAPTER 9

Storage devices

OVERVIEW

Computers provide us not only with the ability to quickly process data, but also to support the storage and rapid retrieval of data. In fact, over the last twenty years one of the major developments that has occurred in the computing world are the advances that have been made in connection with storage media. Hard disks (which are pivotal in the operation of the modern computer) have developed not only in terms of their storage capacity but also in their ability to support high-speed access. In parallel, an ever-greater emphasis is placed upon the networking of computer systems and the development of network architectures that operate at ever-greater speeds. We have now reached a position whereby it is possible to access a vast amount of data stored on remote machines very quickly.

Learning outcomes At the end of this chapter you should be able to:

- Distinguish between primary and secondary storage devices
- Discuss the basic characteristics and operation of storage devices that are based on magnetisation techniques
- Discuss the basic characteristics and operation of storage devices that are based on optical techniques.

9.1 Introduction

A major part of this chapter focuses upon secondary storage devices. In this context, we consider the operation of the hard disk, floppy disk, and CD-ROM. In each case we briefly review the underlying principles of operation, and comment on the capabilities and performance of each technology. As we will see, the hard disk and floppy disk operate in a similar manner (although the latter offers much lower performance). On the other hand, the principle of operation of the compact disc is somewhat different, and in our discussions on this technology we consider CDs that support only read operations, and those which allow us to both read and write.

The floppy disk has a long history of association with computer technologies. However, this storage technique is now reaching the end of its useful life. Not only are the storage capabilities of floppy disks quite small (when considered in the context of the great volumes of data and file sizes that are associated with today's computer systems) but also transfer times (the time needed to for read or write operations) are relatively long. Both writable CDs and 'memory sticks' massively outstrip floppy disks in terms of their storage capacity and provide reduced read and write times. However, we include discussion on floppy disks as they are still quite frequently encountered.

9.2 Primary and secondary storage

We can broadly classify storage devices as providing either 'primary storage' or 'secondary storage'. Primary storage refers to systems that store instructions and data that can be directly accessed by the processor and so they store the program(s) in execution. Main memory (RAM), cache memory and read only memory are primary storage devices. As we have discussed in previous chapters, cache and main memory differ in terms of speed and cost per unit storage capacity. However, they are both able to support read and write operations but do not retain their contents once the machine is turned off.

Devices such as the hard disk drive, floppy disk drive, writable CD and so-called 'USB flash cards' or memory sticks provide us with examples of secondary storage devices. These are characterised as offering greater storage capacity than primary storage devices, but operate more slowly. (Recall the memory/storage hierarchy that we have previously discussed – faster devices tend to be more expensive in their cost per unit storage capacity.) Furthermore, when the power to the machine is turned off, these types of storage device retain their contents.

In the case of the modern computer, the hard disk forms the main secondary storage device. The performance of the hard disk has increased dramatically over the last twenty years. Not only have hard disk drives become much smaller, but also they are able to store much more data – and support read and write operations at higher speeds. In the next section, we will briefly consider the operation of the hard disk drive.

Activity 9.1

The concept of primary and secondary storage

Distinguish between primary and secondary storage devices.

Activity 9.2

Primary and secondary storage devices

State two forms of primary storage device and two forms of secondary storage device. In each case, indicate in relation to the modern desktop computer which device you would expect to offer the highest storage capacity.

Activity 9.3

Storage capacity

Determine the capacity of the hard disk that is fitted to your computer and the amount of this capacity that is presently in use.

9.3 Secondary storage using magnetisation

In this section we consider secondary storage devices whose underlying principle of operation is the magnetisation of a medium. Here we briefly examine the hard disk and floppy disk, and in the next section we turn our attention to the compact disc (CD), which employs optical techniques for the recording of digital data.

The hard disk

The hard disk represents the most important secondary storage mechanism used in the modern computer. In this section, we will briefly consider the structure and operation of this device.

Essential components within a hard disk unit are illustrated in Figure 9.1, and a photograph of a disk assembly is provided in Figure 9.2. As can be seen from these illustrations, the hard disk consists of a series of disks or platters that are mounted on a common drive shaft. Typically, the disks have diameters in the range 1.8 to 5.25 inches, and their rotational rate is in the range of 60 to 150 rotations per second. (Earlier hard disks were considerably larger – for example, in the mid-1980s, the DEC R81 employed 4 platters, each of which was 14 inches in diameter and offered a storage capacity of 456MB.)

The two surfaces of each disk are coated with either a ferric oxide material or a metal alloy (the coatings are of the order of 2,000 atoms in thickness). Above this material is an extremely thin lubricating layer – a fluorocarbon. The underlying technique that is used to record binary 1s and 0s on the surface of the disk relies upon the magnetisation of the surface coating. This is achieved by means of read/write heads, one of which is positioned adjacent to each disk surface. In fact, these read/write heads essentially fly across the surface of the disk, being separated from it by a remarkably small distance – of the order of a fraction of a millionth's of a metre (e.g. 0.01 micrometres)! The spacing between the read/write head and the disk's surface is in fact critical and it is remarkable that this precise spacing can be achieved in a reliable way.

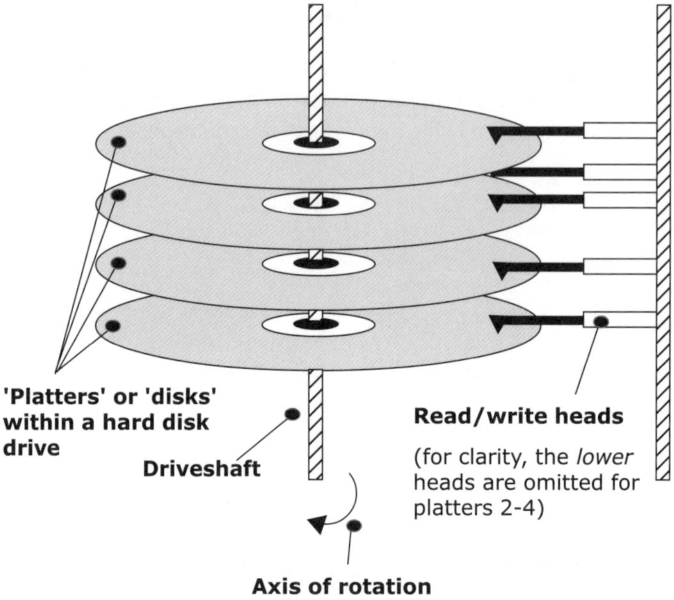

Figure 9.1: Main components within the hard disk. A number of read/write heads are able to simultaneously read or write from a set of rotating disks.

Given the close proximity of the read/write head to the disk's surface, even the smallest contaminants, such as minute dust particles, can have catastrophic consequences and cause what is called a 'head crash'. If this occurs, it results in total failure of the device.

As indicated above, there is a small read/write head adjacent to each surface. Within the head there is a minute coil of wire and when current is passed through this coil, locations on the adjacent disk's surface can be magnetised and thereby 1s and 0s recorded. The read/write heads are attached to a common 'actuator'. This is shown in Figures 9.1 and 9.2 and enables the read/write heads to be moved across the disk's surface – from the periphery towards the centre and vice versa. Here it is important to note that all read/write heads move together – they are not individually driven.

The read/write head is also able to sense the magnetisation of the disk surface; changes in magnetisation induce minute voltages into the coil of wire that is within each head assembly. These are amplified and the signal generated enables read operations to be performed.

Figure 9.2: A hard disk removed from its sealed container. A disk platter can be seen, together with a read/write head

Vinyl records, which for many years provided an essential approach to recording music, employed a spiral recording technique. In this case, the single track along which music is recorded gradually spirals towards the centre of the record. The recording technique used on both hard and floppy disks is somewhat different to this approach. As shown in Figure 9.3, data is recorded on the disk in a series of tracks or concentric rings. The read/write heads can be positioned over a track, and then data can be either written to, or read from the track. The use of multiple read/write heads (and multiple disks, which are usually referred to as 'platters') enables data to be written simultaneously to more than one disk and so increases throughput. Here, another technical term needs to be introduced – the 'cylinder'. Tracks on each disk which are at an equal radius from the centre of the disk are said to form a cylinder. A final term that is commonly employed in connection with both hard and floppy disks is the 'sector'. Each track is divided into a series of sectors – as shown in Figure 9.3.

Individual bits are not read or written to the disk drive, but rather we read or write groups of bits. The smallest group of bits that can be written is called a 'block' and typically a block may contain, say, 512 bytes.

Let us suppose that we wish to read a file from a hard disk. The processor will provide the hard disk controller (electronic hardware associated with the disk drive) with information concerning the identity of the file that it wishes to access. In turn, the disk controller will use information stored on the hard disk to relate the identity of the file that we wish to access to its physical location on the surfaces of the disks. This will involve identifying the cylinder number (and thus obtaining information on the tracks where the file can be found), and the sector number indicating at what point (or points) on a track the blocks that comprise the file may be found. Once this information has been obtained, the read/write heads will be positioned over the appropriate set of tracks. Subsequently, it is likely that it will be necessary to wait for a very brief amount of time as the disk rotates and the appropriate sector comes around. Once the sector appears under the read/write heads, then the read operation can commence.

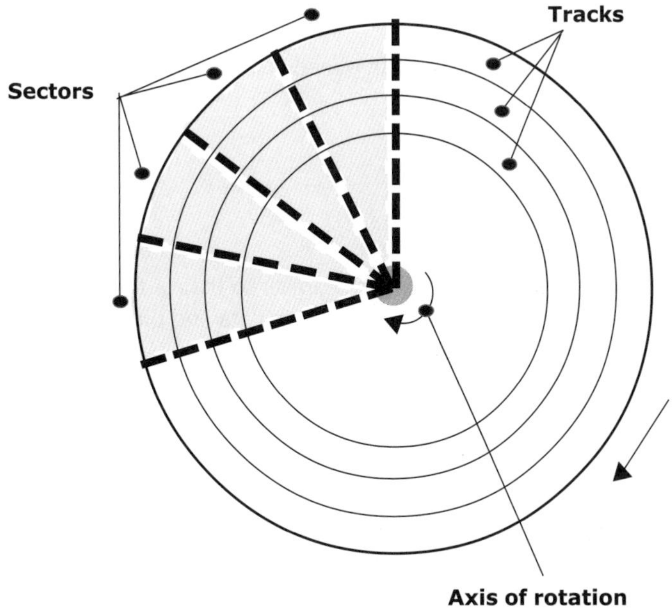

Figure 9.3: The storage format that is used on the surface of each disk

When we read or write to a hard disk, there are two key latencies (delays) that occur. The first of these corresponds to the need to move the read/write heads to the appropriate set of tracks (or cylinder) – this is called the seek time. The second is called the 'rotational latency' and corresponds to the time we must wait for the relevant sector(s) to pass beneath the read/write heads. In addition to these there is the 'settle time' (the time that it takes for the read/write heads to stop vibrating when they reach the desired track) and the 'read/write time' (the time taken to actually perform the read or write operation). When you use your computer, you may sometimes hear a slight sound from the hard disk during read or write operations. This is the noise made by the actuator responsible for moving the read/write heads to the appropriate cylinder. Naturally, we wish to reduce delays as much as possible, and so the heads should move as fast as is practical. Similarly (to reduce the rotational latency) the disks should rotate at the highest possible speed.

Modern laptop computers contain small hard disks with the capacity to store many gigabytes of data (remember that a gigabyte is actually 10,243 bytes, whereas 'giga' means 10^9). This miniaturisation of hard disk technologies is a relatively recent occurrence; in the early 1980s a typical hard disk storage capacity was in the order of 20 to 40MB. The hard disk unit itself would have been quite large – larger than a shoebox. Earlier still, hard disks were built so that it was readily possible to remove the disk assembly and replace it with another. However, this is no longer a possibility because of the very close spacing between the read/write head and the disk's surface, and the consequent need for absolute cleanliness. Today's hard disk drive assemblies are constructed within sealed units and require clean-room conditions for their assembly or repair (although repairs are not really practicable in terms of repair cost versus replacement price). If you have in your possession an unwanted hard disk drive assembly, then you might try opening it – but do remember that once you have opened the case, it will not work again! In an attempt to dissuade users from opening disk drives, unusual screws are often used and these are difficult to undo but, with a little ingenuity, this difficulty can be overcome!

Activity 9.4

Hard disk performance

Describe two latencies associated with a read or write operation to a hard disk.

The floppy disk

The underlying physical operation of a floppy disk is similar to that of the hard disk. However, floppy disks were designed to provide a method by which data and programs can be easily transferred between machines. The original floppy disk, first developed in the 1960s, was housed in a sleeve that was some eight inches square; this was reduced in size, in the 1980s, to a 5.25-inch diameter disk and eventually the 3.5 inch disk became the norm (it is said that this size was chosen by measuring the typical size of a shirt pocket!)

The floppy disk is constructed from a flexible material (Milar) that is coated with a magnetic surface material such as ferric oxide. As with the hard disk, a read/write head is used to write data to a series of concentric rings (tracks). However, the floppy disk does not employ precision engineering and the requirement that it should be possible to remove and insert disks within the disk drive means that the mechanical components used operate in a more rudimentary manner. The read-write head employed in a floppy disk does not (as is the case with the hard disk) fly over the disk's surface, but rather is in contact with it. Over time, the read-write head can therefore erode the surface layer (and so give rise to a bad disk) and the head itself is gradually contaminated by particles that are eroded from the disk's surface. This means that the read/write head must be cleaned from time to time.

As the read/write head is in contact with the surface of the disk, the high rotation speed that is associated with the hard disk cannot be employed in the case of the floppy disk. Typically, a floppy disk rotates at around six times per second, and naturally this therefore increases the rotational latency that we discussed above.

The format used in reading and writing data to a floppy disk closely follows that used in the case of a hard disk, in as much as data is written to a series of concentric tracks and the minimum unit of data that can be written is again referred to as a 'block'. If you have access to an unwanted floppy disk, it is worthwhile to spend a few minutes dismantling it.

Flash memory

As already indicated, floppy disks are now rapidly being superseded. Although older machines will still have the 3.5-inch disk drives, they are now rare to find on a new computers. For reasons of cost, storage capacity and portability, the 'USB flash cards' or, more commonly, 'memory sticks', are increasingly the norm. A typical memory stick will hold between 256MB and in excess of 2GB and can cost less than £10.

9.4 Secondary storage using optical techniques

In this section, we briefly review the operation of systems that employ optical techniques for the storage of digital information. At the present time, the four most commonly used forms of optical storage device are:

- The **CD-ROM**: compact discs of this type contain pre-recorded digital data. This data is loaded onto the disk at the time of manufacture – it cannot be deleted or overwritten. The capacity of a CD-ROM is up to 680MB.
- The **WORM**: in the case of this type of media, a user may write to it, but once written, the contents cannot be deleted or overwritten. The acronym WORM stands for 'write once, read many' – indicating the single write operation and the freedom to repeatedly read the content
- The recordable CD (**CD-R**): this type of CD (which is a special form of WORM) can support both read and write operations. For this type of device, the reading speed is higher than the writing speed and this is often indicated by manufacturers who may quote figures such as 8x32. The ratio of these figures provides us with an indication of the relative read/write speed (i.e. 32/8=4 indicates that the device can be read four times faster than it is able to perform write operations)
- Digital versatile (video) disc (**DVD**): these are able to store very large amounts of digital data, typically up to 8.5GB. As a consequence of their enormous storage capacity, they are now the preferred media for the storage of video images and support the desktop computer's increasing role as a multimedia machine.

These different types of compact disc (and others such as Sony's mini-disc and the laser disc) all provide optical storage techniques. In the case of the WORM, writing to the disc is achieved through the use of a highly focused laser beam that is able to change the physical properties of the disc at the point at which the beam impinges upon it. The beam in fact changes the reflectance characteristic of the disc material, i.e. where the disc is 'burned' by the laser, a spot that is non-reflective is created. In other regions the disc is reflective. The difference between reflective and non-reflective locations upon the disk corresponds to the storage of digital values (0s and 1s).

In the case of a CD-ROM, a master disc is produced and from this copies are made by injection moulding such that bumps in the mould (created via the master disc) are formed in the copies. This allows discs to be manufactured at an extremely high rate and at low cost.

As indicated above, the CD-R allows both read and write operations. This is achieved by using an alloy (formed from silver, indium, antimony and tellurium). This can be in two states – crystalline or amorphous. The former state is used to record a binary zero and the latter a one. Typically, a high laser power is used to convert spots on the disk from the crystalline to amorphous states. A lower power is needed to reverse this process. Thus the spots can be converted between the two states so supporting repeated writing operations. Reading from the disc is achieved with a laser whose power is insufficient to impact on the state of the alloy.

You will recall that in the case of the hard disk, data is stored along a set of concentric circular tracks and we compared this to the spiral storage technique traditionally used for audio recordings (records). Interestingly, the compact disc does not use the concentric ring storage format, but rather the single spiral track that is associated with the traditional audio record on vinyl, but this time recorded from the centre outwards. Along this spiral track, digital data is stored in the form of changes in the reflectance property of the CD material. Here we should mention that although we say that the underlying techniques used for the storage of data on the CD are optical, this is a slight misnomer. In fact, the focused laser beam heats the disc material at the point of contact, and it is this heat that changes the optical characteristics of the disc. Consequently, and more precisely, the underlying physical technique used for the recording of data on a CD is thermal rather than optical.

The optical technique used for reading from a CD is illustrated in Figure 9.4. Light from a laser diode is collimated and passes through a tilting, semi-silvered mirror or glass plate. Subsequently, the light is focused by a lens onto the CD. Depending on whether the light impinges upon a 'pit' or 'bump' (corresponding to a 1 or a 0), the light is reflected or otherwise. In the case of light that is reflected, it travels back through the lens and is reflected to the right by the semi-silvered mirror (or glass plate). The function of the semi-silvered mirror/glass plate is therefore to direct reflected light to the right-hand side where another lens is used to focus the beam onto a photodetector. This converts the light signal into an electrical signal. In practice, more efficient optical arrangements are used.

The electromechanical systems used for both writing and reading from a CD have to operate with great accuracy. For example, the optics required to read data from the CD must accurately follow the spiral track as the CD rotates. In principle – because when the CD is being read no mechanical read head is in contact with the CD – the CD should provide a very reliable form of storage. However, the surface of a CD is very easily marked (e.g. scratched) and as a consequence considerable emphasis is placed upon error detection and correction. Special electronic hardware is used for this purpose within the CD controller and in principle this hardware should be able to detect and often recover contaminated data. The error detection and correction mechanism naturally slows down the rate at which data can be retrieved from the CD. Both reading and writing speeds for a CD are less than those associated with a hard disk.

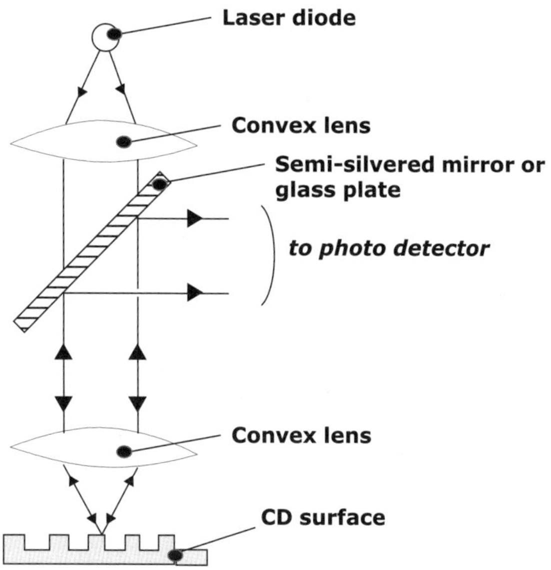

Figure 9.4: A simplified schematic showing the principle of operation of a CD read mechanism

Activity 9.5

Hard disk and compact disc formats

'The hard disk and compact disc have the same data storage format.' Briefly discuss the accuracy of this statement.

9.5 Summary

In this chapter we have outlined the operation of several forms of storage media. Each has associated strengths and weaknesses. None provide a perfect solution, and as we have seen, with the exception of flash cards, they are based upon electromechanical systems. Thus, even in the case of the modern computer, we cannot describe it as a wholly electronic device: mechanical systems are still required.

9.6 Review questions

Review question 9.1

Why is it desirable that a hard disk should rotate at the maximum possible speed?

Review question 9.2

Why does a floppy disk rotate at a lower speed than a hard disk?

Review question 9.3

In the case of a hard disk or floppy disk, two main latencies are associated with any read or write operation. Briefly explain these latencies.

Review question 9.4

In the case of a WORM device, how are the bits written onto the disc?

Review question 9.5

In the case of the CD-R, what are the two physical states of the alloy used for data storage?

9.7 Feedback on activities

Feedback on activity 9.1: The concept of primary and secondary storage

The main memory within a computer (RAM) represents primary storage. This memory supports rapid transfer to and from the processor, however its contents are lost when the power is turned off or the computer reset. The hard disk provides us with an example of secondary storage. Unlike main memory, the contents of the hard disk are retained even when power is turned off. Floppy disks and the CD-ROM provide additional examples of secondary storage devices. Primary memory is commonly used for memory that is to be directly addressed by the processor; secondary storage devices store programs and data on a more permanent basis (e.g. outside program execution).

Feedback on activity 9.2: Primary and secondary storage devices

The main memory and cache memory within a computer are generally referred to as providing primary storage capability. The hard disk, floppy disk, and CD-ROM are generally referred to as secondary storage devices.

Feedback on activity 9.3: Storage capacity

Under Windows you may find the disk capacity and the space in use by selecting (from the 'Start' menu) 'Programs', 'Accessories', 'System Tools', 'Drive Space'.

Feedback on activity 9.4: Hard disk performance

The first latency corresponds to the time it takes for the read/write heads to move to the appropriate track. The second latency corresponds to the time it takes for the appropriate sector within a track to pass beneath the read/write heads. This is often referred to as the rotational latency. Naturally, if the disk rotates at higher speed, then the rotational latency is reduced.

Feedback on activity 9.5: Hard disk and compact disc formats

In the case of the hard disk, data is stored on tracks. These tracks take the form of concentric rings on the surface of each disk. On the other hand, in the case of the CD-ROM data is held on a track that spirals from the disc's centre towards the periphery. The form of track therefore represents a fundamental difference between the way data is physically stored on the hard disk, and the way it is stored on the CD-ROM.

Further reading

- Clements, A (2006), *Principles of Computer Hardware*, Oxford University Press
- Englander, IRV (2003), *The Architecture of Computer Hardware and Systems Software*, John Wiley, 3rd Edition
- Wilson, J & Hawkes, J (1998), *Optoelectronics: an introduction*, Prentice Hall, 3rd Edition

CHAPTER 10

From reset to operation

OVERVIEW

Today's computers employ a 'layered architecture' in which low-level layers offer services to the higher-level layers. Within this chapter we highlight aspects of this layered approach. As we will see, at the highest levels we have applications programs that perform tasks such as word processing and at the other extreme the PC uses the 'BIOS' – a collection of programs that communicate directly with the computer's hardware systems. Thus if a word processing application needs to print a document, it need not be aware of (or involved in) direct communication with the printer – this is achieved by other, lower-level, software.

Learning outcomes At the end of this chapter you should be able to:

- Describe the use of the reset vector
- Describe the nature of a layered computer architecture and discuss the role of a PC's BIOS and operating system within such a framework
- Explain key functions of the BIOS
- Describe main functions of an operating system.

10.1 Introduction

When discussing computers, it is important that we have a clear understanding of the difference between hardware and software. The former consists of a set of electronic circuits able to perform a variety of tasks. These tasks are defined by software – instructions and data that are provided, and describe what is to be done. In itself the hardware is passive; it is the software that controls what happens. By changing the software, we can change the functions performed by the hardware – this denotes the essential power of the computing machine.

By way of analogy, consider the various parts of our bodies (the 'hardware'). Tasks that we perform (such as breathing, speaking, hearing, etc) are all controlled by the brain. Some actions are automatic, in the sense that we do not consciously think about them. For example, we do not need to remember to breathe! Other actions – such as speaking – are voluntary and require thought. Computers can be considered in a similar way, but always remember that people, their bodies and brains are a great deal more complex than any computer yet conceived (or likely to be conceived).

Some actions of our bodies are quite basic, for example the contraction of a single muscle in the arm. You may think 'I will reach for that pencil', but a basic part of your system controls the muscles that move your arm so you can reach the pencil. You do not need to 'think' about each muscle, you only 'think' about reaching for the pencil. In fact, your request to reach for the pencil is broken down into a set of more basic tasks, each one undertaken by a simpler part of your system. Without pushing this comparison too far, the request: 'reach for the pencil', is analogous to a high-level software instruction, and each individual muscle contraction that results from this request is analogous to a low-level software function. The action is actually carried out by the muscles – the hardware.

Computers have similar basic functions: there is the need, for example, to detect whether a single keyboard key has been pressed and to identify the function of the key. Such basic functions are usually built into the basic input/output system (BIOS) as a set of low-level software routines, and are briefly discussed in Section 10.4. However, before this, we will examine the events that occur when a process receives a 'reset' signal – or is powered on. We then discuss the nature of the layered architecture – as employed in today's computers.

In Section 10.5 we briefly consider aspects of a computer's operating system which provide services to programs executing on a computer, and interfaces with the hardware and BIOS.

10.2 Processor operation following a reset

When a processor is reset, or powered on, it must be able to locate the address of the very first instruction that it should execute. Most processors identify the location of this first instruction in a similar manner and in the following description we will continue to employ our simple 8-bit model microprocessor. However, it is important to note that the ideas introduced below can be applied to more complex processor architectures.

In Figure 10.1, we illustrate a processor connected to a memory device that contains the program that is to be executed when the computer is powered on or reset. We will arbitrarily assume that the very first machine code instruction that should be executed is located at address D000 (hex).

When reset or powered on, the processor automatically performs two read operations. Typically, it will read the contents of address FFFE and FFFF (hex) – which are the highest addresses in the processor's address space (recall the address space is the name given to the range of addresses that can be accessed by the processor).

The data that is read from these two locations is brought together to form a 16-bit address. This address is assumed by the processor to correspond to the address of the first instruction that it should now execute.

In setting up the software within the computer, the developer decides where in the processor's address space to locate the boot program (this is the name commonly given to the program that is initially executed following power on or after the computer has been reset). In the above example, we have assumed that the program begins at address D000 (hex). The developer must therefore store this address at addresses FFFE and FFFF (hex) respectively. You might ask why this address is stored in two memory locations. The answer is quite simple: in our simple processor model, we have assumed the use of an 8-bit data bus and a 16-bit address bus. Therefore, every memory location can store only 8 bits, and so a 16-bit address will need to be stored across two memory locations. Hence, in our above example, address FFFE (hex) will store D0 (hex) and address FFFF (hex) will store 00 (hex). The processor reads these two memory locations, forms the address D000 (hex) and then reads the contents of address D000 (hex) – where it expects to find the first instruction that it should execute.

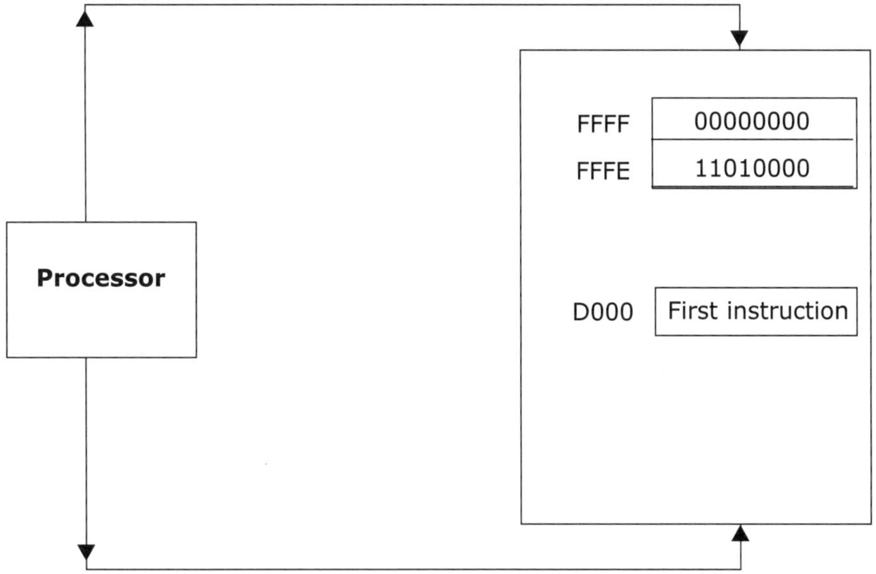

Figure 10.1: The reset vector is located at addresses FFFE and FFFF.

Addresses FFFE and FFFF are said to store the reset vector, a pointer to the first instruction that the processor should execute. Why is a pointer necessary? The answer is simple: by using this approach if we change the location of the boot program, we need simply modify the reset vector accordingly. This gives us great flexibility and parallels the approach used for accessing the interrupt service routine – see Chapter 8.

Activity 10.1

The reset vector

Explain what would happen if a computer's reset vector were to become corrupted.

10.3 A layered architecture

As we have seen, computers are machines that perform operations in binary (base 2). All computation is carried out on numbers and it is perhaps difficult to visualise the connection between these statements and the ability of a computer to carry out, for example, word-processing tasks.

To illustrate the difficulty of conceptualising between a machine that works according to the rules of mathematics, and its ability to perform apparently non-mathematical tasks, imagine you are given the job of explaining the concept of a 'city' to someone who has only ever lived on a desert island and has never had need of permanent housing. If you started by describing a brick and then immediately described the construction of a whole town (constructed entirely from bricks), the connection between the small hard brick and the warm and comfortable rows of houses would be a very difficult to visualise.

Bricks and towns	Computer hardware	Computer software
Bricks. Study what a brick is made of, how it is made, how strong it is, what it will cost.	1s and 0s, simple digital circuits and how logical arithmetic can be performed with a circuit.	Boolean logic.
Walls. Study how to mix cement, how to lay bricks to make a wall, how strong a wall is.	How a sequence of logical operations can be achieved with a circuit, how to add, subtract, perform logical AND and OR operations, etc.	How to perform arithmetic with simple numbers.
How to make several walls into a building with spaces for windows and doors, etc. How to build a roof.	How to store many logical instructions and feed them in sequence to a circuit that can execute them.	How to perform arithmetic with multiple digit numbers.
How to install all the services a building needs, water, electricity, gas, heating etc. and to move in the carpets, furniture etc.	How to accept human inputs by devices such as a keyboard and to display outputs using devices like a colour monitor.	How to handle data such as text and to edit it, i.e. move a sentence within a paragraph.
How to build a row of houses, provide street lighting, public access etc.	How to provide a complete set of devices such as a mouse, keyboard, printer, CPU etc. and to make them all connect correctly.	How to present a complete set of facilities in a word processor.
How to plan a town, provide libraries, shops, hospital, bus station etc.	A complete PC.	How to control the entire machine: the operating system.

Table 10.1: A layered architecture

If you then took the view of a town planner and spoke of where the hospital should be in your town or how to route a road around a village, any connections with bricks would be entirely lost. The problem is in understanding the creative ways in which large numbers of bricks can be used!

The connection between the binary 1s and 0s used in, and manipulated by a computer, and the varied tasks that the machine can perform is equally difficult to visualise. One way of gaining an insight into this type of conceptual problem is to develop 'layers' of knowledge – as indicated in Table 10.1.

Computers are designed and organised using a layered architecture. A traditional way of identifying the layers employed in a typical personal computer (PC) is:

- **Hardware:** which actually performs each task
- **BIOS:** controls simple or basic operations such as reading a key from the keyboard
- **Operating system:** controls what software runs in the machine and provides an environment in which applications programs are able to execute. (It also performs various other tasks that we will discuss later)
- **Application software:** the name given to user programs such as word-processing software, spreadsheets, e-mail, etc.

Generally, each layer communicates with the adjacent layers, such that the BIOS acts directly on the hardware; the operating system 'asks' the BIOS to read the keyboard; the BIOS in turn 'asks' the hardware for data, etc.

In the next section we will discuss some of the functions of the BIOS, and in Section 10.5, the functions of an operating system.

Activity 10.2

Understanding a layered architecture

A computer operates entirely on arithmetic and logical operations, which are performed in binary. How is it therefore possible for a computer to perform tasks such as the storage and manipulation of text that is associated with everyday word-processing activities? You should answer this question within the context of a layered architecture.

10.4 The BIOS

In today's world we expect appliances such as the radio and television, or machines such as the car, to be available for instantaneous use. In fact, not so long ago, it was necessary to wait for a television or radio to 'warm up' before it could be made to operate – perhaps for thirty seconds or even longer.

In the early days of cars, some designs employed steam power. Although the performance characteristics of steam-powered cars were quite impressive, their greatest drawback was the need for the driver to wait for the steam to be created, i.e. they were not available for immediate use and the driver would need to wait for a few minutes before setting off. The development of appliances and machines that were available for immediate use has denoted a major advance.

Interestingly, in the case of today's PC, users seldom question the need to wait for some time between powering on the machine, and the machine's availability for use. In fact, since the advent of the PC in the early 1980s, this waiting time has increased. Developers have chosen not to attempt to reduce this waiting time (something that could have been easily achieved), and of course there is a similar waiting time when a computer is shut down.

During the time that we must wait between a computer being powered on and its being available for use, a number of tasks are performed. These include hardware diagnostics, the identification of hardware configurations and the transfer of some program code from the hard disk into the computer's main memory.

When a PC is powered on, special programs stored in ROM located on the main circuit board (the motherboard) begin to execute (recall Section 10.2 which describes the way in which the processor locates the first instruction that it should execute). These routines are collectively referred to as the BIOS (basic input/output system) and BIOS software is responsible for performing the 'boot' sequence (power-on sequence).

Software must be loaded from storage media (usually the hard disk) into main memory and then control must be passed to it. However, we need some form of software to load the initial software from disk (traditionally this was called 'the loader', because the 'loader' is contained in the BIOS and this program accesses the storage medium and reads from it additional code). The BIOS then passes control to this code – which in turn loads into memory the relevant portions of the operating system. Gradually, the computer performs a boot sequence – pulling into memory the code needed to establish an environment in which applications can run and with which a user can interact.

The first task performed by the BIOS is the POST (power on self test). Code, stored in the BIOS ROM, tries to obtain a response from each of the main system components, such as the video card, main memory, keyboard. It performs limited tests on each in turn and if a communication problem is encountered an error is reported. This may be reported to the user via a sound ('beep') or by a screen message.

The next task undertaken by the BIOS is the initial program load. Here the BIOS loads into main memory a program located at a certain (pre-defined) place on the hard disk (usually the first sector). Once this code has been placed in main memory the BIOS passes control to it. (The first sector on the hard disk is generally referred to as the boot sector because it contains the bootstrap loader for the operating system.)

One of its first tasks concerns the configuration of any add-on boards using a 'Plug and Play' technique. This means that the settings to be associated with each add-on board are determined during the boot-up process – they not pre-configured. (Previously, devices were pre- configured at the time of installation, switches on each board being used to set various parameters.)

Summary of the boot sequence

- POST, the power on self-test
- Initialise the system board and load the interrupt vectors
- A check is made for other devices plugged into the main board of the PC and to link the BIOS information in those devices to the main BIOS code. (This is called daisy-chaining.)
- Initial program load, then BIOS hands over control to whatever operating system loader is stored on your disk
- Set up 'plug and play' devices.

Other parts of the operating system are now loaded (not always Windows).

The BIOS has various additional functions. These include:

- Read a single keyboard key
- Read system clock and return date and time
- Set 'Caps lock' key on or off
- Send a single character to the printer
- Read a single character from a serial port.

You cannot normally access the BIOS directly yourself; the layered architecture implies that the operating system will communicate with the BIOS for you. For example, as the BIOS forms part of the layered architecture of the PC, the next layer above the BIOS – the operating system – may request a service such as a reading the keyboard: the BIOS will 'talk' to the hardware layer, obtain the keypress data and send it back to the operating system. This is summarised in Figure 10.2.

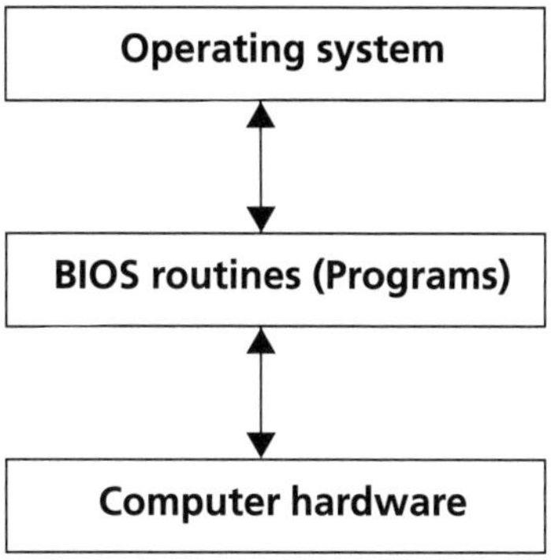

Figure 10.2: The BIOS acts as an intermediary between the OS and the hardware.

Activity 10.3

BIOS functionality

Explain why the BIOS plays such an important role in today's personal computer.

Activity 10.4

The function of the BIOS software

Using the Internet or your local library, research and describe one essential role fulfilled by the BIOS software.

10.5 Operating systems

An operating system (OS) comprises a set of program modules that undertake a wide range of tasks and provides a variety of services to both the user and the applications programs running on a computer. For example, it acts so as:

- To act on commands provided by the user
- To provide output to the user
- To create environments in which a user program can execute
- To manage the file system (including the directory structure)
- To enable programs to share resources
- To provide resources for a user program via special instructions – often referred to as 'system calls' – see Figure 10.3
- To interface with hardware such as the keyboard, display screen, printers, hard disc drives, etc. Often such interfaces are implemented using programs called 'device drivers'
- To provide security (e.g. password protection, the protection of files belonging to each user, etc.)
- To provide network communications and thereby allow computers to communicate
- To provide a convenient user interface (using menus, icons etc.)
- The provision of text editing facilities
- The provision of various utilities that may be accessed by a user such as 'system tools', 'calculator', 'calendar', etc
- The provision of back-up facilities.

An operating system (OS) is designed in a layered architecture. The layers in a typical OS are:

- **Layer 4: User interface and control of applications**

  Applications are the programs the user wishes to run in the machine. The OS must load them into memory, start them running and control access to them and their access to the hardware. For example, a word-processor may need to print a document. The operating system will take the request for printing and provide that service – the word-processor does not need to 'know' how to do this in detail. The user interface determines how you communicate with the computer and the ways in which the computer communicates with you.
- **Layer 3: Kernel**

  This organises the way that processes are controlled: for example, if an application requests service from a printer, other application requests must not interfere. If you are running a wordprocessor and a spreadsheet at the same time, they must not be allowed to use the same memory (otherwise important data may be corrupted and the programs will fail). In fact when programs are allowed to share computer resources, controls must be put in place to ensure that the resources are properly distributed and are used in an orderly way.

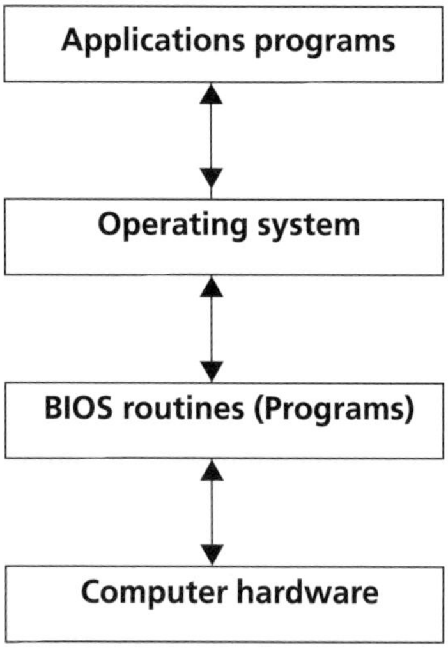

Figure 10.3: An operating system provides resources to applications programs.

- **Layer 2: Drivers**
  This refers to software that communicates with specific device types such as disk drives. For example, in a PC, a CD-ROM needs a device driver because the operating system at layers 3 and 4 has no knowledge of CD storage formats, or the services that need to be supported in order to make use of this storage media. The device driver provides this interface. The operating system simply 'asks' the device driver for a service such as 'access a file' and the device driver does the work. A different device driver is required for each type and brand of device
- **Layer 1 – Hardware communication (in PCs via the BIOS)**
  This represents aspects of the OS that communicate with the hardware (not the hardware itself). In the case of PCs, this generally takes the form of the BIOS.

The internal part of the OS is not readily visible to the user but if you look at what is loaded on a PC, you can find parts of it. In the case of Microsoft Windows, this is done by the Windows API (Application Programme Interface). Application software can ask for service from the Windows API. The actual code for this is stored in .DLL files (Dynamic Link Libraries). Each .DLL file is written to store the code that provides a particular set of routines or services. There are .DLL files to control the video graphics, others to control the printers, others to control the mouse, etc. The ones specific to Windows itself are stored in directories such as c:\windows or c:\windows\system or c:\winnt – depending on the version of Windows that you have.

Until the mid-1980s, computers generally used a command line interpreter. Here, the user was presented with a command prompt such as: C:\>. This 'prompted' the user to type a command such as DIR to gain a service. (The command DIR requests a listing of the files on the current disk drive.) This style of user interface is called a CLI or command line interpreter, because the text typed at the prompt (the command line) is interpreted by the CLI and either a request made to the kernel for a service, or an error message is issued. In Microsoft's DOS, the CLI is called COMMAND.COM. In the Unix world there are many different command line interpreters; they are called 'shells' but do essentially the same thing – provide a command line user interface.

Modern PC operating systems use a graphical user interface or GUI. This is used in conjunction with the mouse so as to allow a user to make selections from a menu system (employing graphical objects such as icons and menu lists).

Other operating system features:

The modern OS must support multi-tasking (whereby a single user is able to run a number of programs in parallel) and often operating systems make provision for multiple users (whereby a number of users may share the resources of a single computer). Below we briefly examine these two features:

- **Multi-tasking**

  Here a computer appears to be able to run a number of programs simultaneously. For example, a computer may be executing a program that is downloading material from the Internet, and at the same time the user may be working with a word-processing package. However, the majority of PCs have a single CPU, which can do only one thing at a time, but when an OS supports multi-tasking then, from the user's perspective, the two programs appear to be executing at the same time. This is achieved by sharing processor resources between the programs – each gets access to the processor (and other computer resources) for very brief periods of time. A number of techniques may be employed to fairly share processor resources between the various programs that may operate 'simultaneously' on a computer.

- **Multi-user operating systems**

  These must provide additional services to allow the identification of users, i.e. they must 'log in'. The OS must also provide security so that malicious or careless users cannot affect the work of others.

The provision of multi-tasking and/or multi-user services necessitates the OS taking responsibility for memory management. This means that the physical memory must be organised so that users and applications cannot write to areas of memory allocated to other users and applications programs. Were this to happen, the consequences might be catastrophic. For example, when using Windows, you may have seen the error message 'This program has performed an illegal operation'. A common cause for this is an application that attempts to write to an address in memory that belongs to a different application or process. If Windows cannot resolve the problem, it shuts down the offending process.

Activity 10.5

Find DLL files

Using Windows Explorer, find out how many .DLL files there are on your PC. To do this, search the C: drive for *.DLL, i.e. any file that has a .DLL file extension.

Activity 10.6

Tasks performed by an operating system

At the beginning of this section we listed a number of tasks performed by an operating system. State two additional tasks.

10.6 The process

The term 'process' is widely used in relation to operating systems. Unfortunately, depending on the O/S under discussion, the term can take on different precise meanings. For our purposes, we will use a relatively straightforward definition:

- **A process is an environment in which a program can execute.**

In the case of a 'multi-tasking operating system' each program has an associated process. The use of processes plays a pivotal role in the architecture of such operating systems. Each program may be considered to be 'encapsulated' within a process and when, for example, an applications program wishes to communicate with a computer resource, it does so via the process – see Figure 10.4.

The general role of the process can be readily understood by means of a simple analogy.

Consider your local bank. This has a number of resources – money, computers, Internet banking facilities, etc. Suppose that these resources were not managed, and that anybody was able to go into the bank and directly manipulate the resources. For example, anybody could help themselves to as much money as they wanted – and it was left to the individual to record how much money they had taken. Obviously there would be a great deal of chaos, and it's fairly certain that after a few hours there would be very little money left in the bank! The resources offered by the bank are therefore managed and, for example, this prevents one person from taking money from another person's account. Here, management is achieved by encapsulating the resources – rather than the individual – and in this respect the scenario is not quite accurate in describing the use of processes within a computer.

Whenever resources are shared, we need to put controls in place to ensure that they are shared properly and equitably. Thus applies to the computer in which the hardware is shared between a number of programs. Without controls, chaos would ensue. For example, in the 'free-for-all' scenario, one program could overwrite areas of main memory containing the code and data belonging to another program! Each process 'encapsulates' a program and ensures that resources are not used inappropriately. However, even in the case of a computer which does not permit multi-tasking, we still have to put controls in place: we would want, for example, to ensure that an applications program could not overwrite areas of main memory in which operating system code (or data) resides.

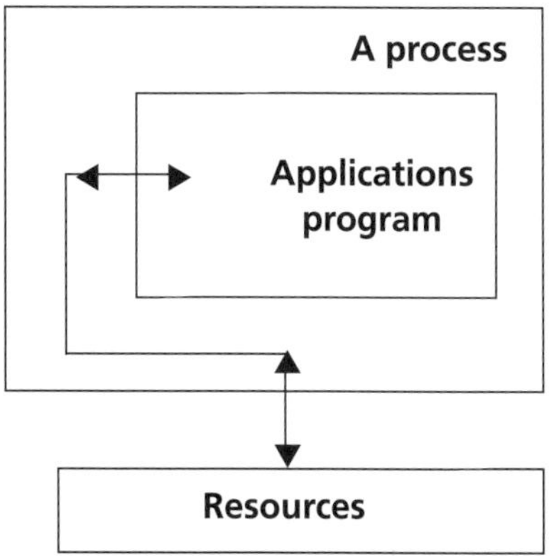

Figure 10.4: In this model, the process encapsulates a program and manages all communication.

10.7 Summary

In this chapter, we have discussed the layered architecture that is adopted in the creation of software systems which underpin the operation of the modern computer. Subsequently, we considered each of the layers commonly encountered in, for example, the PC, and emphasised the functions of the BIOS. The functionality of a typical operating system has been briefly considered and we have outlined the implementation of both multi-tasking and multi-user operating system characteristics.

10.8 Review questions

Review question 10.1

In terms of your body, give examples of high-level operations? How do these relate to computers?

Review question 10.2

In terms of your body, provide an example of a low-level operation?

Review question 10.3

In terms of a computer, give some examples of high-level operations.

Review question 10.4

In terms of a computer, give some examples of low-level operations. What part of the PC provides these operations?

Review question 10.5

List five important tasks carried out by a typical OS.

Review question 10.6

What is a process?

Review question 10.7

What is meant by the acronym POST?

Review question 10.8

What is meant by the acronym BIOS?

10.9 Feedback on activities

Feedback on activity 10.1: The reset vector

The corrupted vector would still be used as a pointer to the first instruction that should be executed by the processor. Depending on the corrupted value of the reset vector, the pointer may still direct the processor to machine code existing in the address space. However, the processor would begin to execute this code from the wrong place and this could lead to unpredictable results. Furthermore, rather than point the processor to an opcode, the processor may be directed to an operand – which it would incorrectly assume was in fact an instruction. By chance, the operand may have a value that could be decoded as an instruction. Computer failure is assured! It is therefore important that the reset vector is not corrupted.

Feedback on activity 10.2: Understanding a layered architecture

Although a computer operates entirely upon binary numbers, we can use these numbers to represent symbols and characters. Thus, at the lowest level, we see the processor manipulating numbers; at a higher level we can use these numbers to represent symbols and characters. The processor is, of course, completely unaware of the meaning that we assign to the results of its low-level computation. Conversely, when operating a word-processing package, a user needs to have no knowledge of the manner in which the processor performs its mathematical operations. Each layer within the architecture of the underlying software that runs on a computer generally needs no knowledge of the way in which the other layers operate.

Feedback on activity 10.3: BIOS functionality

The BIOS performs a number of varied functions. Some of these such as the 'power on self test', are not vitally important. On the other hand, there are two areas in which the BIOS is indispensable. Firstly, when a computer is powered on, the BIOS provides a way via which critical software is moved from secondary storage devices, such as the hard disk, into main memory. Having moved this software across from the hard disk, the BIOS passes control to it. This is a critical part of the boot sequence. In the days of early computers, this was a task often carried out manually. The second critical function of the BIOS concerns its interface with various hardware. In this role the BIOS is acting as the lowest layer in the layered software architecture model.

Feedback on activity 10.4: The function of the BIOS software

Various answers may be given – for example: When a personal computer is turned on, the operating system will not automatically run as it is stored on the hard disc. Consequently, we need a way of bringing a portion of the operating system into the main memory. This is one of the essential tasks carried out by the BIOS software. Usually, entry to the BIOS is gained by means of the reset vector, and BIOS software executes. This is contained in ROM on the motherboard. The BIOS is able to access the hard disk and bring a portion of the operating system into the main memory area. The BIOS then passes control to the operating system.

Feedback on activity 10.5: Find dll files

No feedback on this activity.

Feedback on activity 10.6: Tasks performed by an operating system

Various answers can be given to this question. For example, multi-tasking (that is, enabling more than one program to appear to execute concurrently), and access to the system clock which enables, for example, a program to determine the current date and time.

Further reading

- Englander, IRV (2003), *The Architecture of Computer Hardware and Systems Software*, John Wiley, 3rd Edition

CHAPTER 11

Interaction hardware

OVERVIEW

A computer that cannot take input from the physical world and return the results of the computational process has little, if any, purpose. The PC, is able to take input from sources such as the keyboard, touch screen and mouse, and provide output to the display or printers. Aspects of these and similar devices are outlined in this chapter.

Learning outcomes At the end of this chapter you should be able to:

- Discuss the need for both input and output devices
- List key input and output devices
- Distinguish between various forms of interaction device
- Discuss the operation of the cathode ray tube (CRT), plasma and liquid crystal displays (LCDs)
- Discuss several display metrics.

11.1 Introduction

The devices that we use to interact with the computer (namely, the screen, keyboard and mouse) have been in existence for many years. The cathode ray tube, which is still commonly used for the implementation of the computer monitor (although it is rapidly being superseded by plasma and liquid crystal thin panel displays), was pioneered in the nineteenth century, so too was the 'QWERTY' keyboard. The mouse has a briefer history and was first prototyped in the 1960s. Interestingly, the basic form of today's human–computer interface (with its reliance on the bitmapped graphical user interface) was put in place during the 1970s and, in essence, this has changed very little during the intervening years. In this chapter we introduce a range of techniques that are used to enable the computer to accept input from its surroundings and to enable it to output the results of the computational process.

In the next section, we discuss aspects of the input/output (I/O) process and summarise the operation of various input devices and in Section 11.3 we discuss the computer display, where we focus on the operation of CRT plasma and liquid-crystal-based displays. Finally, in Section 11.4 we summarise the operation of several types of printer.

11.2 Input and output devices

The process of communicating with computers involves converting signals from the physical world into signals that can be acted upon within the digital domain. As we discussed previously, ASCII (American Standard Code for Information Interchange) codes and Unicodes are commonly used for the representation of symbols within a computer, and the keyboard provides us with a simple means by which these characters may be entered.

The type of keyboard we use today (in countries where English is the first language) is known as the 'QWERTY' keyboard (as a result of the top row of letters). The QWERTY keyboard was originally designed for typewriters over 100 years ago; the layout of the characters was devised to ensure that frequently used characters were not adjacent to each other and would not, therefore, be likely to hit each other in the mechansism and jam the machine. This layout is far from optimal for today's purposes and there are several other designs for keyboards such as the Dvorak keyboard, the Tony keyboard and the Maltron keyboard.

Another commonly used input device is the mouse, which allows us to move a cursor around the screen. In addition, it has one or more buttons on the top that can be used to click (or double-click) and so define some operation that we wish the computer to perform.

Output devices translate bits and bytes into a form that users can understand. The purpose of output devices is usually to display processed data and information in a way that is readily understandable to people. The most commonly used output devices are the computer screen (the monitor) and the printer.

Input and output devices vary greatly in size, performance and functionality, and we now discuss a few of them.

We can simply divide input/output (I/O) devices used in conjunction with computers into two major types:

- Those that interact with people
- Those that do otherwise.

Below, we briefly summarise the operation of various devices that enable input to be supplied to the computer. These devices are largely concerned with the translation between human-readable and machine-readable forms.

We can further divide the human-interactive devices into two categories:

- **Direct I/O devices**
- **Indirect I/O devices.**

Direct I/O devices must respond to human action and display information in real-time, at a rate that complements the capabilities of people. Indirect I/O devices accept input or produce output where the human is not directly involved. Examples would be a scanner or a printer – these devices perform the human–machine translation, but they do not need to react directly to a human in real-time.

The keyboard

The keyboard is an assembly of switches logically arranged in a matrix. When a key is pressed (i.e. when a switch closes) a specific row and column of wires are energised and this combination identifies the particular key pressed. The electronic circuitry of the keyboard has two functions to perform:

- It must 'debounce' the signal (whenever a mechanically based switch closes, it has a tendency to produce a brief set of pulses rather than a single voltage transition). The 'debounce' process improves the quality of the signal
- It must translate the row and column pair into a standard code and then make this available to the CPU.

Most keyboards also provide circuitry to detect when a key is held down for longer than a normal period; when this happens, the keyboard hardware automatically start to repeat the transmission of the corresponding character code. In some systems, the keyboard may also have special keys that bypass the usual translation step and connect directly to the computer, providing a means of getting the computer's attention (generating a high-priority interrupt). The typical keyboard produces bursts of character codes at a rate of up to 10 per second (120 words per minute).

When a key is depressed, a scan code (a number) is generated. The circuit stores the number in the keyboard's own memory buffer and then loads it to the computer's BIOS so it can be read. The circuit sends an interrupt signal to the CPU telling the CPU that there is a stored scan code. A BIOS software routine reads the scan code and on completion sends a signal to the keyboard buffer to tell it to delete the scan code from its buffer memory. The BIOS then translates the appropriate scan codes into ASCII code/Unicode equivalents, as used by the computer and places it into its own buffer until it is retrieved by the operating system or the application software.

The mouse

The mouse is one of the few I/O devices that originated solely within the computer industry. It has a burst data rate of 20 bytes per second (when sending counts) and slightly higher when sending raw pulses, but its average data rate is much lower. Typically, the counts are sent to the processor in the same serial manner as the keyboard, and in some systems the mouse even shares the same I/O lines with the keyboard.

A mouse can be either mechanical or optical in nature. With a mechanical mouse, a ball rotates under the housing and as it is rolled across a surface it turns a perpendicular pair of shafts inside the housing. These shafts drive encoders consisting of a clear plastic wheel with radial lines printed on it. An LED (light emitting diode) shines through this wheel onto a phototransistor and, as the lines pass between them, the variation in the light reaching the phototransistor causes it to generate pulses. The pulse train is either counted in the mouse or sent to the computer to be counted.

In the case of a first-generation completely optical mouse (this type of mouse had no moving parts), a pair of LEDs shone onto a special reflective pad that is printed with a grid of lines that had two different colours (commonly, blue lines that run horizontally, and black lines that run vertically). Two phototransistors sense the reflected light and determine (as the mouse is moved across the pad) the direction and extent of motion. This is achieved by ensuring that each of the two phototransistors are sensitive to only one of the two colours printed onto the mouse pad. Thus, for example, one phototransistor can 'see' the blue lines and the other the black lines.

The second-generation optical mouse is a much more complex device and operates on normal desktop surfaces – without recourse to a special pad. A light emitting diode is used to illuminate the surface beneath the mouse and this is captured by a two-dimensional sensor array. As the mouse is moved, the image captured by this array changes and special purpose image processing hardware compares consecutive images. Differences in images are used to determine the direction of motion and distance of displacement. Typically, images are captured every 1/2000 of a second! Naturally, this all-optical mouse has a number of advantageous characteristics – no mouse pad is required, there are no moving parts to wear out or become damaged and surface friction is low. The wireless mouse is becoming increasingly common, removing the need for a connecting cable.

The trackball

A trackball is very much like an upside-down mechanical mouse, but the ball is typically larger. Here, the user rolls it with his or her fingers or hand. A version of this type of mouse is commonly employed in laptops.

The track pad

Here, you use your finger to point to a particular position on the screen. The movement of a finger on the pad corresponds to a location on the screen. Tabs at the bottom of the pad serve the same functions as the mouse buttons.

The joystick

The traditional joystick makes use of two variable resistances (potentiometers) – the change in their resistance corresponding to the degree to which the 'stick' is deflected. The stick turns the shafts of two potentiometers (one for X, one for Y) and the voltage resulting from the potentiometer's resistance at that particular position is converted into a corresponding number by an analog-to-digital converter (ADC). The output of the ADC is serialised and sent to the computer – in the same ways as keyboard or mouse data. Alternatively, some joysticks sense force and in this case strain gauges are used, rather than the potentiometers mentioned above.

The touch screen

This type of screen allows users to select the desired item directly by placing a finger at (or above) an image on the screen Frequently found in shopping, tourist or manufacturing environments, they allow the use of computing when either the environment may be unfriendly or when users may have limited awareness or ability to use a conventional computer. The next activity requires you to discover more detailed information about this item.

The microphone

A microphone turns acoustical pressure into a signal of variable voltage that is sampled at a regular rate and converted into numerical values. This digitised signal can simply be recorded, or it can be processed by voice recognition software and turned into corresponding text. The recognition process requires a combination of signal processing and artificial intelligence techniques to extract phonemes and whole words.

The scanner

A scanner consists of a controlled linear light source that is passed over a piece of paper, where a corresponding linear array of photo sensors known as a charge-coupled device (CCD) are used to detect the light reflected from the paper. The contents of the CCD are read out and sent to the computer. Scanners typically operate with resolutions of 100 or more dots per inch and with up to 24 bits of colour information.

Activity 11.1

The touch screen

Using library and/or Internet resources, describe the operation of the 'touch screen'. What are the strengths and weaknesses of this interaction technique?

11.3 The monitor

Traditionally, the computer monitor was based on cathode ray tube (CRT) technology. However, in recent times alternative thin panel display techniques are becoming more usual, particularly those based on gas plasma and liquid crystal technologies. These latter two approaches enable the creation of thin panel displays.

In this section, we briefly outline the operation of these three display modalities.

Cathode ray tube (CRT) based displays

The major elements within a cathode ray tube are depicted in Figure 11.1 – see also Figure 11.2. At the back of the cathode ray tube (CRT) there is an 'electron gun' (see Figure 11.3). Central to this gun is the cathode, which consists of a small piece of metal that is specially coated and heated with a hot wire filament. The heating of this cathode causes it to emit electrons, and these are rapidly accelerated away from the cathode towards the anode (electrons are negative and are attracted towards a positive potential). As the electrons travel towards the anode, they pass through a series of 'electron lenses'. These lenses focus the electron stream into a fine beam. By the time this beam reaches the anode it is travelling at a very high speed. Typically, the anode takes the form of a metal cylinder with central holes machined in its two flat faces. Rather than the striking the anode, the electron beam is targeted at these holes. At this point, it is travelling so fast that it simply passes through both holes and continues on its voyage towards the screen of the CRT. The CRT screen is coated with special materials known as 'phosphors'. When a high-energy electron beam impinges upon the phosphors, it causes them to emit light. In the scenario described above, we would simply observe a visible dot at the centre of the display screen. In order to generate a display, we need to scan the electron beams across the surface of the screen. In the case of CRTs used for computer monitor and television applications, the electron beam is scanned by means of electromagnets arranged around the 'neck' of the CRT close to the anode.

These electromagnets take the form of four coils of wire through which rapidly changing currents are passed. These coils create a magnetic field which interacts with the negatively charged electrons, causing them to be either attracted or repelled. By suitably adjusting the currents that pass through the coils, it is possible to scan the electron beam across the surface of the screen. Usually the electron beam is first deflected to the top left-hand corner of the screen, and is then swept across the screen horizontally (this gives rise to a visible horizontal line). The electron beam is then returned to the left-hand side of the screen but is now in a position slightly below its starting position. Again, it is swept across the screen to form a second horizontal line. This process is repeated and a series of horizontal lines are formed. Ultimately, the electron beam reaches the bottom right-hand side of the screen and it is then rapidly swept back across the surface of the screen to the top left-hand corner. The process is then repeated.

In this way, we are able to sweep the electron beam across the entire surface of the screen and in the scenario we have just explained we would see the screen as being uniformly illuminated. In order to actually generate a visible image, the last step we must take is to modulate the electron beam current. This means that we adjust the electron beam current during the sweeping process – see Figure 11.4. Thus, by way of a simple example, if as the beam sweeps out one of the horizontal lines we briefly turn off the beam, then we would observe a break in the line. Alternatively, if – rather than turning the beam off – we simply reduce its strength, then we would see a lowering of the intensity of the line during that period. The modulation of the beam current is achieved by a further electrode within the electron gun, which is referred to as the 'grid'. This is placed close to the cathode and by applying a voltage to it we can adjust the beam current.

The cathode ray tube principle was first invented in around 1890, and the application of this remarkable device to television was first proposed nearly one hundred years ago.

The CRT described above is capable only of generating monochrome images. In order to generate full-colour images, three electron beams are normally used. Each of these beams is responsible for the production of one of the three primary colours (one beam is responsible for the production of red light, one beam for blue light, and one beam for green light). These three beams are scanned across the face of the screen in unison, and each is directed to dots of phosphor on the screen which will give rise to the appropriate primary colour.

Activity 11.2

The shadow mask

Using library and/or Internet resources, discuss the use of a shadow mask in a colour CRT.

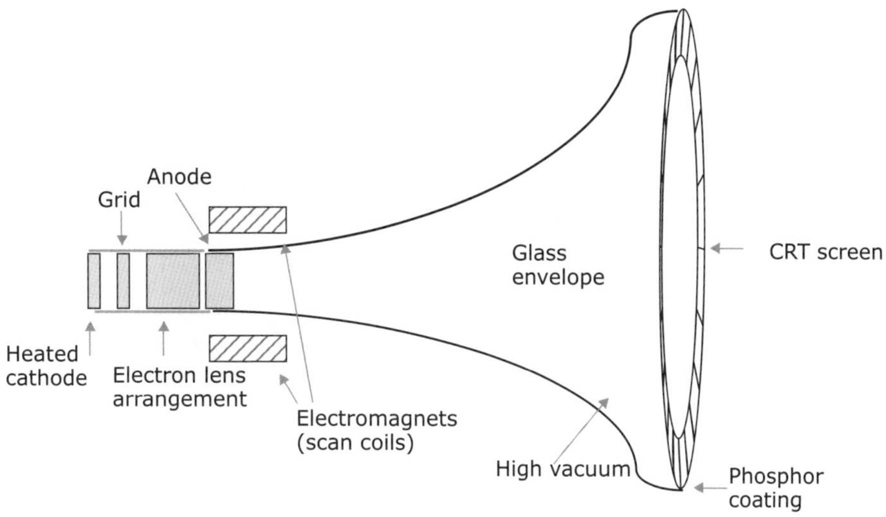

Figure 11.1: Simplified drawing of a cathode ray tube (CRT)

Figure 11.2: The type of cathode ray tube encountered in computer monitors and television sets. It is constructed from a thick glass vessel which contains a high vacuum. In fact, a cathode ray tube is potentially a very dangerous device and must be handled with great care (to avoid implosion caused by the difference between atmospheric pressure and the internal vacuum).

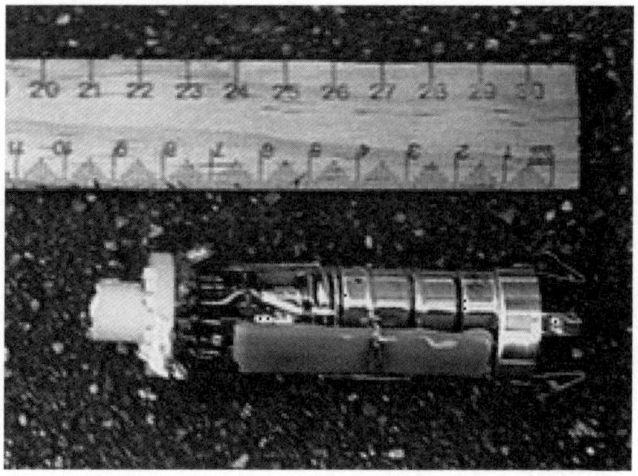

Figure 11.3: An electron gun used to generate an electron beam

Electron guns must be handled with care as the electrode responsible for the production of the electron beam (the cathode) is coated with toxic materials. The electron gun operates via a process of thermionic emission whereby a heated cathode is made to emit electrons. These electrons are accelerated by high voltage (typically, in the case of a computer monitor, ~25,000 volts). Note: the high voltages used within a monitor are potentially lethal.

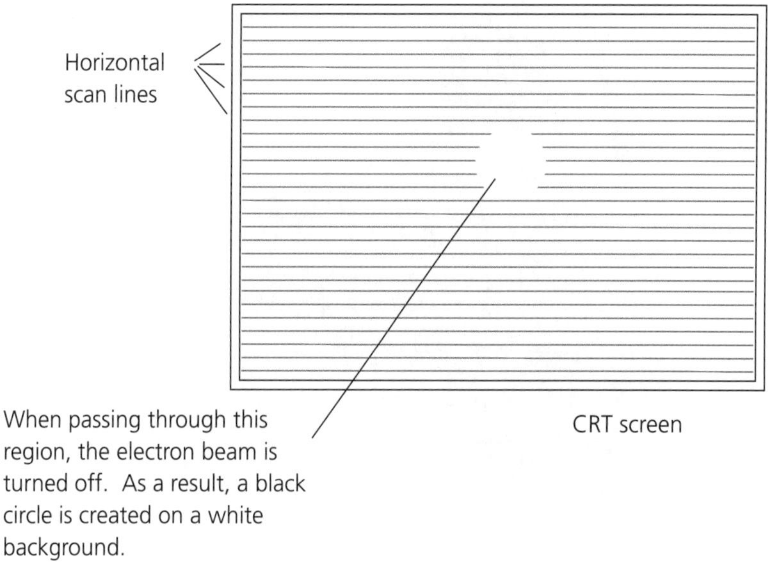
Horizontal scan lines
When passing through this region, the electron beam is turned off. As a result, a black circle is created on a white background.
CRT screen

Figure 11.4: The use of a raster scan to create a black circle on a white background

The images displayed on a computer screen are comprised of pixels. The word 'pixel' is derived from the words 'picture' and 'element'. An average performance computer monitor is able to depict approximately one thousand pixels horizontally, and eight hundred pixels vertically. Thus, during each refresh of the screen, some 800,000 pixels may be addressed.

The scanning of the electron beam across the surface of the screen is carried out at regular intervals – the rate at which this occurs is referred to as the 'refresh rate' (or 'frame rate'). If the scanning process does not take place sufficiently rapidly, the image may be seen to flicker. However, if the refresh frequency is greater than 25Hz, we do not perceive image flicker. Even in this case though, flicker may be subconsciously perceived (subliminal flicker) and this can impose strain on the visual system. It is therefore common practice to refresh monitors at a much higher rate and so ensure that subliminal image flicker is not problematic. Higher-performance monitors achieve refresh rates of the order of 120Hz.

The screen's parameters include resolution (horizontal and vertical, ranging from 320 x 200 to 1,600 x 1,200 in typical monitors (640 x 480, 832 x 624, 1,024 by 768, 1,152 x 870, and 1,360 x 1,024 are common intermediates), colours (depth – 8 to 24 bits), pitch (dots per inch – typically 72 to 100), and size (measured diagonally including a portion of the tube that can't be seen, and typically 12 to 21 inches). Monitors can also vary in refresh rate – the number of times the beam scans the screen each second. In a TV set, the screen is scanned at a rate of 25Hz per frame. However, a frame is divided into two fields that are interlaced: the lines of the two fields alternate on the screen. The fields are scanned in sequence and the effective scan frame rate is 50Hz. Computer monitors are scanned at a slightly faster rate (ranging from 50 to over 120Hz) and are not interlaced.

Bitmapped graphics

Spend a moment closely examining the image depicted on your CRT computer screen. If you have very good eyesight, you will see that it comprises an enormous number of tiny dots. These dots are arranged in groups of 3 to form pixels (an abbreviation of 'picture elements'). In each group of three, one dot is responsible for the production of green light, one for red, and the third for blue light (the three primary colours). Typically, a computer screen comprises 1,000 pixels horizontally and 800 pixels vertically. Each pixel can be set to a different colour (by software) and to a different level of brightness (again by software). Consequently, by changing the colour of the individual pixels ,and their intensity, we can create the images on the computer screen.

Each pixel has a corresponding location in memory where its attributes (colour and intensity) are defined. Thus, by writing a binary value to a particular memory location, we cause a particular pixel on the computer screen to be illuminated to a certain level of intensity and colour. The area of memory used for this purpose is called the 'video memory', and is often located on a special card (circuit board) within the computer that is called the 'video card'.

Employing a direct mapping technique between screen pixels and memory locations is referred to as 'bitmapped' (or more accurately 'pixmapped') graphics. This approach is also used by plasma and liquid crystal displays.

Activity 11.3

The role of the display in both input and output

The computer display provides a window into the digital world enabling us to see the results of the computational process. Explain why the computer display performs a pivotal role in the interaction process?

Activity 11.4

The raster scan

Consider a computer display that measures 40cm horizontally and 30cm vertically. Assuming that it has a display bandwidth of 1,000 by 800 and supports a refresh rate of 50Hz, determine the speed that the electron beam sweeps across the screen (you may neglect the time that the electron beam spends performing retraces (flyback) and therefore can assume that all the time is spent in drawing the horizontal scan lines).

Gas plasma thin panel display

As with the CRT, images generated via plasma displays comprise a rectangular array of pixels (each pixel consisting of red, green and blue sub-pixels). In Figure 11.5 we illustrate a glass tube containing a gas such as argon. At either end of the tube these is a metallic electrode and we maintain a high voltage between these two electrodes. We assume that the tube is connected to a vacuum pump and, as we lower the gas pressure within the tube, light will eventually be seen to emanate from the gas. This is the effect that underpins the operation of fluorescent-tube-based room lighting, so-called neon signs, etc. and is referred to as a gas discharge process.

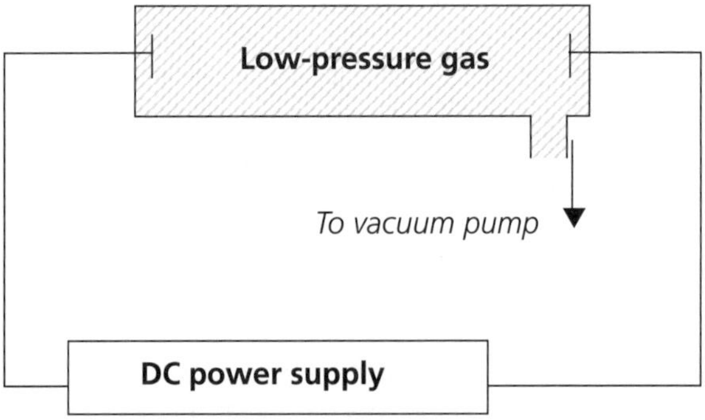

Figure 11.5: A discharge of light occurs when the gas is at an appropriate pressure. Note in practice a current limiting resistor must be inserted into the electrical circuit

The gas discharge process underpins the operation of thin panel plasma display systems. Consider the apparatus depicted in Figure 11.5. The voltage applied to the two electrodes gives rise to an electric field. Free electrons and positive ions (atoms from which one or more electrons have been removed and which exist in small numbers in any gas) experience a force – the electrons are pulled towards the positive electrode and the ions to the negative electrode. As they move, they accelerate and gain energy. When they collide with gas atoms, energy is transferred and this can cause the formation of more ion–electron pairs (which also undergo acceleration) or simply the excitation of atoms. In this context, an atom is said to be excited when one or more of its electrons move from a low-energy level to a higher-energy level. Eventually, such excited atoms 'decay' to their natural ('ground') state and in doing so give out electromagnetic radiation. This may be in the form of visible or non-visible light. In the case of the plasma display, non-visible (ultraviolet) light is produced. This in turn impinges on a phosphor material (as used in a CRT) and visible light is generated. As in the case of the CRT, different phosphors are used for the generation of red, green and blue sub-pixels.

A typical 'cell' (responsible for the formation of a single sub-pixel) is illustrated schematically in Figure 11.6.

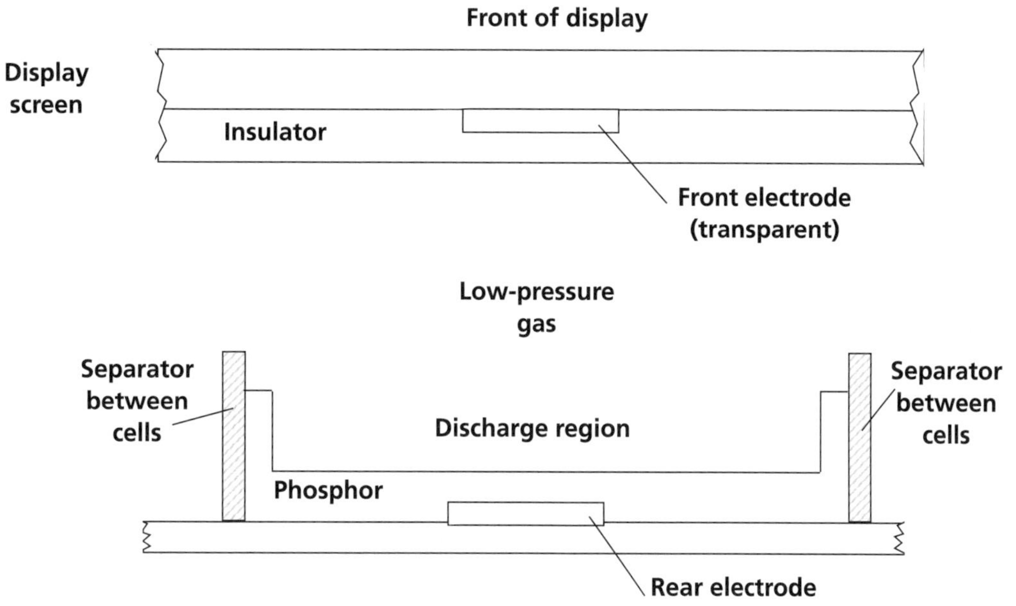

Figure 11.6: A simplified cross-sectional view of a cell used in a plasma panel. A gaseous discharge is initiated by applying a voltage between the two electrodes. The gas mixture is designed to maximise the production of non-visible (ultraviolet) radiation. This stimulates the emission of visible light from the phosphor which radiates from the cell.

Liquid crystal thin panel display

In a liquid, molecules are not locked into a rigid structure but are able to move relative to each other and therefore a liquid can take the shape of the vessel into which it is poured. However, in the case of a solid, molecules vibrate about fixed positions and there is a degree of order in their relative positioning. Liquid crystal materials possess these two characteristics: the molecules are free to move relative to each other but also exhibit a degree of ordering in their alignment.

Liquid crystal molecules have a rod-like shape and their alignment can be controlled by subjecting the material to an electric field or by the nature of the solid surfaces in which the material is in contact.

As with the plasma display, a liquid crystal display comprises a rectangular array of pixels – each of which is formed from red, green and blue sub-pixels. A thin layer of liquid crystal material is sandwiched between two glass plates (see Figure 11.7). The inner surfaces of these two plates are treated so that each is scribed with a set of very fine lines (grooves). In addition the glass is coated with a layer of a transparent conductive material. The coating on either plate forms an electrode and, when a voltage is applied between the coatings on the two plates, the liquid crystal material is subjected to an electric field.

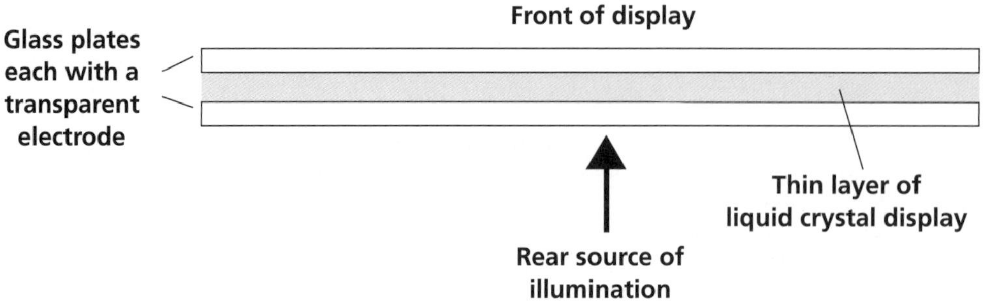

Figure 11.7: A cross-sectional view of a part of a liquid crystal display panel

The set of parallel lines that are scored onto the inner surfaces of the two glass plates lie at right angles to each other. Thus, if we imagine one set of lines as being arranged horizontally, the other set of lines would be arranged vertically. These lines suggest an alignment arrangement to the rod-like liquid crystal molecules that are in immediate contact with them – the rod-like molecules tend to line up in the direction of the grooves. If we continue to think of one set of lines being arranged horizontally and the other set of lines being arranged vertically, then it follows that the rod-like molecules in contact with one plate will be aligned in a horizontal direction, and those in contact with the other plate in a vertical direction. In turn this influences the direction of the molecules within the bulk of the material – and these tend to twist around in a manner akin to a spiral staircase so that they gradually move from the horizontal to the vertical alignment. However, when we apply a voltage to the transparent electrodes, we create a field within the liquid crystal material that overrides the natural alignment that we have introduced through the presence of the scored lines – the molecules no longer gradually spiral between vertical and horizontal states, but tend to align themselves in the direction of the electric field.

To create a thin panel liquid crystal display we position two polarisers – one is in contact with either of the glass plates. The direction of polarisation of the two polarisers is crossed – the directions of polarisation being aligned with the grooves in the glass plate.

In the absence of an electric field, if we now shine non-polarised light through the arrangement that we have just described, then when it passes through the first polariser it will be polarised in a particular direction. The liquid crystal material acts as an optical waveguide and as the light passes through the material its plane of polarisation is gradually rotated through 90 degrees, and so it is able to emerge from the second polarising filter. (Recall a simple experiment that you may have carried out in which you get two polarising filters from sunglasses – if the directions of polarisation of the two filters are aligned, then light passes through the two filters, but if their directions of polarisation are at 90 degrees to one another, light is not transmitted through the combination. In the case of the liquid crystal structure arrangement that we have just described, although the two polarising filters are orthogonal, light passes through the arrangement because of the effect of the liquid crystal molecules which gradually change the plane of polarisation of the light.)

If we apply a voltage to the electrodes, the light's plane of polarisation is no longer gradually moved through 90 degrees; when it impinges on the second polarising filter, its plane of polarisation is at 90 degrees to that of the polarising filter – consequently it is absorbed.

Through the application of an electric field we can therefore prevent the passage of light through the combined arrangement of filters, glass plates, and liquid crystal material. Without any field being applied, the light source behind the liquid crystal panel can be seen; when an electric field is applied, light from the source is absorbed.

In order to create a rectangular array of pixels (and for the production of a colour display sub-pixels) we need to deposit on the glass plates a corresponding array of transparent electrodes, thus allowing us to individually address each pixel or sub-pixel. Liquid crystal displays are frequently referred to as being either 'passive matrix' or 'active matrix' displays. The performance of the latter is greatly superior to that of the former – however, they are more difficult to manufacture. The essential difference between the two is that active matrix displays have a transistor associated with every pixel/sub-pixel. These transistors are deposited onto the glass plates and, when we apply a signal to turn on a particular sub-pixel, the electric field associated with the sub-pixel will be maintained until the application of a further signal which indicates that the field should be removed. In the case of a passive matrix display, transistors are not used in this way and the electric field is only present for short periods of time. Active matrix displays produce higher-quality images than the passive matrix approach, and furthermore they exhibit a wider field of view.

In the case that we are implementing a full-colour thin panel liquid crystal display, each pixel comprises three sub-pixels and colour filters are used so as to allow the generation of red, green, and blue sub-pixels.

One final point to note: in the case of the CRT and the gas plasma display, the material responsible for the production of pixels emits light. However, in the case of liquid crystal displays, the liquid crystal material does not emit light – its role is to cause a change in the plane of polarisation of light passing through the panel. Consequently, thin panel liquid crystal displays for use with computer systems and TVs are 'back lit'. This means that behind the panel there is a light source that is cunningly arranged so as to uniformly illuminate the entire rear of the liquid crystal panel.

Activity 11.5

Display characteristics

Imagine that you are purchasing a computer display. Describe the characteristics that you would consider to be particularly important.

11.4 Printers

A printer is a device that produces information (hard copy) on paper. There are many different types, such as laser printer, inkjet, impact dot matrix and dye sublimation; each uses a different technology:

- In an impact dot matrix printer, needles are driven by electromagnets to strike an inked ribbon against the paper (the computer sends a series of hexadecimal ASCII codes (or Unicodes) to the impact printer to represent characters and printer movements)
- An inkjet printer uses a non-impact method, where the ink is squirted from a column of holes by piezoelectric crystals or by thermal expansion
- In a laser printer, a selenium-coated drum is charged with static electricity and then scanned by a laser beam that is rapidly deflected and modulated – the laser beam 'writes' the image onto the drum. Wherever the light strikes the selenium, the charge is dissipated. The drum then passes over a cartridge with black (toner) powder. Where the static charge remains, the toner is drawn to the drum. The drum then applies the toner to the paper (and is then cleaned of any residue). The paper passes through a heater that fuses the toner particles onto it and then a static discharge brush before being ejected from the printer.

11.5 Summary

In this chapter we have introduced a number of devices that can supply input to a computer. Devices such as the keyboard and mouse provide the means by which the human operator can pass data, instructions etc to the computer. Other input devices such as the scanner convert physical forms of expression (such as writing) into digital form. We have outlined the operation of the CRT, plasma and liquid-crystal-based display and the important concept of 'bitmapped' graphics. Additionally, we have distinguished between several forms of printer (these convert digital signals into 'hardcopy' output).

11.6 Review questions

Review question 11.1

What do we mean by the 'QWERTY' keyboard layout, and why was this particular layout initially adopted (rather than, for example, laying out keys in alphabetical order)?

Review question 11.2

Distinguish between the mechanical and non-mechanical forms of mouse.

Review question 11.3

What is a pixel?

Review question 11.4

Why does a colour cathode-ray tube based monitor employ three electron beams?

Review question 11.5

What is the purpose of a 'shadow-mask' within a colour CRT?

Review question 11.6

Why are some forms of mouse equipped with two motion detectors and how are these arranged?

Review question 11.7

State one advantage to the use of liquid crystal technologies in display implementation.

Review question 11.8

Describe the basic principle of operation of a laser printer.

Review question 11.9

What do you understand by the term 'bitmapped graphics'?

11.7 Feedback on activities

Feedback on activity 11.1: The touch screen

No feedback on this activity

Feedback on activity 11.2: The shadow mask

A shadow mask comprises a sheet of metal within which a very large number of very small holes are machined (slits may also be used and provide greater efficiency (brighter images)). This is positioned just behind the face of the CRT and ensures that each electron beam can only strike phosphor dots which emit the appropriate colour of light.

Feedback on activity 11.3: The role of the display in both input and output

When we interact with a computer, we make considerable use of the mouse and this allows us to move the cursor to any location on the screen and make selections from the menu system. The computer screen plays a very important role in ensuring that we properly navigate the cursor, i.e. move it to the correct position. Try navigating the cursor with your screen turned off! Without the screen it would be impossible to move the cursor to the correct position necessary to make the required selection. Thus, the screen not only provides a window into the digital world, but also plays a very important role in allowing us to interact with this world.

Feedback on activity 11.4: The raster scan

If we neglect the time spent in performing flyback, then in a single raster scan of the screen the electron beam moves 40 x 1,000cm = 400m. The electron beam performs 50 scans per second and therefore the total distance travelled (per second) is 400 x 50 =20,000m. Thus the deflection speed is 20km.s-1. In fact, the speed is somewhat greater than this as, for example, we have not taken into account the additional distance moved as a result of flyback.

Feedback on activity 11.5: Display characteristics

Here are some of the criteria that may influence your selection of a display:

- **The size of the display.** This is normally measured as the length of the diagonal across the screen. Unfortunately, manufacturers of CRT displays also include in their measurement the part of the display screen that is hidden behind the plastic surround! Flat panels displays are generally exactly as described.

- **The resolution of the display.** This provides a measure of the number of pixels per unit length (e.g. so many pixels per centimetre or inch). Displays have different resolutions in the vertical and horizontal directions (generally). The higher the resolution, the better.

- **Colour palette.** This provides an indication of the range of colours and greyscales that may be assigned to each pixel. Typically, monitors offer a 24-bit colour palette.

- **Refresh rate.** This indicates the frequency at which the display can be refreshed. The higher the refresh rate, the better as this avoids any problems that we may experience as a consequence of flicker.

- **Physical 'footprint'.** How much space it takes up on your desk. Modern flat panel displays require significantly less space than the CRT, and are much more easily moved to adjust to changing light conditions. (They are also much easier to despatch or collect.)

Notice that the characteristics of the display must be supported by the performance of the video card through which the processor is connected to the display.

Further reading

- MacDonald, LW, & Lowe, AC (eds) (1997), *Display Systems: Design and Applications*, John Wiley & Sons Ltd
- Sherr, S (1998), *Applications for Electronic Displays: Technologies and Requirements*, John Wiley & Sons Inc
  Although dated, these books contain a wealth of information concerning the variety of display system technologies.

CHAPTER 12

Connectivity and the multimedia machine

OVERVIEW

The modern desktop computer is commonly referred to as a 'multimedia machine'. Although this title is often assigned different meanings, in general terms a multimedia machine is one which can take a variety of forms of input, process this input, and produce appropriate output. For example, the desktop machine can typically accept audio, images, video, etc, can process and store these different forms of media and generate various forms of output. This is made possible because each form of input can be represented within the computer numerically. Consequently, an audio clip or scanned image can both be represented as a series of binary numbers. The computer is able to process these numbers, and has no knowledge of their significance.

The computer's ability to process different forms of media provides many exciting opportunities. For example, whereas audio and video media can be processed within the computer independently, they can also be brought together, enabling us to (for example) create multimedia documents. This permits the incorporation of a variety of media within a single framework. An encyclopaedia no longer needs to be limited to text and static images – we can (for example) include image animations, video clips, sound files, etc. This provides the opportunity to extend the 'dimensionality' of documents. Furthermore, the interconnection of computers via the Internet provides many interesting opportunities for linking documents together and enabling them to be accessed from practically any part of the world.

Learning outcomes At the end of this chapter you should be able to:

- Discuss aspects of the multimedia computer
- Describe methods of connecting a computer to peripheral devices
- Describe the use of a communications protocol
- Describe the interconnection of computers via a LAN
- Discuss file formats used on a multimedia computer and understand the basic concept of file compression.

12.1 Introduction

We begin this chapter by briefly examining the concept of a multimedia computer. Although the term 'multimedia computer' has no single, well-defined meaning, we shall assume that such a machine is able to accept different forms of input media (sound, video, scanned images, etc), process and store the material, and output in a suitable form the results of the computational process. Here, we introduce the analogue-to-digital convertor (ADC), which is able to convert analogue signals into a digital form. We also discuss the digital-to-analogue convertor (DAC). This is able to convert digital data into analogue form. Thus, the ADC and DAC perform opposite roles. In this section, we also consider the important issues of sampling rate and precision.

In Section 12.4 we describe ways in which a computer can be connected to local devices such as the printer, scanner digital camera and the like. Here, we introduce serial and parallel forms of interconnect.

Today's computers do not work in isolation – they are generally interconnected via some form of network. In Section 12.7 we discuss issues relating to the communication of computers across a local area network (LAN). Here we introduce the concept of a communications protocol, which provides clearly defined rules according to which computers communicate. We examine some of the basic issues that must be incorporated within a communications protocol.

In Section 12.8, we briefly discuss file formats used for the storage of different forms of media, briefly summarising the general purpose and characteristics of different file formats; we also examine file compression and introduce two basic forms of compression – lossless and lossy compression. In the case of the former, when a file is compressed, no information is lost. However, in the case of a lossy compression technique, some content is lost when a file is compressed. This can lead to the degradation of (for example) image or audio quality.

Finally, we turn our attention to the Internet and the World Wide Web (WWW). Although these two names are commonly used in an interchangeable manner, they do have a different meaning. In this section we clarify their usage, and also briefly refer to HTML (hypertext markup language). HTML is not used for writing programs, but provides us with a way of specifying the layout of web pages.

12.2 The multimedia machine

Over the centuries we have developed techniques to advance self-expression, extend the varied forms of human creativity and develop additional techniques by which we communicate. By way of example, consider the Renaissance period which flourished in Italy between the 14th and 16th centuries. During this time, artists discovered (or, more accurately, rediscovered) the techniques needed to enable the accurate and realistic rendition of 3D imagery upon a 2D medium (the artist's canvas). In fact, the perspective techniques developed at that time underpin modern computer graphics. Once these techniques had been learnt and gradually refined it became possible for artists to not only create photorealistic images but also surpass photorealism and be bounded only by the limits of an individual's imagination. In the 19th century, our ability to capture images was further advanced by the development of photographic techniques and, in the 20th century, apparatus was developed by means of which images could be directly captured and stored in electronic form.

The written word also supplies us with a further example of the way we have developed our skills, not only in terms of expressing ourselves, but also in providing a means whereby history is no longer passed from generation to generation orally, but by static record.

The invention of the printing press denoted a major landmark, and permitted both writing and images to be rapidly reproduced. Books were therefore no longer confined to a very limited audience, but became more widely available. The development of the typewriter provided a means of more rapidly producing printed material. However, until the latter part of the 20th century, paper represented the primary medium upon which written material was stored.

The modern computer is able to support the storage and manipulation of a wide variety of forms of human expression and creativity. It is for this very reason that today's desktop computer is often referred to as a multimedia machine. However, the term has different meanings to different people. For our purposes we will consider a multimedia computer to be a machine which:

- Is able to support the acquisition of different forms of material relating to, for example, human creativity and expression. This includes video imagery, audio, text and graphics
- Is able to support the manipulation of such material
- Is able to store these materials
- Is able to display the results of the computational process (often in real-time, e.g. the replay of video images).

Note, that within the computing community the term 'multimedia machine' has no single well-defined interpretation.

12.3 Input and output

As we have seen, one important characteristic of the multimedia machine is its ability to accept different forms of input, process this input, and provide some suitable form of output. The text that follows briefly reviews aspects of these processes.

The input process

In order to acquire input from its surroundings, a computer employs one or more transducers. A transducer is a device able to convert one form of energy into another. For example, a transducer may convert light or mechanical energies into electrical energy. In Figure 12.1, we illustrate the use of a transducer. Here, sound energy (air vibrations) is converted into electrical energy, which takes the form of an analogue signal. As discussed previously, an analogue signal is able to take on any value between two limits – for example, any value in the range 0-10 volts. Consequently, analogue signals differ from digital signals in as much as the analogue signal is usually continuous, whereas the digital signal can only exist in one of two states. As we have seen, computers operate on binary (digital) numbers, so we must have a means to convert the analogue signal into an equivalent digital form. As illustrated in Figure 12.1, an ADC (analogue-to-digital convertor) is used for this process. An ADC is able to sample an analogue signal and represent the signal's instantaneous value by a binary number.

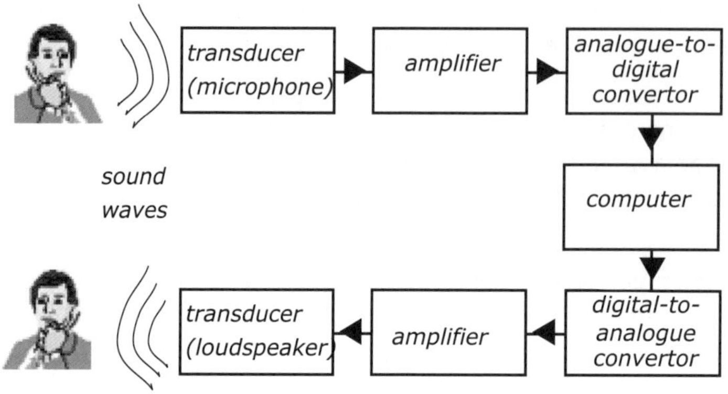

Figure 12.1: The acquisition, processing and output of an audio signal

There are two key aspects to this conversion process – the sampling rate and the precision. Let us briefly look at these in turn:

- **Sampling rate:** this determines how frequently the ADC samples the analogue signal. There is an optimum rate at which a signal should be sampled; if a signal is sampled more frequently than is necessary, then we will generate an unnecessarily large amount of data. (If we are, for example, processing an audio stream into a computer, this will result in an overly large audio file.)

  On the other hand, if a signal is sampled too infrequently, content within the signal will be lost. In turn, this will degrade the quality of, for example, an audio recording. Here, higher-frequency sounds will be lost.
- **Precision:** this relates to the range of binary values that may be used to represent an analogue signal. The ADC converts the instantaneous analogue value into digital form, and therefore produces a series of binary numbers. ADCs are chips which are readily available, and one way in which ADCs vary is in their sampling precision. If, for example, we bought an 8-bit ADC, this would mean that the input analogue signal could be represented by 256 (2^8) different binary values. On the other hand, a 10-bit ADC could represent an analogue signal by 1,024 different values. Let's take a simple numerical example. Suppose that we have an analogue signal that can take on any value between zero and ten volts. Additionally, let's consider that we use an 8-bit ADC for the conversion process. Since the output of the ADC can take on 256 different values, it follows that the minimum voltage change that can be accurately detected by the ADC is 10 divided by 256 (i.e. approximately 0.04 volts). Consequently, the higher the precision of the ADC, the more accurate the conversion process. On the other hand, higher precision ADCs are more expensive.

Returning to Figure 12.1, as you can see, a transducer converts the sound energy into electrical energy (providing an analogue waveform) and this signal is then amplified before being presented to the ADC. The ADC samples the analogue waveform (at a suitable rate) and converts it into a series of binary numbers (which are of the desired precision). Thus, as we talk into the microphone (the transducer) our speech is converted into a series of binary numbers. The computer is therefore able to process and store our speech.

The fact that the binary numbers correspond to speech or music is irrelevant to the computer – the computer has no knowledge of the significance of the numbers that it is processing.

Activity 12.1

Analogue-to-digital conversion

Let us suppose that a 4-bit ADC is used to convert an analogue signal into digital form. Consider that the analogue signal may take on any value between 0 and 6 volts. Estimate the minimum voltage change of the analogue signal which can be detected by the ADC.

The output process

Here we continue with the example shown in Figure 12.1 concerning the processing of an audio data stream. Having captured the audio, and having processed it in some way, it is natural that we should wish to play back. We therefore have to convert the binary number representation of the audio signal into an audible form. This conversion process is illustrated in Figure 12.1. Whereas the ADC converts analogue signals into a digital form, another electronic component – called a digital-to-analogue convertor (DAC) – provides the converse operation. The DAC takes digital values and produces from them an equivalent analogue representation. It therefore converts from the digital domain to the analogue domain. As we generate an analogue waveform from the digital values applied to the DAC, the waveform is fed through amplifier to a loudspeaker. The loudspeaker represents another form of transducer which serves the opposite function to the microphone. Whereas the microphone converts sound energy into electrical energy, the loudspeaker converts electrical energy into sound energy.

As with ADCs, DACs have a certain precision and, again, this impacts upon the accuracy of the conversion process. The higher the precision of the DAC, the greater the accuracy of the conversion.

12.4 The digitisation of images

In the previous section we considered the processing of an audio stream, and in this section we briefly review the digitisation of static images – such as photographs or text. Today's computers are often equipped with a flatbed scanner, by means of which we can scan documents and images and subsequently manipulate and store these on our computer. In the previous section we discussed the use of a transducer able to convert sound energy into electrical energy. In the case of the scanner, a transducer able to convert light energy is used. The next time you use a scanner, notice that during the scanning process a light source is gradually moved down the page that is being scanned. The light from this is reflected from the surface of the page and the amount and wavelength of reflected light determines the luminance/colour of points (dots – small regions) on the page. As shown in Figure 12.2, a page being scanned is divided into a number of small rectangular areas. The number of 'dots' into which a page is divided can generally be controlled by the operator, who defines the scan resolution in terms of the number of dots per inch (dpi). For example, we may elect to use a scan resolution of 100dpi. This means that for each inch of the page (vertically and horizontally) we will take 100 samples. Thus, one square inch of the page will be represented within the computer by 10,000 samples. The amount of light reflected from the page in each region that is to be sampled determines the luminance/colour of the region.

If we are scanning in colour, then the amount of red, green, and blue light reflected from each sample area on the page is measured.

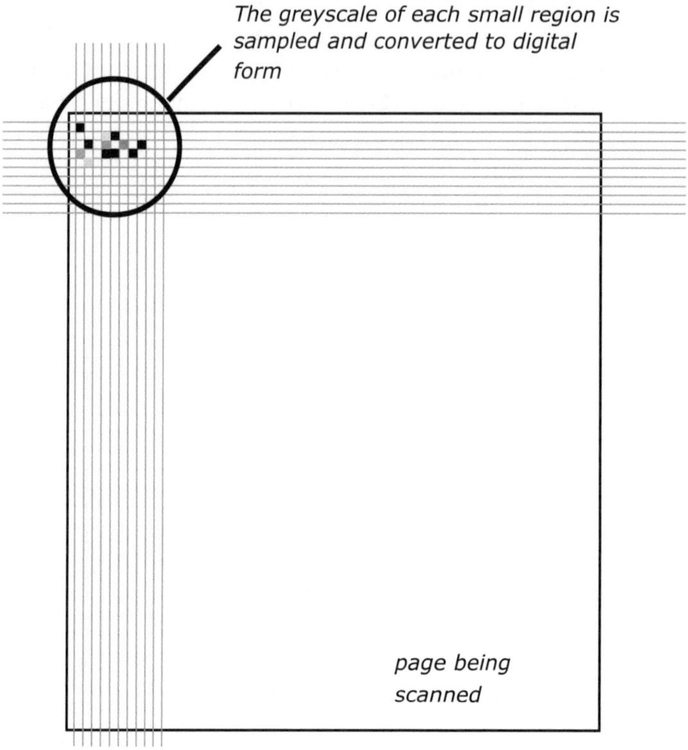
The greyscale of each small region is sampled and converted to digital form
page being scanned

Figure 12.2: The scanning of a page. The size and number of regions are defined by the number of 'dots per inch' (dpi)

Each sample taken from the page is converted (via an analogue-to-digital convertor) into digital form, and passed to the computer. Consequently, as with the earlier example of audio sampling, the computer receives a series of numbers. In the case of the audio example, these numbers represented the instantaneous loudness of the sound being supplied to the microphone. When we scan an image, the binary numbers correspond to the greyscale/colour of small regions of the page being scanned. In sampling an audio stream and an image, we have converted from two quite different forms of media, but in either case, the result within the computer is simply a series of numbers.

The ability to convert different forms of media into numerical data enables the computer to process a range of different entities. However, it is important to remember that the computer has no knowledge of the meaning that we assign to the numbers that it stores and manipulates. By this, we mean that the form of a binary number corresponding to a sample of an audio waveform is no different from a binary number that relates to the scanning of a document.

Activity 12.2

Signal sampling

Using the Internet or your local library, research and explain what is meant by the Nyquist Criteria relating to signal sampling.

Activity 12.3

Scanning a page

A page measuring 8 inches horizontally by 10 inches vertically is scanned at a resolution of 200dpi. Each sample is stored as a 4-bit binary number. Calculate the size of the file created on the computer (you should assume that compression techniques are NOT used).

12.5 Serial and parallel connectivity

The I/O devices connected to the central processing unit (CPU) are collectively called the I/O system. A single device controller with its attached devices is called an I/O subsystem; a device controller can be a simple interface between CPU and I/O device, or control a number of devices that are independent of the CPU. Device controllers are connected to the CPU via the system bus, and the simplest device controller consists of two parts:

- **The host port**
- **The device port.**

There is one 'device port' per device. The host port presents the status and control information to the CPU and receives the commands and addresses from the CPU. The device port takes care of the transfer of data to and from the I/O devices (e.g. printers). To the CPU, the I/O device ports appears as a block of memory locations, and the device controller independently implements the protocols required to communicate with (external) I/O devices.

Serial and parallel ports

We are able to connect computers to peripheral (external) devices, such as keyboards, monitors, printers, scanners by use of the sockets (called ports) that are usually located at the back of computers (see Figure 12.3).

There are several different types of port:

- **Parallel port:** if you have a printer connected to your computer, it probably makes use of the parallel port. Parallel ports can be used to connect various commonly used computer peripherals such as printers, scanners, external hard drives, network adapters
- **Serial port:** this has been an integral part of most computers for more than twenty years. In fact, modems often use this interconnect – as do some printers. Traditionally, computers have two standard serial ports. Essentially, serial ports provide a standard connector and protocol enabling us to attach devices to our computers. Parallel ports support faster data transfer than do serial ports
- **USB port** (universal serial bus): this is now a widely used standard for connecting a range of multimedia devices to a computer. A USB port can be connected to a 'hub device' which provides, for example, up to 127 other USB ports to which peripherals may be attached. Thus a USB port is expandable. When devices are connected via USB connections, they communicate with the computer's operating system and the appropriate device drivers and device parameters are established using the 'plug and play' technique. Consequently, as long as the operating system has the required device driver, a peripheral that is connected to a USB port will be recognised and communication will occur. A USB interconnect comprises four wires – two transmit power (5 volts) and the other two support the transfer of data.

Figure 12.3: Various ports (connections) on the back of a computer

The name 'serial' comes from the fact that a serial port 'serialises' data. A serial I/O port can be used to send data along a single cable in the form of a succession of logic 1s and 0s (a single bit at a time).

On the other hand, a parallel I/O port can handle data directly in byte form – enabling a number of binary digits to be transferred simultaneously along a number of wires, and is thus much faster than serial transmission. On the other hand, serial transmission (such as a USB connection) needs only one pair of transmission wires per communication channel, making the serial port less expensive than the parallel port, which requires the use of multiple wires. Serial ports are usually used for longer distance transmission while parallel ports are only used for transmission of data over a distance of few metres, at the most.

Before sending each byte of data (e.g. an ASCII character), a serial port sends a 'start bit' – which is a single bit, usually with a value of 0. After sending each byte of data, it transmits one or more 'stop bits' to signal that the character is complete. It may also include a parity bit, used for error detection. Serial ports (also called communication (COM) ports) are usually bidirectional. As we have seen, bidirectional communication allows each device to receive data as well as transmit it. Serial devices use different electrical wires to receive and transmit data.

Serial ports are generally implemented using a special controller chip such as the universal asynchronous receiver and transmitter (UART). The UART chip takes the parallel output of the computer's system bus and transforms it into serial form for transmission through the serial port. Most UART chips have a built-in buffer of anywhere from 16 to 64 kilobytes in size. This buffer allows the chip to 'cache' (temporarily store) data coming in from the system bus while it is processing data going out over the serial port.

12.6 I/O device properties

Properties of an I/O device that directly influence computer system operations are:

- **Access time**
- **Data transfer time**
- **Error rate.**

These are briefly discussed.

- **Access time** corresponds to the time period required by a storage unit to respond to an access request. How rapidly data can be accessed is important, as it impacts on system performance. The access time of secondary storage devices is significantly longer than the access time of main memory. Hard disks are relatively slow and hold lots of data, but are also relatively cheap. RAM is a lot faster but, unfortunately, is more expensive per unit of storage capacity
- **Data transfer time** of an I/O device depends on the amount of data to be transferred (the block size) and data transfer rate. The block size is determined by the device type. Character-oriented devices send their data on a byte-by-byte basis, and block-oriented devices transfer blocks (chunks) of data. There are many forms of I/O device. In Table 12.1 we provide a list of some devices, together with their typical data transfer rates (amount of data per second). Note that such performance figures often become quickly dated
- **Error rate** refers to the average frequency at which errors occur. During transmission, signals are exposed to electromagnetic interference and this can cause individual bits and groups of bits to be corrupted. Error detection and correction schemes are often employed in the transfer of data between peripheral devices.

Device	Behaviour	Data Rate
Keyboard	input	10 bytes/s
Mouse	input	20 bytes/s
Scanner	input	0.2 MB/s
Laser printer	output	0.1 MB/s
Graphics display	output	30 MB/s
Floppy disk	storage	50 KB/s
CD-ROM	storage	0.5 MB/s
Magnetic disc	storage	2 MB/s
Magnetic tape	storage	2 MB/s

Table 12.1: I/O devices and example data rates

12.7 Networking computers

The ability of the computer to accept different forms of input (audio, video, scanned images, etc) represents only one aspect of the modern multimedia desktop machine. Of equal importance is the fact that computers can be connected together to form a computer network. Whereas some years ago the desktop computer was often used as a stand-alone machine, today there is an ever-increasing requirement to interconnect computers and so enable them to share material. Networking is therefore a vital aspect of modern computing.

Within a building, computers are commonly connected together via what is called a 'local area network' (LAN). This form of network allows, for example, workers within offices, libraries, etc, to share information.

Material stored on one computer can be accessed and downloaded via the network onto other computers. LANs are generally connected to other networks, so we are not confined to the resources available on the computers within, for example, an office, but can 'go out' and download material stored upon other networks. In fact, today we are able to access (assuming we have the authorisation to do so!) material stored upon computer systems located in practically any part of the world.

In order to permit computers to communicate, we have to devise 'communication protocols'. Such protocols precisely define the way in which computers and computer-based technologies communicate. Below we briefly describe why protocols form such an important part of intercomputer communication, and so underpin network operation.

Communications protocols

Let us imagine for a moment that we attend a meeting in which we are to discuss some topic. We'll imagine that everybody at the meeting sits around a large table. The meeting can be carried out in two ways:

- **Without rules and guidelines:** in this scenario, any of the participants at the meeting can speak at any time and for as long as they want. They can speak in whatever language they wish to use, can shout, or even whisper. Everybody can speak at the same time. Because rules or procedures are not laid down and enforced, it is likely that the meeting will be a complete waste of time. Since more than one person may speak at any one time, it will indeed be difficult to understand what is being said, and even if the meeting goes on for an extremely long time it is doubtful that progress will be made. Certainly, anyone trying to record what is said will have an impossible task!
- **With rules and guidelines:** clearly, holding a meeting as described above is not going to be profitable activity and so when we attend a meeting we follow rules, guidelines, and procedures. For example, we assume that the participants will use a common language. We also assume that only one participant will speak at one time, and they will indicate that they wish to do so in some way (e.g. by raising an arm). We may also impose a rule that no one speaker should speak continuously for, say, more than one minute – in this way we ensure that everybody has the opportunity to talk. If these rules, guidelines and procedures are followed, then the meeting has a greater chance of being productive.

The above analogy applies not only to situations where people communicate, but also to the way computers communicate. If we are to create mechanisms by which a number of computers can share a communications medium and pass data to one another, then we have to specify a communications protocol: a clearly defined set of rules that govern the techniques that will be employed in implementing the communication. A communications protocol therefore underpins computer communications and, just as in the case of a meeting held without rules or guidelines, computer systems that do not strictly adhere to a common protocol have no chance of communicating effectively.

In fact the communications protocol that must be used in order to achieve effective computer communications is far more rigid and tightly specified than the type of protocol that we may lay down for situations in which people communicate. We are able to apply our considerable intelligence to inferring correctly what others mean when they communicate (or hopefully so!). When somebody speaks, we listen not only to the words but also to the tone, or the emphasis they place upon words. We may also infer additional information from, for example, facial expressions.

Computers, however, are machines with no innate intelligence – they perform a task without emotion and without understanding. It is, therefore, extremely important that the protocol to be followed in order to permit communications is absolutely defined, because there is no room for ambiguity.

In the early days of computer networking – dating back to the 1960s and 1970s – a range of communications protocols were developed. By the 1980s individual computer manufacturers had devised their own communications protocols and there was a lack of standardisation: computers developed by one manufacturer could not easily communicate with those produced by another. This led to a drive for standardisation and, particularly, the development of a communications protocol that would act as a standard and to which computer manufacturers would be expected to conform (as a consequence of market forces). Unfortunately, standards take a time to evolve and often reflect many compromises, with the result that standards put in place do not always reflect the best solution. Frequently they could be greatly improved upon.

On the other hand, the establishment of standards – particularly in the area of computer communications – has facilitated the creation of computer networks upon which computer systems created by different manufacturers can reside and communicate.

Protocol functionality – and some terminology

There are various forms of computer network, with the name given to a type of network often providing an indication of its physical extent. The smallest type is referred to as a 'local area network' (LAN), and this is commonly used to connect computers within offices or buildings (the use of the word 'local' implies that the extent of the network is restricted). The computers and computer-based equipment connected to a network are commonly referred to as 'nodes'. Thus, a local area network comprises a set of nodes connected together via some form of medium. The medium enables signals to be passed between the nodes.

The computers (nodes) within a LAN can be interconnected in various different ways. The interconnection scheme used is referred to as the 'network topology'. In Figure 12.4, we illustrate several forms of network topology: a bus topology, a ring topology and a fully connected topology.

Let us now imagine that you were given the task of developing a communications protocol in relation to the implementation of all aspects of a local area network. Let's think about some of the issues that you would have to consider in the development of such a communications protocol.

Topology

Here you would have to think about the interconnection scheme that you would use to join together the nodes within the LAN, and so support the passage of data between them. You may choose to use, for example, a fully connected topology – although here you will recall that a fully connected topology involves much more wiring, and the number of wires (or other types of media) rapidly increases with the number of nodes. For simplicity, let's assume that you decide to make use of a bus topology as illustrated in Figure 12.4(a).

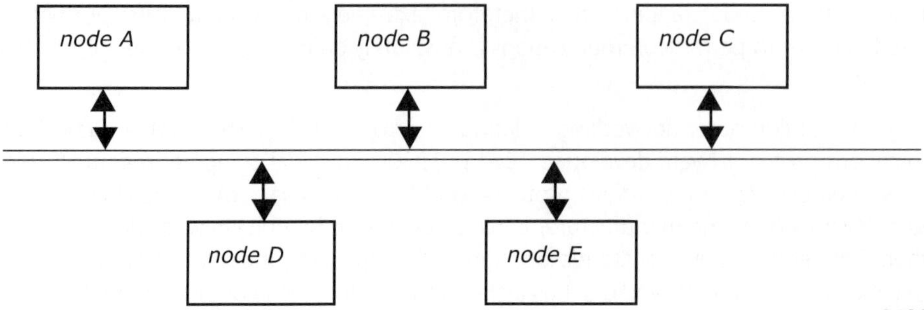

12.4(a)

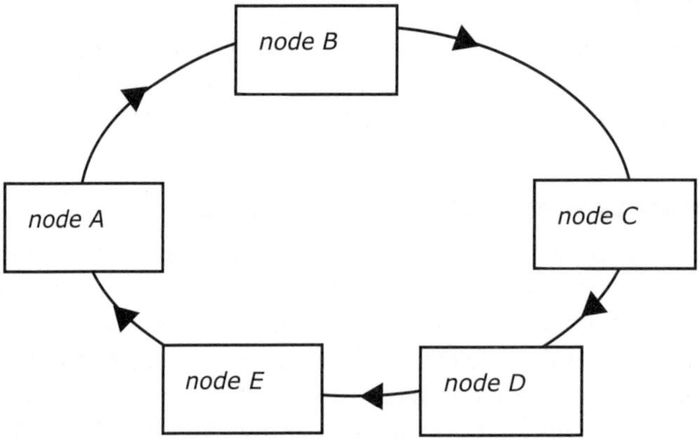

12.4(b)

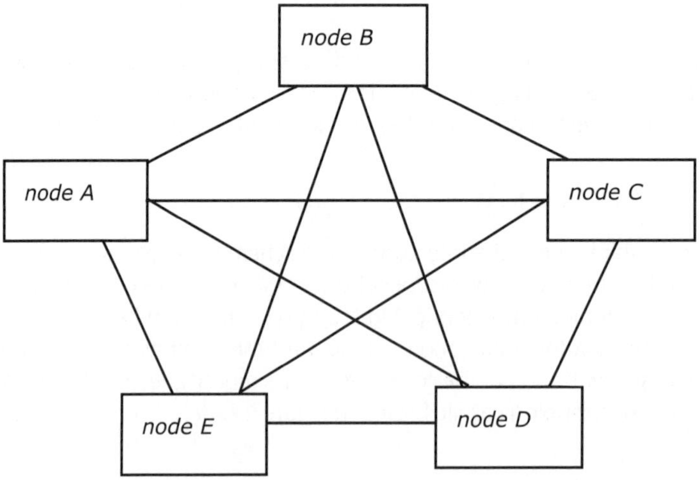

12.4(c)

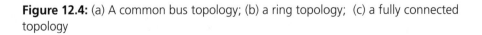

Figure 12.4: (a) A common bus topology; (b) a ring topology; (c) a fully connected topology

Media

Having decided upon the interconnection scheme, you will now need to consider the type of medium that you will use to support the passage of signals. Here various options are available to you. You may decide to use metallic conductors (such as coaxial cable or twisted pair cable), or you may choose fibre optic cable. If you decide to use the latter, then the signals that pass between the nodes will take the form of pulses of light, rather than electrical signals. A further option is for you to use a wireless link, and here you will no longer have to provide a physical connection between each node, since nodes will be able to broadcast signals via radio waves. Each type of media has its own advantages and disadvantages. For example, fibre optic cable is able to support the passage of enormous volumes of data and provides greater immunity to interference than do metallic conductors. The use of a wireless link avoids the necessity of routing cables through buildings. On the other hand, radio signals are very susceptible to electrical interference, and it is easy for third parties to intercept signals and therefore 'tap in' to the network. Let's suppose that at the end of the day you decide to make use of standard wiring to connect the nodes on your LAN.

Computer interface

Having decided on the type of topology to use, and the type of medium that will connect the nodes together, you will now have to turn your attention to the development of hardware enabling each node to be connected to the LAN. In this context, you would develop a 'network interface card', which would connect between the computer's internal bus and the medium. The network interface card (NIC) would be designed to support the transmission of signals of certain voltages, and its architecture would determine the upper limit to the rate at which data could be transferred between nodes.

The NIC is responsible for outputting signals onto the LAN and receiving signals from the LAN. The hardware on the NIC determines the voltages transmitted onto the medium, and the maximum bit rate (i.e. number of bits per second that can be transmitted onto the medium). Commonly, a network interface card contains memory to allow the buffering of data. This is a process we have encountered on previous occasions, and you will recall that the buffering technique enables, for example, a processor to send a certain amount of data quickly to a peripheral device. This data is then temporarily stored in the peripheral device's buffer, and can be utilised by the peripheral device as and when it wishes. The NIC also provides each computer with its own 'address'. In a LAN, this address is unique and is used to direct data to the correct destination. Thus, a node that wishes to send data to a particular machine will append to the data the address of the intended recipient (in much the same way that we provide an address when mailing a letter). Each NIC on the LAN will view the address specified in any transmission. Only the NIC whose address matches the specified address will read the data.

Sharing the media

The issues discussed above all relate to hardware. In developing a communications protocol we now have to turn our attention to aspects of the protocol that can be implemented in software. One important consideration concerns the way in which the nodes will equitably share the medium. In the previous example, we decided to make use of a bus topology. This means that all the nodes connected to the LAN share a single common medium. Naturally, therefore, we must ensure that all nodes are able to share this in an orderly manner, and various issues arise. For example, let us suppose that one node is outputting data onto the medium when a second node also begins to transmit.

If this occurs, the signals on the medium will become corrupted, so we must make sure that either:

- When one node is transmitting, no other node can transmit or
- Should two or more nodes transmit at the same time – we have a well-defined strategy to deal with this situation'.

This is rather like the situation that we described in our analogy earlier, concerning a meeting attended by a number of participants. As indicated, we need to make sure that order is maintained among speakers – only one person should talk at any one time. It is no different with computers – if they are sharing a common medium, then we must exercise controls to make sure that the medium is utilised properly by all nodes.

A further problem that can arise when a medium is shared relates to the volumes of data that individual nodes may wish to transmit. For example, let us suppose that a computer on a network wishes to transmit a VERY large file to another computer.

Consider that we implement our protocol in such a way that when one node (we'll call this node A) gains access to the medium and starts to transmit, no other node can access the medium. Now let's suppose that node A wishes to transmit a very large file – the result is that for some time (and this could be quite a long time) no other node can use the network. Thus, node A has locked out all the other nodes and this is a most undesirable situation. Returning to the earlier analogy concerning the meeting, this would be akin to speakers being able to talk for any length of time and so monopolise the meeting. Naturally, this is undesirable and therefore the protocol must allow the network medium to be equitably shared.

Other issues

The communications protocol is responsible for many other aspects of the communications process. For example, it is likely to provide security – thus ensuring that it is difficult for unauthorised recipients to access a message and perhaps interfere with its content. The protocol must also deal with error checking; in the case that transmitted data becomes corrupted, procedures must be in place to deal with this situation. There are many other issues that are dealt with by the communications protocol. In general the activities of the protocol in providing reliable and secure data transmissions are hidden from applications programs that wish to communicate across a network. For example, an applications program that communicates across a network does not need to know how network nodes are interconnected, nor does it need to know the techniques that will be used when errors in transmission occur. These are issues that are handled by the communications protocol software.

Activity 12.4

Communications protocols

List six key functions of a typical communications protocol used for a LAN.

Activity 12.5

Network transmission media

Using your local library or Internet, research and discuss two advantages of fibre optic media for the implementation of a computer network, as compared with the use of traditional metallic conductors.

12.8 Multimedia storage formats

Multimedia content is saved in various standard file formats to allow it to be viewed on many computer platforms and browsers. The format of a file refers to the way the numbers in the file are arranged. Multimedia files come in a wide range of formats: images can be arranged in the GIF, JPEG or PNG format (and others). Sound can arrive in the Audio Interchange File (AIF) format, or the QuickTime format. Video files can, for example, appear in the Windows Media, RealVideo, or QuickTime format. We summarise various file formats next.

Graphics/image file formats

- **BMP** (Bitmap) Uncompressed file format
- **GIF** (Graphics Interchange Format). This bitmapped format is one of the most common image compression file formats for graphics and animations. Suited to graphics that have no more than 256 colours
- **JPG** (Joint Photographics Expert Group). This format is one of the most common image compression techniques and file formats for still graphics. Designed for compressing either full-colour or greyscale digital images of 'natural', real-world scenes
- **TIFF** (Tagged Image File Format). A file format used for still-image bitmaps, stored in tagged fields. Standard choice for scanned images. Universally accepted format designed to be easily transferred across different computer operating systems. Tiffs retain their original high quality because they are not compressed when saved
- **PNG** (Portable Network Graphic). A more recent format being used for graphics, instead of the GIF format. An image compression technique suited to graphics that have a large colour palette and where there is low information loss
- **WMF** (Windows Metafile Format) often used for vector graphics. Not appropriate for the web.
- **CGM** (Computer Graphics Metafile) for vector graphics. Used for multimedia requiring line drawings
- **PCX.** Filename extension for images created with the IBM PC Paintbrush tool. A popular format for storing graphics
- **PDF** (Portable Document Format). Stores a compressed file containing text, images and active links.

Sound/audio file formats

- **MIDI** (Musical Interface Digital Instrument). A method for storing musical information such as notes, musical sequence and the instrument intended to play the music. A hardware specification and protocol used to communicate information on notes and effects between synthesisers, computers, keyboards, controllers and other electronic music devices

- **WAV** (Wave files). Digitised audio file of varying levels of quality which can be played directly by a sound card
- **Real Audio.** Used to transfer sound data across the Internet. Requires a real audio player (integrated with most browser software)
- **MP3** MPEG standard – compressed audio sound. Currently requires a software player
- **AU.** An audio file name extension for digital audio first developed for the Sun Unix platform. It is a popular format for digital audio on the World Wide Web.

Video/animation file formats

- **MPG** (Motion Picture Experts Group) Common file format for video. This format uses an inter-frame compression scheme – only one frame every half-second is fully recorded, and only the changes between frames are then noted
- **AVI** (Audio Video Interleave). Common file format for streaming video. Developed by Microsoft to play back digital video on Windows-based machines
- **DVI** (Digital Video Interactive) is a compression technique for data, audio and full-motion video from Intel. It provides up to 72 minutes of full-screen video on a CD-ROM with up to 100:1 compression ratio
- **MOV** (QuickTime movie). Available for both Macintosh and Windows and handles animation.

Compression

Data compression allows us to store data in a format that requires much less space. Here, a process of encoding is used and results in a reduction in file size, so enabling files to be transferred between machines more rapidly. This is achieved by means of a compression/decompression algorithm (CODEC).

There are two types of compression:

- **Lossless:** this is a compression scheme that does not lose information when a file is compressed. Although this is the least effective form of compression for image files, it can still achieve around a 40% reduction in original file size
- **Lossy:** this is a compression scheme where some image information is lost each time a file is compressed. Most JPEG algorithms are 'lossy' compression algorithms. A lossy compression technique results in a degradation of quality – although this is usually quite small and is therefore generally acceptable.

Streaming

This technique allows elements such as audio and video to be heard or viewed while a file is downloading, as opposed to waiting for the entire file to download. Real Audio is a well-known streaming audio format; as a file is being downloaded, playout can commence.

Plug-ins

A plug-in is a file used to alter or enhance an application program. Usually downloaded from the Internet without cost. Often plug-ins are used to improve animation, video and audio.

Activity 12.6

File compression

Explain two important advantages associated with file compression. Do you think that there are any disadvantages associated with the use of compression techniques?

12.9 Internet and the World Wide Web (WWW)

The Internet is a worldwide system of interconnected computer networks; it makes it possible for a computer user anywhere in the world to exchange text, pictures, movies, sound, computer programs, and anything else that can be stored in digital form with anyone else in the connected world.

It is important to remember that the Internet and the World Wide Web are not the same thing. The Internet is a collection of computers and devices connected by equipment that allows them to communicate with each other. On the other hand, the web is a collection of software and protocols that have been installed on the computers on the Internet. The web can be thought of as a vast collection of documents, some of which are connected by links. We can access these documents by web browsers such as Microsoft Internet Explorer or Netscape.

Browsers are clients on the web and they initiate the communication with the server, which waits for a message from a client before doing anything. When you requests a document using a web browser, the browser requests the document from a server and the server locates the document and sends it to the browser, which displays it on the user's computer.

The web supports various protocols, but the most common one is the hypertext transfer protocol (HTTP); the most commonly used tools and programming languages include HTML, Java and JavaScript .

HTML (hypertext markup language) is not a programming language and cannot be used for computations. It is used to describe, or code, the general form and layout of documents to be displayed by a browser.

Java was designed by, and is still controlled by, Sun Microsystems. It provides a powerful way of solving the problem of HTML not being a programming language. Instead of running programs on the Web server, a special kind of Java program called an applet can reside on the server computer and a compiled version of the applet can be downloaded to the browser when requested by the HTML code being displayed by the browser.

12.10 Summary

In previous chapters we have, in the main, focused on internal aspects of the computer and in this chapter have turned our attention to more general characteristics. We have reviewed aspects of the multimedia computer and, as you have seen, while the modern computer is able to accept different forms of communications media, within the computer itself sound, video, etc is represented in a similar manner, i.e. numerically. Irrespective of the form of media, the computer has no knowledge of the meaning that we will ultimately assign to the results of its computation. Thus, in processing an audio stream the computer is not aware that it is producing something that we can ultimately hear, nor when processing a video stream does it know that it is processing something we will eventually see. The vital point to understand is that within the computer all forms of media are simply stored as a set of binary numbers. You have been introduced to the ADC and DAC, both of which play a pivotal part in converting between analogue and digital signals.

We have also briefly reviewed aspects of computer networking. Here we have referred to interconnection topologies, and this discussion paralleled material presented in a previous chapter concerning bus topologies. We have also described the need for the development of clearly defined communications protocols which provide the rules that computers follow when communicating. When we communicate, we often apply our communications skills in an imprecise manner. In this sense, we are able to communicate without the need for precise rules. However, this is certainly not the case with the computer, and in a communications protocol every aspect of the communications process must be defined without any ambiguity. Within this chapter, we have reviewed some of the general functions of a communications protocol. We have also summarised the file formats frequently encountered on the multimedia computer and have introduced the concept of file compression.

Finally, we have briefly discussed the Internet and World Wide Web. These form a vital aspect of the modern computer – which is no longer an isolated desktop machine. In fact, from our desktop computer we are able to access and download material stored on computers located in practically every part of the world.

12.11 Review questions

Review question 12.1

Explain the function of a transducer.

Review question 12.2

When scanning a document, why is it often not best to make use of the highest scanning resolution (dpi) supported by the scanner?

Review question 12.3

A computer is able to process and store various forms of media (e.g. text, images, video, audio.) State one key factor that makes this possible.

Review question 12.4

State one advantage and one disadvantage associated with the use of a fully connected network topology.

Review question 12.5

In the context of computer networking, what is a 'node'?

Review question 12.6

Data compression allows you to store data in a format that requires much less space. What are the two general categories of data compression? Define each of them.

Review question 12.7

Write down the similarities and differences between the file types given below:

1: gif, jpg, png

2: midi, wav

Review question 12.8

HTML is referred to as a markup language. Can this language be used for the creation of computer programs?

12.12 Feedback on activities

Feedback on activity 12.1: Analogue-to-digital conversion

A 4-bit ADC is able to produce 16 different binary outcomes. The minimum change that can therefore be detected by the ADC is approximately 6 divided by 16 volts (i.e. approximately 0.4 volts).

Feedback on activity 12.2: Signal sampling

If a signal is sampled by an analogue-to-digital convertor too infrequently, information within the signal may well be lost. Take, for example, the case of an audio signal. Such a signal comprises a rich mixture of different frequencies. These all add together to produce a complex waveform. As we reduce the sampling rate of such a signal, higher-frequency components within the signal are ultimately lost. Even in the case of a pure signal (such as a sinusoidal wave), if the signal is not sampled with sufficient frequency it will be impossible for us to reconstitute the signal. The Nyquist Criteria tells us that in order to reconstitute a signal, it must be sampled at least twice as frequently as the highest-frequency component within the signal. Thus, for example, if we consider a sine wave with a frequency of 100Hz, we must sample this signal at least 200 times per second.

Feedback on activity 12.3: Scanning a page

Horizontally – 8 x 200 = 1,600. Vertically 10 x 200 = 2,000.

Total number of samples is therefore 1,600 x 2,000 = 3,200,000.

Each sample is stored as 4 bits.

Therefore the total number of bits is 4 x 3,200,000 = 12,800,000, so the file will be approximately 13Mbits.

Feedback on activity 12.4: Communications protocols

Various important functions are summarised in this chapter. These include:

- Specification of voltages that will be used for signal transmission
- Specification of the speed at which bits will be output onto the transmission media
- The splitting of data to be transmitted into smaller 'chunks'
- Appending destination address and other information to each data 'chunk'
- Checking for transmission errors – and dealing with these
- Ensuring secure data transmission.
- The re-assembly of data 'chunks' at the destination
- Ensuring that the transmission media is equitably shared between computers.

Feedback on activity 12.5: Network transmission media

Fibre optic cable has much greater immunity to noise (electrical interference) than do traditional metallic conductors (e.g. coaxial cable or twisted pair cable). Fibre optic cabling is also able to support a much greater signal transmission bandwidth than traditional forms of interconnect. Thus greater volumes of data can be transmitted (per unit time interval) along an optical fibre.

Feedback on activity 12.6: File compression

Compression techniques reduce file sizes and so result in less storage space being consumed on the hard disk (or other forms of storage media). (This is important as multimedia files are often quite large.) Furthermore, since files become smaller when compression techniques are used, they can be more rapidly transmitted across a network. One disadvantage generally associated with compression techniques concerns the processing that must be undertaken in the compression and decompression activities. Consequently, although compressed files can be more rapidly transmitted across a network, additional latency is introduced at the receiving end – as a file must be decompressed. This may offset the transmission advantage. On the other hand, the transmission of smaller files results in a decrease in network traffic and so is generally advantageous.

Further reading

- Englander, IRV (2003), *The Architecture of Computer Hardware and Systems Software*, John Wiley, 3rd Edition
- Clements, A (2006), *Principles of Computer Hardware*, Oxford University Press

Glossary

We list here the main terms for each chapter; space is allocated for any notes you may wish to make, alongside each

Chapter 1

Computer

Computer architecture

Input device

Output device

Hardware

Software

Computer memory

Chapter 2

Hex

Bit

Byte

Binary

Chapter 3

Truth table

Logic gate

NAND gate

NOR gate

NOT gate

Invertor

Logic low

Logic high

Propagation delay

Combinational logic

Sequential logic

Chapter 4

Bus

Address bus

Data bus

Control bus

Program counter

Register

ALU

PC

Mainframe computer

Minicomputer

Client–server model

Read/write signal

Microprocessor

Microcontroller

Chapter 5

System clock

Cache memory

Common bus

Latency

RAM

ROM

Non-volatile RAM

Spatial locality

Temporal locality

Chapter 6

Opcode

Operand

Machine code

Assembly language

High-level language

Assembler

ASCII

Unicode

2's complement

Fetch/execute cycle

Chapter 7

Condition code register

Program counter

Memory address register

Memory buffer register

ALU

Control unit

Microcontroller

Microprocessor

Embedded controller

Chapter 8

Interrupt

Non-maskable interrupt

Maskable interrupt

Interrupt priority

Interrupt controller

Interrupt vector

Interrupt overheads

Chapter 9

DVD

WORM

CD-R

Track

Cylinder

Sector

Platter

Primary storage

Secondary storage

Chapter 10

BIOS

Reset vector

Boot sequence

POST

Layered architecture

Operating system

Kernel

.DLL files

Multi-tasking

Process

Chapter 11

Mechanical mouse

Optical mouse

Joystick

Display resolution

Refresh frequency

Active matrix LCD panel

Passive matrix LCD panel

QWERTY keyboard

Trackball

Trackpad

Shadow mask

Bitmapped graphics

CRT

Plasma display

LCD

Laser printer

Chapter 12

DAC

ADC

Sampling rate

Precision

LAN

Lossless compression

Lossy compression

Multimedia machine

dpi

USB port

Parallel port

UART

Communication protocol

Network topology

NIC

Streaming

JPEG

TIFF

GIF

BMP

HTTP

Additional notes

Additional notes

Answers to review questions

Chapter 1

Question 1.1

A general purpose programmable machine is a machine that can be used to carry out a wide range of different tasks. It can be told to do a specific task by means of a computer program.

Question 1.2

The Difference Engine was intended to perform calculations, whereas the Analytical Engine would (in principle, had it been constructed) have been able to perform computation. In this sense, instructions could have been executed in sequence, by selection and by iteration.

Question 1.3

Previous computing machines were programmed by connecting circuit elements together in particular ways and by setting switches. The stored program concept provided a model via which the program that was to be executed was stored within the computer's memory. Thus, when users wished to run a different program, it was no longer necessary to reconfigure the computer's hardware, but rather simply load a new program into memory.

Question 1.4

Prior to the use of transistors in computer systems, throughout the 1940s until the late 1950s valve (vacuum tube) technologies were used. In comparison to a transistor, valves are quite large and dissipate quite a lot of heat. Transistors offered a more effective solution, being smaller and also working at lower temperatures. With the advent of the silicon chip it became possible to fabricate electrical components (particularly transistors) on a single piece of silicon. Transistors could therefore be placed in close proximity, allowing signals to pass between them at very high speed. Three key aspects of the silicon chip are therefore (a) high density fabrication of components, (b) high speed operation, (c) low power dissipation. Gradually as techniques improved, the manufacturing costs of silicon chips fell, and this was a major factor in the proliferation of the modern computer.

Question 1.5

A computer is able to execute instructions in sequence (following the order in which they are stored within memory), by selection and by iteration.

Question 1.6

The abbreviation CPU stands for central processing unit. The CPU in the modern computer takes the form of a silicon chip upon which, typically, millions of transistors are fabricated. The CPU is responsible for controlling the computer hardware, and for executing program instructions. It is as the name implies the 'central' part of the computer.

Chapter 2

Question 2.1

The answer is 27.

Question 2.2

The smallest number represented by the bits is zero. The largest number represented by the four bits is when they are all 1s. In this case, the binary value represents 15 (in base 10). Thus, four binary digits can represent values from 0 through to 15, corresponding to 16 different numbers.

Question 2.3

Hexadecimal (base 16) provides a simple and efficient way of compacting binary strings. It reduces the number of digits that we need use to represent a binary number.

Question 2.4

The symbol 'A' represents the decimal (base 10) value of 10, and 'D' represents the decimal value of 13.

Question 2.5

The answer is 87.

Question 2.6

A digital signal can only take on certain values. For example in the case of a binary digital signal, the signal can only represent two states.

Question 2.7

The answer is 10110010

Question 2.8

The answer is 35

Question 2.9

A bit is a binary digit.

Question 2.10

Three hexadecimal digits are needed.

Chapter 3

Question 3.1

A	B	C	D	Output
0	0	0	0	1
1	0	0	0	0
0	1	0	0	0
0	0	1	1	0
0	1	0	1	0

Question 3.2

A	B	C	Output
0	0	0	0
0	1	0	0
1	0	0	0
1	1	0	0
0	0	1	1
0	1	1	1
1	0	1	1
1	1	1	0

Question 3.3

When the signals applied to a gate are changed, it takes the gate a finite time to respond and produce a new output corresponding to the change in input. This time delay is referred to as the 'propagation delay' and is typically a few nanoseconds.

Question 3.4

The circle signifies that the gate has an inverting function. Thus the symbol for a NAND gate includes such a circle indicating that it is in fact a 'NOT AND' gate.

Question 3.5

A truth table shows the outputs corresponding to the combinations of possible input conditions. It may also be used to summarise the logic states of connections within the circuit.

Question 3.6

NAND - Any low gives a high.

AND - Any low gives a low.

Question 3.7

These have the same functionality other than when both inputs are a logic high. In this case an OR gate produces a logic high and an XOR gate a logic low.

Chapter 4

Question 4.1

This approach allows the program that is to be executed to be stored within the internal memory of a computer. This contrasts with earlier computer architectures in which the operation of the computer was defined by the setting of switches, and the interconnection of computer components using cables.

Question 4.2

The CPU is the 'heart' of the computer, meaning that it is central to all computer activity. The CPU is responsible for reading instructions from memory, and for executing these instructions. The CPU is also responsible for controlling almost all hardware activity.

Question 4.3

The ALU is the 'arithmetic and logic unit' located in the processor. It is responsible for performing arithmetic operations such as addition and subtraction, together with logical operations.

Question 4.4

Electricity flows through wires at a finite speed – the longer the wire, the longer it takes for an electrical signal to pass through the wire. In order to maximise computer performance, it is desirable to have the key components of the computer close together. In this way, the length of electrical connections is reduced and therefore signals are able to pass between components in a shorter time.

Question 4.5

This work was carried out at Xerox PARC in the US during the 1970s. The work included both hardware and software developments.

Question 4.6

Signals flow on the address bus only in one direction - from the processor to devices such a memory. This contrasts with the data bus in which signals can flow from the processor to memory and vice versa.

Question 4.7

This term is used when referring to a group of connections that serve a common purpose.

Question 4.8

This wire indicates to devices such as memory whether the processor is wishing to perform a read or a write operation.

Question 4.9

This coordinates all the low-level activity of the computer. For example, it interprets (decodes) program instructions and directs both internal operations and the flow of data to and from memory (and other devices).

Question 4.10

This is the name given to a group of eight binary digits.

Chapter 5

Question 5.1

A wider data bus allows more data to be transferred in each bus cycle, whereas a larger address bus allows access to a larger number of memory locations.

Question 5.2

Firstly the backplane bus which connects processor, memory and I/O devices by one single bus. Secondly, a high-capacity bus called the processor memory bus, which connects the processor and memory. The third is the I/O bus, which connects low-speed I/O devices.

Question 5.3

Data, address and control buses. The data bus carries data from CPU to memory or I/O and also to CPU from memory or I/O. The address bus carries the address to which the processor wishes to write or from which it is to read. The control bus primarily carries control information from the CPU to select memory or I/O devices and to select read or write functions.

Question 5.4

The different components inside and outside CPU are kept in step by use of a 'clock signal'. This plays a crucial role in the timing of all computer operations.

Question 5.5

A PC employs various types of bus, each being most suited to different data transfer requirements (e.g. speed). As discussed, one type of bus may be used to connect the processor to main memory and another bus to connect to devices such as the hard disk.

Question 5.6

The need to distribute the clock signal to all devices that are connected to the bus limits its physical length. The clock signal is not instantaneously transmitted to each component that is connected to the bus – its propagation occupies a finite time. The longer the bus, the greater is this time. In the case of high-speed buses, this can cause timing problems and ultimately limits bus speed or bus length.

Question 5.7

We are currently reaching the basic physical limitations of semiconductors. Unless fundamentally new techniques are developed for the implementation of key components comprising the computer, this model is likely to be no longer applicable.

Question 5.8

Frequency=1/period of oscillation. Thus the frequency = $1/10^{-6}=10^{6}$Hz.

Question 5.9

In a fully connected topology, each device is connected to all other devices. As a result the number of physical connections rapidly increases with the number of components that are to be connected. The number of interconnects is given by $n(n-1)/2$

Question 5.10

A protocol is needed to ensure that communication takes place in an orderly manner. This must ensure that each time data is transmitted, appropriate address information is included so as to specify the intended recipient. Additionally, only one device can be allowed to communicate at any one time.

Chapter 6

Question 6.1

High-level languages allow us to construct programs that consist of recognisable (and often meaningful) words and constructs. This assists in the programming task and makes it easier for us to examine code and understand its operation. However, a high-level language program cannot be directly executed by a processor - first it needs to be converted into machine code.

Question 6.2

This term dates back to the early days of computing and stands for 'operation code'. An operation code is a machine code instruction that can be executed by the processor.

Question 6.3

Although this is common, various machine code instructions can allow the processor to break away from the execution of sequentially stored instructions. In this way the processor can 'jump' to different locations within its address space.

Question 6.4

We return to the original number.

Question 6.5

By using the 2's complement approach to represent negative integers, it is possible to perform subtraction operations using the same hardware that is employed for addition. This simplifies hardware design.

Question 6.6

001100

Question 6.7

ASCII: American Standard Code for Information Interchange.

EBCDIC: Extended Binary Coded Decimal Interchange Code

Question 6.8

Add the hexadecimal value 20 – for example, 'A' is represented as 41 (hex) and 'a' as 61 (hex). The addition of the binary number 00100000 (20 (hex)) converts between these two symbol codes.

Chapter 7

Question 7.1

The ALU (arithmetic and logic unit) performs mathematical and logical operations. It is here that all the arithmetic undertaken by the processor is carried out. The ALU makes use of various registers.

Question 7.2

Various answers possible, including the support for a very small instruction set, the presence of on-board ROM, the provision of control lines that allow the microcontroller to readily control hardware, the provision of input lines via which the microcontroller can detect external events.

Question 7.3

This ROM enables the program to be stored on the CPU chip and so simplifies the wiring of the microcontroller. When accessing program instructions, the processor does not need to perform external fetch/execute cycles; these are performed internally within the CPU.

Question 7.4

The MBR interfaces the data bus with several sub-units within the CPU that deal with the processing of opcodes and operands. Thus when data is to be written to memory, or when a read operation is performed, the MBR serves as a temporary buffer.

Question 7.5

The individual bits that comprise the CCR have different meanings and are set or reset according to the outcome of the last operation performed by the ALU. When conditional branch operations are encountered (e.g. 'branch if zero' – meaning that the action taken depends on whether or not the outcome of the previous instruction that was executed was zero or otherwise), the CU will obtain this information from the CCR.

Chapter 8

Question 8.1

This is an abbreviation for the 'interrupt service routine' - the program that executes following an interrupt request.

Question 8.2

The interrupt vector is a pointer to the address of the first instruction in the interrupt service routine.

Question 8.3

The interrupt controller enables the CPU to accept interrupts from several sources. It is also able to prioritise interrupts.

Question 8.4

A maskable interrupt can be disabled. If, for example, the processor is undertaking critical operations, then it can disable maskable interrupts.

Question 8.5

A non-maskable interrupt cannot be disabled. Non-maskable interrupts are often used to deal with time-critical situations. Thus a non-maskable interrupt will be served rapidly. However, it is important to note that priorities can still be applied to sources of non-maskable interrupts.

Question 8.6

No. Only a higher priority interrupt can do this.

Question 8.7

Polling refers to continuously checking to see if an event has taken place (e.g. the pressing of one or more keyboard keys).

Chapter 9

Question 9.1

During a read or write operation, the read/write head must be positioned over the appropriate sector(s). This necessitates waiting until the sector lies underneath the head and consequently there is a corresponding rotational latency. The rotation of the disk at a higher speed reduces this rotational latency.

Question 9.2

The floppy disk drive does not make use of high precision technology. Furthermore, in the case of a floppy disk the read/write head does not fly across the surface of the disk, but rather rests upon it. Since there is no separation between the read/write head and the surface of the disk, lower rotational speeds must be employed.

Question 9.3

The first latency corresponds to the time needed to move the read/write head to the correct track. The second latency concerns the need to await the sector on the track rotating to be beneath the read/write head.

Question 9.4

They are written using a highly focused laser beam. This heats the material within the disc and causes the optical properties of this material to change. In this way it is possible to record binary digits on the CD-ROM.

Question 9.5

Amorphous and crystalline.

Chapter 10

Question 10.1

Executing requests such as 'stand up', 'sit down', 'drink tea'. The key point about high-level operations is that no attention has to be paid to simpler operations, these can be left to other systems. It relates to computers because when designing or using high-level systems such as a word processor, no consideration need be given to low- level operations such as how the digital signals travel around the computer. Computers use a layered architecture to achieve this.

Question 10.2

A low-level operation is, for example, the contraction of a single muscle in your leg, which helps you to stand up.

Question 10.3

Examples of high-level operations would be running a spell check in a word processor, adding a column of numbers in a spreadsheet, sending an e-mail or browsing a web page.

Question 10.4

Examples of low-level operations would be reading a keypress from the keyboard, sending a character to the printer etc. The BIOS is able to provide these operations - the basic input/output system.

Question 10.5

Memory management

Interface creation via which a user is able to interact with the digital world

Multi-tasking

Security

Network access.

Question 10.6

A process is a software environment in which a program can execute.

Question 10.7

Power on self-test

Question 10.8

Basic input/output system

Chapter 11

Question 11.1

The QWERTY keyboard layout is used widely in countries where English is the first language and indicates the order of six alphabetic keys on the keyboard. This layout was originally devised over a hundred years ago in connection with keyboards intended for use with mechanical typewriters. The keyboard layout was designed to reduce typing speeds by increasing the distance through which the fingers have to move when typing. In this way it was hoped to reduce the frequency with which mechanical typewriters jammed. Attempts have been made to develop a better keyboard layout (which would actually increase typing speeds), but they have been unsuccessful. There are a number of reasons for this, one of which is that there are too many people who are trained on the normal QWERTY keyboard and who are therefore reluctant to move to alternatives.

Question 11.2

Movement of the mechanical mouse causes the rotation of a ball, which in turn rotates two wheels. These are arranged at right angles (orthogonal) to each other. As these wheels rotate, their movement is encoded electrically and transmitted to the computer. In one form of non-mechanical mouse a special mouse-pad is used, upon which vertical and horizontal lines are printed in two different colours. Optical sensors within the mouse are able to detect the passage of the mouse over these lines. As the mouse moves over the lines, signals are passed to the computer and in this way the computer is able to monitor the direction of mouse movement and the distance that it has travelled.

In the case of an alternative approach, an image sensing array is employed together with an image processing system. Differences in successive images are used to measure distance travelled and direction of motion.

Question 11.3

The name pixel is an abbreviation for 'picture element' and is the fundamental 'particle' from which images are generated on a computer display. A computer image is formed from a set of pixels that are illuminated (under computer control) in different colours and at different levels of brightness. Individual pixels may be seen by looking very closely at a computer monitor – a better view will be obtained if a magnifying glass is used.

Question 11.4

The colour of each screen pixel is created by mixing together different amounts of the three primary colours (red, green and blue). Each electron beam is made responsible for the generation of one of these primary colours, thus one electron beam generates shades of red, the next shades of green, and the third shades of blue. The three electron guns scan the screen together in a series of horizontal lines.

Question 11.5

The shadow-mask ensures that each of the three electron beams referred to in the previous review question can only excite a phosphor of a certain colour. This is achieved by defining the geometry by which the beams strike the phosphor dots that are printed onto the surface of the CRT screen.

Question 11.6

A mouse may be equipped with two motion detectors arranged at right angles (orthogonal) so as to be able to measure the vertical and horizontal components of motion.

Question 11.7

This approach supports the implementation of thin panel displays. Additionally, these displays weigh much less than their CRT-based equivalent.

Question 11.8

A selenium-coated drum is charged with static electricity and then scanned by a laser beam that is rapidly deflected and modulated – the laser beam 'writes' the image onto the drum. Wherever the light strikes the selenium, the charge is dissipated. The drum then passes over a cartridge with black (toner) powder. Where the static charge remains, the toner is drawn to the drum. The drum then applies the toner to the paper (and is then cleaned of any residue). The paper passes through a heater that fuses the toner particles onto it.

Question 11.9

Each pixel has a corresponding location in memory where its attributes (colour and intensity) are defined. Thus, by writing a binary value to a particular memory location, we cause a particular pixel on the computer screen to be illuminated to a certain level of intensity and colour. The area of memory used for this purpose is called the 'video memory', and is usually located on a special card (circuit board) within the computer that is called the 'video card'.

Employing a direct mapping technique between screen pixels and memory locations is referred to as 'bitmapped' (or more accurately 'pixmapped') graphics.

Chapter 12

Question 12.1

A transducer converts one form of energy into another. For example, a temperature transducer will typically convert temperature into an electrical signal.

Question 12.2

This will generally result in the creation of very large files. Such files consume storage space and their transmission across a network may be time-consuming. The scanning resolution used should reflect the nature of the activity (i.e. the way in which the material being scanned will be used) and the information content of the document/image. If, for example, a document contains only fairly coarse handwriting (and little, if any, fine detail), then it is best to use a low scan resolution.

Question 12.3

These different forms of media may be represented numerically within a computer. Thus an audio clip or video image may both be represented as a series of binary numbers. The computer is able to process such numbers and thereby process the different forms of media.

Question 12.4

Since each node is directly connected to each other node, communications can be achieved rapidly and the topology contains considerable redundancy (should a network connection fail, data may be routed along alternative paths). Unfortunately, when a fully connected topology is implemented, the number of network connections rapidly increases with the number of nodes.

Question 12.5

A node is a computer or a piece of computer-based hardware that is connected to a network. (Computer-based hardware encompasses specialised network components such as bridges and routers.)

Question 12.6

- Lossless: A compression scheme that never loses information when a file is compressed. This is the least effective form of compression for images.

- Lossy: A compression scheme in which some image information is lost each time the file is compressed. Most JPEG algorithms are lossy compression algorithms. About 5% reduction in original file size once it has been compressed. Good for sound, images and video. Multimedia, networking and the Internet.

Question 12.7

1 **gif, jpg, png:** these are all graphics file formats.

- **gif** is common for graphics and animations. Bitmapped format that uses lossless compression. Limited to 256 colours

- **jpg** - superior lossy compression. Smaller file sizes can be achieved than with gifs.

- **png** - allows for a larger colour palette than a gif's 256 colours.

2 **midi, wav**: these are both sound file formats:

  - **Midi** is used for storing a vast range of musical information - hardware specification and protocol. Requires a synthesiser to replay.

  - **Wav** is more commonly used than **au** files. Varying levels of quality and can be played directly by a sound card.

Question 12.8

No! A markup language does not contain the type of constructs that are used in the creation of computer programs.

INDEX